T0400161

"In describing the analytic process as 'intimate fiction,' Joye Weisel-Barth, writing about her clinical work like a good novelist, captures why I have for years avoided reading much of the psychoanalytic literature and embraced in its stead, contemporary novels. Perhaps it takes someone like Dr. Weisel-Barth and her background in literature, to bring to life what actually transpires in the intersubjective clinical situation, unencumbered by allegiances and obeisance to jargon-filled and overly intellectualized theoretical religions. I hope that this rich and vital book serves as an exemplar, inspiring a new era of readable and vivid psychoanalytic writing."

—**Irwin Hirsch, PhD,** NYU Postdoctoral Program in Psychoanalysis and Psychotherapy, The William Alanson White Institute

"What Joye Weisel-Barth offers us in this beautifully written collection of essays is an original approach to understanding the work we do. Joye contends that over the course of their hours together, patient and analyst write and rewrite the patient's life narrative in such a way that the emerging story feels both true and acceptable, and capable of supporting a more expansive sense of future possibility. This unique vision of therapeutic process is vividly portrayed in numerous clinical vignettes where troubled lives are seen to deepen with new meaning and potential. I love this exquisitely rendered book especially for the hope it engenders for our patients and our profession."

—**Estelle Shane,** Institute of Contemporary Psychoanalysis

"In this collection of beautifully written, often dramatic, clinical stories, Joye Weisel-Barth emerges as one of our psychoanalytic pioneers. Combining a complex grasp of contemporary theory with the courage always to be thoughtfully authentic with her patients and readers, Weisel-Barth pushes the limits of analytic acceptability in the service of giving her most challenging patients what they truly need from her. Moreover, she is as open about treatment failures as she is about her successes, always seeking to learn from her experience, and help us do the same. In short, *Theoretical and Clinical Perspectives on Narrative in Psychoanalysis* deepens and complicates our understanding of what it means to work relationally."

—**Steven Stern, PsyD**, Clinical Associate Professor, Tufts University School of Medicine and Maine Medical Center

Theoretical and Clinical Perspectives on Narrative in Psychoanalysis

This book is of and about psychoanalytic stories. It describes the personal, theoretical, and cultural stories that patients and analysts bring, create, and modify in analytic work. It shows how the joint creation of new life narratives over time results in transformed senses of self and relationship.

Flowing from the tradition of narrative theory, these stories seek to recast the creation of analytic narratives in social contexts and contemporary relational theories. They depict ongoing therapeutic process and heightened interactive events and moments that together expand personal scope and change life directions for both partners in the analytic dyad. Its stories illuminate sometimes difficult and arcane analytic theory, bringing the meanings and utility of theory into living action. They also show how familiar emotions such as love, hate, envy, and loneliness, and active human values such as empathy, generosity, and good faith function in psychoanalytic interaction. In short, these analytic stories are useful teaching tools.

The narrative tales in this book address a wide range of history and emotions in both patients and analyst. The patients, fictionalized characters from a lifetime of analytic practice, are protagonists with backgrounds of trauma, loss, relational and geographical dislocation, but also successful adaptations and struggle toward self-development. Some of their stories describe intense short-term work and others long-term analytic relationships. The subjective experience and responses of the analyst are also central parts of the analytic fictions.

The book will be invaluable to readers curious about psychoanalysis, for therapists, and especially for teachers of therapeutic issues and process.

Dr. Joye Weisel-Barth is a senior instructor, training analyst, and supervisor at the Institute of Contemporary Psychoanalysis in Los Angeles. Her psychological and analytic practice is in Encino, California. Joye is a frequent contributor to major psychoanalytic journals and serves on several editorial boards.

Theoretical and Clinical Perspectives on Narrative in Psychoanalysis

The Creation of Intimate Fictions

Joye Weisel-Barth

LONDON AND NEW YORK

First published 2021
by Routledge
2 Park Square, Milton Park, Abingdon, Oxon OX14 4RN

and by Routledge
52 Vanderbilt Avenue, New York, NY 10017

Routledge is an imprint of the Taylor & Francis Group, an informa business

© 2021 Joye Weisel-Barth

The right of Joye Weisel-Barth to be identified as author of this work has
been asserted by her in accordance with sections 77 and 78 of the
Copyright, Designs and Patents Act 1988.

All rights reserved. No part of this book may be reprinted or reproduced or
utilised in any form or by any electronic, mechanical, or other means, now
known or hereafter invented, including photocopying and recording, or in
any information storage or retrieval system, without permission in writing
from the publishers.

Trademark notice: Product or corporate names may be trademarks or
registered trademarks, and are used only for identification and explanation
without intent to infringe.

British Library Cataloguing-in-Publication Data
A catalogue record for this book is available from the British Library

Library of Congress Cataloging-in-Publication Data
Names: Weisel-Barth, Joye, author.
Title: Theoretical and clinical perspectives on narrative in psychoanalysis:
the creation of intimate fictions/Joye Weisel-Barth.
Description: Abingdon, Oxon; New York, NY: Routledge, 2021. |
Includes bibliographical references and index. |
Identifiers: LCCN 2020031203 (print) | LCCN 2020031204 (ebook) |
ISBN 9780367542528 (hbk) | ISBN 9780367542511 (pbk) | ISBN
9781003088356 (ebk)
Subjects: LCSH: Psychoanalysis. | Psychotherapist and patient. |
Psychoanalysis and literature.
Classification: LCC BF173 .W4175 2021 (print) | LCC BF173 (ebook) |
DDC 150.19/5--dc23
LC record available at https://lccn.loc.gov/2020031203
LC ebook record available at https://lccn.loc.gov/2020031204

ISBN: 978-0-367-54252-8 (hbk)
ISBN: 978-0-367-54251-1 (pbk)
ISBN: 978-1-003-08835-6 (ebk)

Typeset in Bembo
by MPS Limited, Dehradun

Contents

Credits	viii
Preface	x
Introduction I: Stories, imagination, language, and the development of mind	1
Introduction II: Sample stories	16
1 On my becoming an analyst: An overview of the contemporary analytic world	23
2 On analytic certainty and delinquent dissembling: The case of Sharon	53
3 Analyst envy in working with an artist: Four scenes	60
4 Thinking and writing about complexity theory in the clinical setting	79
5 Waking sleeping beauty in the case of Emily: Mutual dissociation from a systems perspective	97
6 Stuck: Choice and agency in psychoanalysis	105
7 Malignant loneliness and its clinical implications	125
8 Bad faith and analytic failure	132
9 Temporal disturbance in the case of Maya: Musical dissonance, and the failure of future vision	139
10 Courting the "real" and stumbling in "reality": Confusions and hazards of relational practice	155
11 Katherine: A long, hard case	165
Index	184

Credits

Material from The Poems of Emily Dickinson: Reading Edition edited by Ralph W. Franklin, Cambridge, Mass.: Reprinted with permission: The Belknap Press of Harvard University Press,
Copyright © 1998, 1999 by the President and Fellows of Harvard College.
Copyright © 1951, 1955 by the President and Fellows of Harvard College.
Copyright © renewed 1979, 1983 by the President and Fellows of Harvard College. Copyright © 1914, 1918, 1919, 1924, 1929, 1930, 1932, 1935, 1937, 1942 by Martha Dickinson Bianchi. Copyright © 1952, 1957, 1958, 1963, 1965 by Mary L. Hampson.

Temporal Disturbance in the Case of Maya: Musical Dissonance and the Failure of Future Vision, Psychoanalytic Inquiry, November 2018, reprinted by permission of the publisher (Taylor & Francis Ltd, http://www.tandfonline.com).

Analyst Envy in Working with an Artist: Four Scenes, Psychoanalytic Dialogues, December 2008, reprinted by permission of the publisher (Taylor & Francis Ltd, http://www.tandfonline.com).
Stuck: Choice and Agency in Psychoanalysis, Psychoanalysis: Self and Context, June 2009, reprinted by permission of the publisher (Taylor & Francis Ltd, http://www.tandfonline.com).

Katherine: A Long, Hard Case, Psychoanalysis: Self and Context, March 2010, reprinted by permission of the publisher (Taylor & Francis Ltd, http://www.tandfonline.com).

The Case of Emily: Analyst Dissociation From a Systems Perspective, Psychoanalysis: Self and Context, March 2020, reprinted by permission of the publisher (Taylor & Francis Ltd, http://www.tandfonline.com).

Credits ix

On Analytic Certainty and Delinquent Dissembling: The Case of Sharon, Psychoanalysis: Self and Context, March 2020, reprinted by permission of the publisher (Taylor & Francis Ltd, http://www.tandfonline.com).

Courting the "Real" and Stumbling in "Reality": Confusions and Hazards of Relational Practice,Psychoanalysis: Self and Context, April 2016, reprinted by permission of the publisher (Taylor & Francis Ltd, http://www. tandfonline.com).

Preface

In psychoanalysis analytic partners create, modify, and destroy emotional worlds. They do this through exploring and enacting the themes and patterns in a patient's life and ordering them into a story. In creating a life story, they mark all the ways the patient's choices and behaviors created a self; that is, there is no self without a story, without a protagonist who does things and, in turn, is done to. I call this process the creation of "intimate fictions."

The created analytic worlds emerge in a larger context—called culture—consisting of imaginative constructs like family, country, democracy, etc.; and the stories we tell about the analytic exploration and its contexts—called theories—are more intimate fictions. Psychoanalysis, then, consists of layers of narratives that exist within and describe and traverse time.

Patients and therapists, fully and dramatically engaged with each other, create emergent space that transcends the individual worlds of the partners. The created analytic space has many names: intersubjective, transcendent, transitional, illusory, dyadically expanded states of consciousness, the two person unconscious, and the third. This book seeks to describe analytic encounters in this space, to tell their stories—personal, clinical, and professional—their intersections, the cultural contexts in which they occur, the nature of the space they create, and the complex, recursive, creative, and destructive processes they may set in motion. It also tells a story about the meanings and purposes of these encounters.

To begin simply, analytic work is fictional because relationships grow out of contextually informed and mutual verbal and non-verbal emotional exchanges that continually recede into the past. The act of interpreting, negotiating, and writing about these past exchanges requires translating them into words. To find those words, the analyst and patient must use their[1] imaginations to filter memories, associations, metaphors, and specific explicit and enacted moments of experience. Then with or without the patient's participation, the analyst must order the experience into a temporal sequence or narrative. This is the process of fictional creation.

Because I love stories, I will mainly describe this process through telling different clinical tales. One story in the book—often operating underground but continuing in real time—is autobiographical. That is, it's about my developing identity and comfort as a psychoanalyst. It's a narrative about my efforts and difficulties in understanding, juggling, and integrating not only the factors that are active in the field and in myself, but also the conflicts and contradictions between those factors: between memory and historical accuracy; recapturing the past and moving into the future; received theories, preferred theories, and new ideas; the self and culture; the self and power structures; the self and the other; the intrapsychic, intersubjective, and intercultural; empathy and authenticity; theoretical convictions and clinical experience; moments of enactment and ongoing contextual processes, etc. In developing my analytic identity, then, I realize how heavily I have relied on—and also struggled against—a multitude of stories to hold and contain all these factors and contradictions. Who I am as an analyst springs from my imaginative interactions with autobiographical, literary, clinical, and theoretical tales.

Another focus in the book, the primary story, is about my patients and me and what we do together in treatment. I emphasize mutual dramatic action as central to development and change. Particularly, I want to describe the creation of relational space and the "intimate fictions" that emerge from the peculiar human interactions in that space. Intimate fictions begin with the patient's historical and familial and personal stories. These accord, clash with, or converge in the analytic relationship with the analyst's own life stories; and in their jointly constructed analytic space, the analytic pair begin to enact, react to, and otherwise play with their common themes. As a result of their mutual recursive interactions, new and enlarged and more comprehensive stories emerge; lives are written anew, and possible futures spring forth. Hence, the stories that I call intimate fictions—jointly created interactive dramas and life narratives that emerge in relational space—are the vehicles both for shifting, and sometimes retiring, old and calcified self-concepts and for initiating new movement into the future. In fact, I argue that these dramatic stories have value to the extent that they advance new forays into the future.

Complicating the process of meeting and melding differing stories is the fact that each of us carries multiple stories about ourselves that reflect differing self-states. This is true for therapist as well as patient. At any given moment, there may be hundreds of potential stories present in the shared therapeutic space. For example, while at times I may be the hero of one personal tale, at other times, in a different tale I may be the victim of cruel forces beyond my control. Which story emerges in any given encounter depends on many factors: the emotional climate in which the original event took place, the narrator's emotional state at the time of the telling, the receptivity of the listener, the way the presented story matches or challenges the dominant story in the listener's mind, and how the listener responds. In the cases here I attempt to describe how each partner in the therapeutic relationship juggles the many interacting stories alive in any analytic meeting.

Both sets of stories—the autobiographical and relational—try to capture moments of understanding and emotional growth. Yet, these moments do not stand alone. Their meaning and emotional value derive from the life contexts

xii *Preface*

and narratives from which they emerge, from the exigencies of the present circumstance, and from their capacity to transform old, usually pathogenic stories. While the autobiographical moments are occasionally about some wonderful personal vision of mine, mostly they describe my ongoing subjective efforts to comprehend the other and my analytic difficulties, everything from therapeutic stumbles and clashes to crushing disappointment and disillusionment. All of this is in the quest of capturing important relational moments that occur within co-created analytic space, moments in which a patient and I separately andor together seize on or are seized by something new or when we experience something old in a new light or from a wider shared angle. It is then that something affectively fresh occurs, something that may alter a life story and change its direction.

In the book I have also tried to integrate a third kind of story, this one about analytic writing. I want to show the pleasures and the difficulties of catching the analytic pursuit in words. How does one tell about an analytic relationship when doing so creates a double fiction, a fiction about fictitious relational space? Like consciousness, psychoanalysis is one of those big subjects that we think we know until we try to describe it. It's frustrating, like trying to catch a meteor shower—too many energy flurries spraying in too many directions and all at once. And besides, we are inside the shower and so can't see its lineaments and boundaries. Historical, political, sociological, theoretical, experiential—all of these perspectives are relevant to the subject and are part of any analytic story. But how to include all of these perspectives in a coherent narrative!

And then there is the language we use. Psychoanalytic conversations between different schools are often like visits between distant relatives. Although there may be strong family resemblance, the cousins don't really know each other. While not remembering the old enmities that caused alienation between their grandparents and great-grandparents, by now the cousins rarely attend the same family parties. They don't share inside jokes or silly songs or made-up language or memorable incidents or small familiarities that make for "kissin' cousins." And separate language usages have developed since the family split; in other words, analysts from different schools no longer share the same tongue.

For example, they often use the same abstract term in different ways—think "the unconscious," "trauma," "the self," and "countertransference" and all the myriad meanings of those terms. Conversely, they also use different terms to convey similar meanings—for example, think "language action" for neo Freudians and "multi-modal nonverbal communication systems" for contemporary analysts. With respect to specific concepts, psychoanalysis is also burdened by abstract terms that are archaic, have lost their original, theoretically linked meanings, or have been adopted by different analytic schools and consequently attained meanings different from their original usage. I think of wonderful extinct psychoanalytic words like "cathexis" and "abreaction"; of terms like "Oedipal and "death instinct" that are dependent on libido theory;

Given these language anomalies, how, then, do we talk to each other as part of a common family about our family issues? And how do we teach candidates and the interested public about the richness and power of psychoanalysis? In constructing my analytic tales here, I have tried to avoid abstract terms, to present theoretical ideas in plain English, and to define the abstract terms I do use.

I also have two received formats to use as writing templates. The first, and most widely used, is the format for journal articles: present a problem, review the literature, present clinical illustrations, and then offer and discuss one's conclusions. This format provides both a scaffold and familiar container for complex exploration.

The second format, after Freud's early cases, are extended case descriptions with relevant theoretical material arising from the clinical descriptions and interspersed and integrated in the ongoing narrative. I like this format best, and it works well in many of my papers. Here I initially register the narratives that patients tell about themselves and their lives; I listen especially for style, structure, themes, details, and tone and draw from relevant theory in order to deconstruct the narratives with my patients. I also try to burrow imaginatively into the life space of my patient, attempting to absorb the textures and the cultural and emotional climates of her life. In addition, capturing my subjective responses to the patient's material is central to any analytic story, and articulating how my subjectivity affects the ongoing process is key to the tale I will tell. Finally, I examine the processes by which my patients and I together author new stories about our analytic relationship and thereby—in successful therapy—also revise our original personal narratives. Such revisions allow for new emotional possibilities and freedoms along with increased senses of efficacy and agency and aliveness.

The layered processes I've described are similar to what the anthropologist Clifford Geertz terms "thick description" (Geertz, 1973). According to Geertz, thick description is a methodology that requires deep immersion in the culture of the other; it requires explaining the meaning of human action from as much detailed description of the contexts, behaviors, and semiotics of the culture as possible. In addition to registering the details of the culture being observed, it also requires the observer's active participation and engagement in the settings being reported, what I would term active empathy, as well as cultural immersion. Thick description is more like a novel than non-fiction in the richness of its narratives. It is also like a novel in that it presents each culture—just as the novelist presents each character—as unique in its approach to dealing with human questions of meaning.

From this definition, it is clear that practicing psychoanalysis—when it is practiced well—is an act of creativity and "thick description." And I suggest that the act of making intimate fictions takes many forms and constitutes the heart of therapeutic action.

Finally, I write in the book from a subjective, developmental point of view, which allows me to describe experiences, observations, and discoveries about

xiv *Preface*

the complex field as I move along. And because I've practiced a long time, I've moved a long way. My adolescent discovery of psychoanalysis and its astonishing promise first lured me into the various wonders and snares of classical and ego psychology. Later clinical experience and growing curiosity led me to some new theories that captivated but in time disappointed me, to others that captivated me and have stuck, and then to the heart of my continuing interest in the work: my encounters with other minds and the creative processes that such encounters set in motion. My favorite stories are told by relational self psychologists, interpersonalists, and relational thinkers, particularly those that hold to field theories and a dynamic systems process. Because development in time is so central to how I think about work and life, I'm also always looking to the future to imagine what is coming next in order both to illuminate what I know and introduce me to what I don't.

This would be an arrogant .enterprise if I .didn't hope that my long experience might be useful to other therapists and analysts and curious lay people. They are my audience. Colleagues have requested and sometimes appreciated my analytic tales for teaching purposes, telling me that they are in need of dramatic stories that illustrate sometimes abstract and arcane psychoanalytic theories. This book is an effort to answer this need. I have tried here to present some dramatic instances of what contemporary analysis looks and feels like in action. I also have tried to integrate important analytic theories and emotional concepts with my clinical stories and to include the ideas I consider the best of my analytic inheritance and most helpful in my work. Beginning with my disillusionment with ego psychology, I'll chart my excitement with and immersion in self psychology, intersubjectivity theory, complexity theory, infant research, attachment theory, neuroscience, and narrative theory. At the same time, I'll describe my attempt to integrate ideas from these different models with both relational theories of trauma, dissociated states of mind, and enactment and interpersonal ideas about counter-transference and authenticity in therapeutic action. More and more it seems that I use theory instrumentally; that is, as it is useful to me in particular moments and in particular cases. Finally, in some of these papers I will try to resurrect and recast some old, useful emotional concepts—such as envy, loneliness, compassion, and love—in contemporary relational terms.

As this book caps my long career as a psychologist and psychoanalyst, I also want it to capture the joy of creation in psychoanalytic interaction. Whatever the metaphors—the easy ecstasy of flow, a soaring jazz riff, a graceful dance, a flight on a trapeze—I want to describe how the meeting, gradual coordination, and then playful interaction of minds not only result in mutually constructed analytic space and transforming experience, but also in the mutual pleasure of jointly created intimate stories.

Of course, people entering therapy are usually anything but joyful. They tiptoe tentatively, trudge, or stumble into our offices. They are morose, dull-eyed, and filled with fear; they are resentful, angry, self-pitying, self-blaming and sad; and they are defensively affable or simply weary and worn.

Reality dilemmas and current losses and memories of ancient pain weigh heavily. Patients often seem like prisoners tethered to and dragging distressingly heavy life stories behind. Manacles of reminiscence, restraints of worry, and chains of repetitive, circular thought and negative self-attributions bind them to old histories and obstruct their life energies. Frequently, I doubt my ability to help them liberate themselves. Sometimes, with the bleakest new patients, I question the possibility of liberation entirely.

But then the relationship begins for both partners: a moment of silent understanding, an attuned comment, an unselfconscious anecdote, a glint of curiosity in the patient's eye. Then, after some time together, a reference occurs to a previous exchange in the therapy or a shared smile of embryonic familiarity flashes—a slight loosening of emotional constraint, which indicates that something old is breaking down and something new, the glimmer of a new history, is in the works. Relational threads of nascent memories have started to knit. What the finished fabric, the analytic story, looks like depends on the desired design, the intricacies of it rhythms and forms, the colors and textures of the threads, the tightness or looseness of the weave, and the warp and woof, the particularities and eccentricities of analyst and patient in creative interaction. That the outcome is so often a surprise, so different from the initial vision and expectation, testifies to the creative dimension of the analytic pursuit and the uniqueness of each of our intimate fictions.

There are many people who are loved parts of my personal analytic story and I want to acknowledge them here. My analysts, Philip Oderberg and Janet Hadda, participated with me in therapeutic relationships that opened worlds of emotional connections and understandings. My mentors and colleagues (among many unnamed) Judith Pickles, Estelle Shane, Kati Breckenridge, Lewis Aron, Steven Stern, Judy Teicholz, Helen Ziskind, Helen Grebow, and Daniel Goldin have helped to hone my psychoanalytic stories. Important teachers, many of them dead, Loewald, Kohut, Mitchell, Stolorow, Lachmann, Beebe, Sander, Daniel Stern, D.B. Stern, Lyons-Ruth, have helped shape my thinking. And friends and family, especially my darling husband Lewis Barth, have supported and encouraged my professional explorations.

Note

1 For simplicity, I will use "she" and "her" for all gender designations.

Reference

Geertz, C. (1973) Thick Description: Toward an Interpretive Description of Cultures. In *The Interpretation of Cultures: Selected Essays*. New York: Basic Books, pp. 3–30.

Introduction I
Stories, imagination, language, and the development of mind

My personal odyssey

I'll begin my book about analytic fictions with some personal memory stories.

In first grade we wrote stories on a folded paper. The part above the fold was for pictures; the part below was for the words. My assignment: write about what I want to be when I grow up and draw a picture to illustrate. My uncle was a cameraman in the movies and often talked about his work. And I loved movie cowboys, especially Hopalong Cassidy. And so, for my school assignment I drew myself as a leather-fringed cowgirl riding a horse, and I wrote about being an actor in western movies. Years later, I found the story in a folder, which my mother had saved. I was surprised to see that in the process of writing about being an actor, I had shifted the time sequence in my story from future to present. From my beginning statement, "When I grow up, I want to be a cowgirl in the movies," the story became, "It only looks like I'm riding when my horse galups. Really, the seenary moves along, and I sit still and don't worry about falling off the horse." This was my first intimation of how outside of my awareness my imagination—in interaction with my desires and ambitions, my uncle's information, my movie experiences, and my surrounding Hollywood culture—created a new story, no longer hypothetical but alive, active, and present. Imagination time trips.

When I was 6 or 7 years old, I wanted a collection of my own. Bobby, the boy down the street, collected stamps. I loved their colors and designs and was excited to identify where they came from on his world globe. But I didn't have any money or know where to buy stamps of my own, and so I decided on a rock collection. Rocks were plentiful and free in my neighborhood. I spent several afternoons after school gathering various specimens: rocks of different textures and colors and striations. But then I felt anxious and flummoxed. What to do with my shoebox full of specimens, how to name and classify them? Bobby had a set of encyclopedias at his house, The Book of Knowledge. *The "R" book had many pictures of rocks. Trouble was my rocks didn't match any of those pictures exactly enough. I couldn't confidently name even one of them and, recognizing my incapacity, felt panic rising inside. Basalt, quartz, obsidian—I couldn't tell which were what, what the names meant, where they came from, and, sadly, there was nobody to ask for help. My aloneness hurt, and I knew I needed somebody else's trained eyes, somebody else's knowing mind, to help me put my collection in some kind of order. I felt*

2   *Introduction I*

small, incompetent, lonely, without a story to tell about rocks, with only a failure story to tell about myself. I aborted my nascent rock collection.

The summer before college I had my first conversations with Dr. Freud. I read An Outline of Psychoanalysis *and from it gleaned an astonishing idea: that in dialogue with an "analyst" I could come to understand my hidden self–my passions and my longings and the reasons for my confusions. Thus fortified, I would always be able to make clear, good choices for myself. At the time my adolescent choices seemed muddled and messy: most of the time I felt confused, paralyzed or brain dead, certainly inadequately prepared to think for myself or else too excitable, impressionable, and impulsive to make good choices. Understanding myself and putting the mess of my mind in order seemed an even more daunting task than organizing my childhood rock collection. But now Dr. Freud was telling me that he could help me make sense of myself, that I could—with some of his magic—both know what makes me tick and control my own mind. I might move into the future with a confidence I could only imagine. A great mind nurturing my little developing one—hopeful and astonishing! I wanted my own analyst, but, unfortunately, all my summer job money was designated for a typewriter for college. Analysis had to wait.*

Stories! Stories about origins: these three memory stories chart discoveries about aspects of my own mind. I have remembered/recreated them in the context of introducing this book, and so my purpose informs what I have remembered. *Nachträglichkeit*, time tripping! That is, these are fictional stories whose relation to veridical happenings in the past is murky and whose place in time is slippery. The best I can say is that the ones I have recovered/created are true to my current subjective states, my need for understanding, and the purposes of this introduction. And these short narratives—like all stories—condense layers of feeling and meaning.

The first vignette tells of discovery about the nature and power of stories. This short memory tale describes the importance of human and cultural contexts in the creation of memory stories, the centrality of interest and desire in the generation of story themes, the ways in which imagination kneads and refashions facts, how identity stories can mix and meld wish with reality, and how the manner of telling reveals the mind of the story teller—all this contained in a few lines. I was a funny little girl who loved movies and that I lived in Los Angeles where movies were made. I was never clear whether I wanted to be a cowgirl or a cowgirl in the movies, but this memory story argues for the latter. I was also a prissy storyteller, too intent on explaining away the magic of movie making to get into much dramatic action.

These days it's fashionable and cliché to remark that words limit and/or flatten emotional experience. As aspects of non-verbal communication garner increased attention in the analytic world, and the subtleties and nuances of non-verbal and sub-symbolic emotional processes are recognized, traditional verbal expression often gets short shrift. Some commentators—like the Boston Change Process Study Group—critique the traditional emphasis on cognitive understanding and verbal interpretation as interfering with non-verbal therapeutic action. Certainly, some of the cognitive excesses of ego psychology deserve such criticism. However, language—especially in its metaphorical and narrative uses—has the power of all art to deepen and expand boundaries of understandings, to complexify human experience, and even to create what previously did not exist. In this book I argue that the stories we tell—and how they alter over time in the context of a psychoanalytic relationship—can provide understanding of the psychological change process itself.

The second discovery is about the slipperiness of experience and the ways in which memory and imagination cause experience and time to shape-shift. At about ten when I first began to observe myself, I puzzled that my inner stories and dialogues often ran in directions sharply afield from actual "facts"; that is, from what I knew to be true about people and events and myself in time. This is when I began to write down the stories of my life in locked, store-bought diaries. Without any thought or rationale, I directed my diary entries to an imaginary person, "Dear Jane." Somehow, writing to Jane—a name obliquely attached to a favorite teacher and an admired aunt—created an imaginary listener and dialogue that deepened the scrutiny of my personal experience.

In the course of writing in my diary I noticed that desire fueled my directional and temporal leaps; that is, shifts and oscillations in my focus and attention somehow related to my hopes and longings about other people and myself. Yet, the fantasies I wrote about seemed propelled from an inner source beyond my awareness or control, and they seemed absolutely real. So out tumbled a sparkling Joye in these stories—a swell protagonist, a Joye I would love to be—savvy, confident, adventurous, articulate, and much beloved; a Joye older than and yet the same age as the dreaming little girl; a Joye very different from the shy and awkward one that accompanied me into the world. I wanted "Dear Jane" to know this expansive me and to like her. Confusing indeed, and I sometimes wondered if I were crazy or had an inner trickster conjuring images and stories in my head. Kohut had not yet explained to me the child's need for affirmation in her experiments to enlarge and deepen her life space.

The third discovery, embodied in the story about my rock collection, was that in order to think I also needed other minds to help me. In creating Jane, I must have known this intuitively. The softly assembled nature of mental development moves along and revises itself as mind fuses with and borrows from other minds. Growing up with a depressed father and a vibrant but self-centered mother—neither of whom had much interest in children—I often felt lost and lonely in my mind. Whether I struggled with rock collections or the confusing social world of elementary school, I had no adult to help me figure things out. As the rock collection episode demonstrates, loneliness of mind is an impediment to curiosity and growth.

And so by adolescence I alternated between, on the one hand, making stories in my head or on paper to ease my loneliness, make sense of my extended world, and clear some of my mental cobwebs and, on the other hand, searching for books and friends and mentors with whom to interact. Writing stories for an interested and responsive audience—if only in my imagination—constituted

4   *Introduction I*

enlarging and consolidating "interactions"; but over time real, live people became increasingly important.

And then Dr. Freud came along with explanations and promises. He confirmed that I wasn't crazy; everyone has hidden sources of desire and conflicts, sources that cloud one's mental hold on reality and relationships and cause our minds to leap and soar into irrational realms. But with analytic help these hidden parts are accessible to consciousness and amenable to clarification and narrative. With an analyst I might lift the curtain on my longings and conflicts and, thereby, figure out the big puzzles of life: how to know what I really want and think, how to talk to people without tripping over my tongue, and how to pursue my heart's desires.

The implication that I might eventually know my own mind well enough that I would no longer need any help from anybody really appealed to me. I've always been one of those "I can do it myself" folks. The lonely little girl, who longed for connection with others, liked the compensatory fantasy of sufficiency in her own mind, the illusion of security through complete independence from others. Alas, life has disconfirmed this particular fantasy! Nevertheless, the promise of psychic autonomy was, in part, the impetus for choosing my life path. Field theories and my life of real human relationships have exploded the wonderful Freudian myth of solitary independence; instead, living in the world validates the continued human developmental need for and usefulness of other minds as well as the value of the analytic pursuit.

Except for the fantasy that our minds can exist and function independently from other minds—that one is cast permanently into my childhood illusion pit—I am still occupied with my early discoveries. Later, I hoped that as an analyst I might facilitate growth processes in others. And so, across many years of psychoanalytic practice, I am still curious about the changes wrought through the imaginative meetings and convergences and expansions of mind that occur for my partners and me, separately and together, in analytic space. Thus, to repeat: this book concerns itself with the stories we bring to analysis and the intimate fictions we create from them.

Stories that open and stories that close: theoretical and clinical narratives in psychoanalysis with literature review

The above memory stories are simply meant to illustrate that we live our subjective lives in stories, organizing our experience with motivated human behavior in temporally structured narratives. From the present moment stories, which Daniel Stern describes, stories of ten seconds or less duration, to great literary epics like the Bible and the Iliad of long temporal sweeps, we shape our life significance in stories of human interaction. This is one way that we become agents, the authors of our lives. In psychoanalysis, too, we make theory stories and clinical stories to convey complex human meaning, meaning reflective of our social contexts and our individual relational worlds.

Introduction I 5

Yet, as I think about the enlarging power of rich narrative, I also think about the limitations of closed stories, the ways in which fixed and rigid stories about our lives, theories, and clinical work limit growth and development both personally, culturally, and professionally. This, too, will be a topic in the book. But before addressing limitations in the stories we tell, I want to illustrate the power of stories using some of the literary stories that grabbed and shook me and expanded my horizons as a child—more autobiography, this time in the guise of literature.

Mostly the childhood stories I loved were surprising, amazing, and had a "present tenseness" about them. By "present tenseness" I mean they pulled me into their world; they created the feeling that I was there in the story, a witness to action—sometimes even an imaginary player—in real time. Even in tales about the past, the best ones created the anxious questions "Next? What comes next?" These questions, then, put me in the action with a forward leaning thrust, a desirable posture, by the way, for analytic work.

My favorite stories had characters I could identify with but who did novel and remarkable things beyond my experience, things that challenged my understanding of how things worked or were supposed to work. Unexpected things happened to these characters, and they faced situations that I didn't understand, that frightened me, or that left me wondering about some larger existential questions—although, admittedly, as a kid I didn't know the term "existential." Most of all, the best stories moved me to question myself: Could I have done that? How did she ever find the courage to do this? In other words, the best stories not only surprised and thrilled me and fostered empathy in me for others, but they also made me confront my own vulnerability, my questionable courage, and my shame.

For example, in kindergarten there was a story about four orphaned children who ran away from the orphan police. The children found and set up house-keeping in an old sidetracked boxcar. Jeopardy and challenges! For a time they survived through hard work and loads of ingenuity. I especially liked the way one of the sisters decorated the boxcar from gathered junk. *The Boxcar Children* delighted and surprised me—and also raised my self-doubts. Could children really survive without parents? What would I have done in that situation, and how did those children gain the cleverness and presence of mind to take care of themselves? This little book awakened in me a passion for agency.

I remember vividly my first grownup novel, *Mrs. Mike*, secreted when I was about 8 from the adult section of my public library. A woman in Northern Canada loses her two little children—they die from diphtheria. After grieving, she adopts two Native children, and at the end of the book she is happy. When the first set of children died, I felt unstrung—shocked and heartbroken that they were suddenly dead. Not only was I terrified of getting diphtheria, I was changed by this fictional confrontation with death—its present tenseness. The story opened other possibilities for me, like empathy, identity, and difference. I realized, "I can understand this grownup and her sadness. Maybe grownups aren't so different from me after all?" And I also wondered, "How/why did

6   *Introduction I*

the mother get better from death? Do parents really get over the death of their children? That's strange!"

Less heavy than *Mrs. Mike* was Nancy Drew whom I loved. Nancy was a girl with no mother, little supervision, and her own blue roadster. And she found interesting people and solved mysteries in her little town. I never knew a girl as free and brave as Nancy Drew. Or as lucky: no mother and a little blue roadster!

And there were Bible boys, Biblical heroes chosen for big tasks. First Moses, who with God's help frees the Jews from slavery and receives God's law; then David, who with God's help kills giants, becomes a mighty general, and rules the Kingdom of Israel; and finally Jesus, who with God's help brings a message of eternal life to suffering people but then, forsaken by God, suffers a creepy and detailed death for reasons my child's brain just couldn't fathom. These stories were strange, full of adventure and challenges and complicated denouements. The Bible Boys did well with God's tasks, but .personally their. endings were sad. Did God really help his favorites do amazing things and then, after they did his bidding, just drop them? Was this really the fate of possessing courage and brave hearts? No fair—the idea distressed me. And what about girls—the Bible Girls in these stories were pretty but mostly passive and bland; any place for bold and gutsy women? Big questions and big ideas grow from specific stories about human action.

These literary memories again emphasize the power of stories to waken and feed curiosity and empathy, to waken us to larger worlds. These are the same tasks we want to accomplish as analysts with our patients. Stories, narratives, actions over time reveal character, quirks, personal standards, human connections, social values, and even universal meanings! Stories do all this and then some, and good ones often cover many of these bases simultaneously. Good stories embody webs of experience that readers and listeners register on different levels and in different modes often at the same time. Good stories also often shake or shatter our conventional assumptions, cultural expectations and received ways of thinking; they open our minds and imaginations, thereby expanding empathy, and maybe they even crack some adamantine shibboleths.

Yes, these are the good stories, ones open to nuance and complexity and change; they are the kinds we hope to cultivate in our analytic relationships. However, in practice we also adopt other theoretical and clinical stories that are not so good, ones that are fixed and immovable, predictable or cliched, stuck in time, and stultifying to growth and development. Our patients, too, often bring calcified stories about themselves that function to maintain defeating life patterns. In short, psychoanalysis has varieties of closed narratives, both theoretical and clinical, that shut down thinking and emotions. Recognizing their limitations and opening them to scrutiny and change is a large part of analytic work.

We love stories and must need them because we make so many of them and invite them into our every encounter: "How was your day?" is an invitation for a story. "Tell me more" is another invitation; and so is our analytic stand by, "Uh Huh?" All of these inquiries convey our curiosity, interest, and our wish to be drawn into, live in, and expand the other's story. Some researchers suggest that language arose so that we could share gossipy stories communally. Certainly, we're fascinated by what A did to B; why X hates Y; and especially how J landed in bed with K (Dunbar, 2004; Hsu, 2008). These same researchers suggest that 65% of all human communication is of the "gossipy story" variety (Dunbar, 2004, p. 100). Evidently, we need such stories about the lives of others in order to enlarge our limited human horizons with empathic imagination.

Neuroscientists describe neurochemical brain processes that issue from good stories and serve to promote empathy and intense emotions—like love and compassion (Zak, 2015). Zak, for example, has demonstrated the causal effects of increasing the level of the molecule oxytocin in the brain; that is, he found that increasing levels of oxytocin promotes prosocial behaviors. He says, "I now consider oxytocin the neurologic substrate for the Golden Rule: If you treat me well, in most cases my brain will synthesize oxytocin, and this will motivate me to treat you well in return" (Zak, 2015, p. 3). For the purposes of this paper, Zak's research has demonstrated that emotionally engaging narratives not only increase the levels of cortisol and oxytocin in the brain, but they also cause voluntary participants to act in prosocial ways after hearing the stories. As an instance, participants made charitable donations after viewing a wrenching tale of a father struggling to stay connected to his terminally ill young son.

Neuroscientists also tell us that stories recruit more parts of the brain—the visual, aural, kinesthetic, motor, and limbic parts of the brain—and create more psychic action than does any straightforward conceptual presentation. For example, fMRI's indicate that brains register the bullet points of a scientific talk in only limited areas: that is, only in the speech centers—the Broca's and Wernicke's areas—and some of the frontal cortex. But when you add to conceptual data feeling, sensation, action and narrative—that is, when you add a soulful story—brains light up globally. Colorful stories wake and enhance emotion, thereby activating the brain and intensifying feeling, enhancing empathy, and encoding memory. Neuronally speaking, stories are like Saturday night neon on the Las Vegas Strip. This may be why some of us snooze through speeches but are riveted and awake for stories.

Freud knew all this and appreciated the value of stories. All those early case histories—those memorable hysterics Anna O., Emmy von N, Katrina, and Dora; the Oedipal child "Little Hans"; the obsessive "Rat Man"; and the depressed "Wolf Man"—are strange and fascinating stories. Freud plays two roles in these cases. First, he is a reader of his patients, exhibiting the imagination and openness of a great reader of literature. Then, he is a guide, as any great writer is a guide, leading us on his narratives of discovery. We feel that Freud is learning and fashioning his ideas in present time as he is getting to know his patients. And best of all, he is taking us along, opening up new worlds for us. Each of Freud's cases is a story within a story. Each narrates a fascinating personal tale while, at the same time, illuminating and "selling" the

8   *Introduction I*

meta-story of psychoanalytic theory. Yes, Freud's storytelling skills successfully "sold" psychoanalysis in ways beyond what any presentation of theory could have done alone.

Freud tells his stories with rich detail, some suspense, and the suggestion of comprehensiveness. With each patient he presents a clear narrative arc that begins with psychic disorder and strange symptoms, moves to his analysis and brilliant analytic interventions, and concludes with symptom relief and resolution. Intermittently, he uses significant moments in the treatment to teach his theory. As a result of these literary gambits, he not only promotes his ideas, but also distracts readers from alternative possibilities and other narratives. In addition, the strange stories that support Freud's strange theories, in accretion and with repetition, transform the strangeness of the theory into something recognizably familiar and normative.

In the late twentieth century there was a period of intense interest in narrative which has since fallen off. Some mid- to late twentieth-century philosophers, psychoanalysts, and attachment theory researchers described human stories as central to the development of mind, relationships, and culture. I'll briefly review their ideas in the context of shifting theoretical and clinical analytic paradigms occurring at the time. My purpose is to revive their ideas and recast them in a relational mold.

For Freud and the ego psychologists, psychoanalysis rests on the related notions of the psyche as an objectively knowable, closed system—driven by internal biological forces—to which the analyst has access, and of the analyst as the neutral observer and purveyor of truth about the patient's mind and self. However, objective, knowable reality; intact but hidden truths buried in the past; the knowing analyst as archeologist and interpreter of the patient's closed psyche—these foundational Freudian ideas about epistemology, the mind, and the analytic pursuit met new challenges during the last decades of the last century. Paul Ricoeur, for example, the Continental philosopher, argued against essentialist versions of the human subject. People, for him, were neither rational isolated Cartesian minds nor decentered postmodern non-subjects, entirely dependent on language for self-definition. Rather, he argues for a hermeneutical phenomenological human who emerges through Narrative. According to Ricoeur, narrative describes the ways in which people experience time, the ways in which we understand ourselves in relation to past, present, and future.

Ricoeur suggests that one way we experience time is "cosmological time," which depicts an objective movement, a linear progression; another way is "phenomenological time," which subjectively captures relationships of past, present, and future as we contemplate the meanings of our life situations. "Human time," according to Ricoeur, occurs when we integrate these two disparate ways of experiencing the past: that is, we establish both causal and subjectively meaningful connections between life events—Ricoeur calls this "emplotment." In other words, we make up the stories of our life in time.

Importantly, we compose our stories from the vantage point of the subjectively experienced present, from a present state that patterns past events and renders them meaningful only from this later perspective. As we move through time, the narratives may change with changing circumstances and states. The future, too, is also grasped from the present as a set of possible but potential narratives. We generate these potential narratives through imagining possible choices, actions, and consequences as these reflect our current sense of self and meaning. That is, we make future stories. Thus, for the storied self of Ricoeur, subjectivity replaces Freudian objectivity, and created stories—narrative truths—replace fixed historical truths (Ricouer, 1983, 1984, 1985).

Several American psychoanalysts and psychologists adopted aspects of Ricoeur's epistemology and sensibility (e.g., Bruner, 1991; Shaefer, 1994; Spence, 1982, 1983). Spence, Shaefer, and Bruner agree that story-making is how humans organize experience, and all three of these theorists moved from Freudian positivism—belief in and reliance on objective reality—to qualified constructivism. By this term I mean a turning from verifiable, historical truth in the psychoanalytic situation to the pursuit of narrative truth. For Spence narrative truth is built up and established through a repetitive telling of one's life story, including the deconstructing, broadening, and elucidating of details of that life story. Spence acknowledges the existence of some extra-subjective reality, but he argues that analytic exploration has no access to such objective, historical truth. Rather, it relies on what he terms "psychic reality." He says,

> Psychic reality may, at any one time, contain elements of both historical and narrative truth, and its power to persuade is apparently independent of which truth is represented. In similar fashion, external reality is usually composed of both fact and fiction, and one consequence of analysis is to make the patient philosophically more sophisticated and less of a naïve realist.
>
> (Spence, 1982, pp. 49–50)

The power to persuade that Spence refers to is the creation of a life story that *feels* coherent and consistent.

Roy Shaefer (1994) is also skeptical of a positivist foundation of knowledge and truth in psychoanalysis and argues that the subjective generation of agency, responsibility, and the choice of a unique narrative of one's life are the goals of analysis. Like Spence, he suggests that the power of narrative rests in the active energy with which it was created and the coherence of the resulting story. Similarly, Jerome Bruner advances the idea that "… we organize our experience and our memory of human happenings mainly in the form of narrative—stories, excuses, myths, reasons for doing and not doing, and so on" (1991, p. 4). He goes on to suggest that "Unlike the constructions generated by logical and scientific procedures that can be weeded out by falsification, narrative constructions can only achieve 'verisimilitude'"(p. 4). That is, it is the felt correspondence of the story with the emotional experience of events that determines

10   *Introduction I*

its power and subjective truth. Hence, Bruner avers that narratives are versions of reality whose acceptance is determined by cultural convention and "narrative necessity" rather than empirical verification and logic.

Interestingly, Bruner, unlike Spence and Shaefer, takes the creation of narrative beyond an individual model and places it in a cultural context. He contends that personal narratives, beyond the personal experiences of their creator, absorb and reflect the particular culture in which they emerge. Bruner also catalogues significant features of narratives such as sequenced durativity (occurring in time), particularity (specificity of detail), intentionality, hermeneutic composability (residing in the domain of interpretation rather than empirical truth), canonicity and breach (good stories challenge or break with convention and expectation), normativeness (good stories pivot on trouble that shakes personal, social and cultural norms), context sensitivity, and narrative accrual (stories in accretion contribute to culture and history).

While Spence, Shaefer, and Bruner applaud the usefulness of coherent and consistent stories, Levenson (1988) argues for the deconstruction of tight, coherent stories to uncover meanings—and perhaps to reconstruct new and more complex tales. He argues that asking questions which deconstruct the patient's prepared text is "the driving force" of the analytic process:

> I am suggesting that the "mystery" (the secret core) of psychoanalysis also lies in the pursuit of the particular, and the peculiar deconstructed mosaic of data (not a coherent narrative) which emerges, whether presented in the form of fantasy, free association or Sullivan's detailed inquiry. The common denominator among experienced psychoanalysts of widely divergent doctrinary beliefs, may well be the ability to elicit sufficient data, under sufficient pressure. (p. 15)

Like Levenson, Daniel Stern (2004) views our lives as an accumulation of stories, some as short as three seconds in duration. Meanings derive from exploration and deconstruction of specific life experiences in time. Breaking large narratives into vivid pieces is akin to shattering glass into myriad shards: the act releases sharpness, sparkle, and shine, all the specific details and feelings that restore life to stale life stories. Therefore, Stern, like Levenson, urges therapists to slow down and focus attention and inquiry on the emotional specificities of our patients' memory tales.

Current attention to narrative emphasizes the relational dimensions in constructed life tales. In the analytic setting this means a two-person, intersubjective co-construction of theoretical and clinical tales. For example, the Adult Attachment Interview—the AAI (Main, 2000)—emphasizes the complicated interactive relational sources and surprising relational functions of the stories we tell about different attachment styles. The AAI traces the intergenerational transmission of attitudes and behaviors relating to human attachment. In the interview, adult subjects respond to questions about their childhood experiences with their parents, and the resulting stories of parental treatment reveal the parents' attachment styles; no surprise there. Yet, it is *how the subjects tell their attachment stories* that determines the attachment categories to which subjects themselves are assigned rather than the childhood memories *per se*. In addition, the linguistic style of subjects also predicts the attachment categories of their own children. Literary form and style here trump content!

The AAI demonstrates that interactive relational processes, many of them implicit, organize attitudes and behaviors with respect to others and also organize how these attitudes and behaviors are expressed in the stories we tell. Although it makes sense that relationally derived attitudes and behaviors in their families might create and reinforce the attachment styles of the interviewees, it is astonishing that they also predict linguistic style and the attachment styles of the subjects' children as well—even pre-birth! Also surprising is the stability of the identified categories over time.

In recent years analytic interest in narrative has mostly waned. Except for pop psychology books—e.g., Gottschall's *The Storytelling Animal: How Stories Make Us Human (2012)*—only a few thinkers like Lichtenberg and Goldin seriously address the importance of narrative in human development and in the analytic process. Lichtenburg has long recognized the power of stories in clinical work. He and Lachmann, for example, identified model scenes as vehicles for organizing puzzling information, integrating previous understanding, and initiating further exploration of experience. Model scenes are highly charged incidents which highlight and encapsulate experiences representative of salient conscious and unconscious motivational themes. Jointly created by analyst and patient, they are imaginative constructs—drawn from literature and/or transference and/or incandescent childhood events—that compress relational stories and convey experience dramatically. In analytic interaction I find model scenes to be very valuable, providing touchstones for understanding organizing patterns.

In addition, Lichtenberg et al. in *Narrative and Meaning* (2017) place story making in a rich matrix of development, time, body, culture, and familial and social relationships. They say, "In normal development story making has the important role of facilitating the daily process of self-definition. The child … is not only defining his past; he is creating his identity" (Lichtenberg et al., 2017, p. 10). In addition, Lichtenberg and colleagues emphasize narrative as "a process of enlivening the breadth and depth of a sense of self constantly attempting to adapt to intersubjective and adaptive possibilities" (p. 11). Finally, Lichtenberg et al. also suggest that story making is a fuller and more action-filled version of representation. I agree with this idea that life narratives are the psychic storage containers for crucial and complex relational meanings, a notion I will try to illustrate in this collection of clinical stories.

According to Daniel Goldin (2019), our sense of personal coherence depends on the kinds of stories we create and tell about ourselves. Borrowing from Aristotle, Ricoeur, Daniel Stern, and especially Bruner, Goldin posits, "When adults come to therapy, they come to tell their stories" (p. 661). The construction of such stories arises from the clash between the canonical ways

12   Introduction I

of an individual's world and "trouble," that is, problems that challenge one's cultural canons. A person's culture is his or her procedural memory of collective values and expectations, such memory organized early in one's first family and then later reinforced or modified in the larger worlds of school, social groups, and societal institutions. Goldin suggests that an event that upends one's cultural expectations, that surprises and foils unspoken predictions, that galvanizes attention and embeds itself in memory—this is the kind of experience that sets our stories in motion.

The descriptions of therapeutic process and narrative development as "trouble" and as a challenge to cultural canons reminds me of a central idea in complexity theory: that is, the idea that change and development occur through perturbations of existing systems. In dynamic systems thinking, culture would be a more or less fixed attractor state, the accretion, abstraction, and stabilization of the rules of procedure and engagement in one's first family and larger social order. Development occurs and memory and stories arise as relational interactions destabilize—challenge, expand, modify, or topple—the established attractor state. We may think of the analytic encounter as one such perturbation to the patient's psychological system. Our stories are about how we manage system perturbations. Over time and in accretion, the stories we tell about this process become increasingly integrated: thick, resonant, and nuanced. In complexity terms, our developed stories reflect larger and larger distributed networks.

The last entry in this short literature review is Stephen Grosz's *The Examined Life: How We Lose and Find Ourselves* (2013). This is an eclectic collection of psychoanalytic stories that depict the richness and strangeness of the narratives we encounter and help to create in our practices. Theoretical ideas also emerge from his well-told tales. Grosz presents himself as the facilitator of the creative process and uses his subjective experience not only to understand his patients but also to feel his way into their subjective worlds. Because my book is also mainly a collection of analytic tales drawn from my professional history, and because I focus on many of the psychic and intersubjective processes that interest Grosz, his model has been helpful to me. Although he and I have very different writing styles, like Grosz, the stories I present here contain relational interaction and personal subjective material. They highlight my commitment to a two-person, intersubjective lens on psychoanalysis.

Current analytic tales

Now I'll turn specifically to our current psychoanalytic tales. There are three kinds of analytic stories—explanatory theoretical stories, the tales our patients tell about themselves, and process stories of mutual clinical interaction.

As meaning-making creatures lusting for coherence but also liveliness, we analysts adore and rely on theoretical stories to help us understand our patients, do our work, and accord meaning to that work. We want to make sense of our encounters with the counterintuitive, irrational, and incomprehensible, and so

Introduction I 13

we create theory stories. In psychoanalysis we have many established, well-loved, and much-used theory stories. Mostly they're about pathology. Among them are the original "libido story"—too much of it and you're a psychological goner; the always handy "bad mother story"—too much of her or not enough of her, and you're a psychological goner; the "trauma story"—any of it and you're a psychological goner; and the "serotonin story"—too little of it ... well you get the idea. We also have some new, less organized stories about dynamic systems, bodymindbrain, and enactments; stories that are gathering but have not yet achieved fixed coherence.

Yet, it seems to me that, compared to great literature, our analytic theory stories are way too simple. In presenting our ideas about dyadic process and the goals of therapeutic interaction, we usually overstate our positions or fail to integrate competing positions. In doing this, we simplify reality. Often, in shining a spotlight on one set of observations, the emergent story may shadow and obscure other relevant and important material. Consequently, our simple story lines miss important complexities, particularly the complexities inherent in integrating competing analytic ideas or in tracking therapeutic interaction over time.

When we encounter a new paradigm or an exciting new lens through which to explore our work, we pounce on it. New theories often recruit interest and emphasis away from more established notions. Currently, ideas about dynamic systems, neuroscience, nonverbal communication, and enactments have captivated me. As a result, I tend to emphasize these ideas to the detriment of ideas about cognitive understanding, the intrapsychic, and explicit interpretations, concepts that are older and more familiar but still central to my work. I call this "the lopsided effect," which occurs when a new theory story diminishes the importance of older ones.

Then, with respect to the stories we do use, through repetition and overuse they tend to contract and lose complexity and surprise. Over time organizations become rigid and conclusions predictable. In other words, a storyline loses its immediacy, its "present tenseness"; and what, at first, seemed brilliant and new and allusive, may over time turn into dogmatic kitsch. Such fixed and familiar stories may then come to absorb data that may not actually fit. For example, the Oedipal story, once so culturally subversive, psychologically disruptive, and persuasive in the "Case of Little Hans," becomes cliched and often stretched and silly when applied universally to every analysand. The casual use of Brandchaft's powerful concept of "pathological accommodation" (Brandchaft et al., 2010) is another case in point. To my mind, commentators have vastly expanded and thus diminished its original meaning. Originally, the concept described a severe disturbance: a child's self-nullifying response to intrusive, emotionally overbearing, and narcissistic parents. Now writers frequently apply the term "pathological accommodation" indiscriminately to any form of child accommodation, even to common or trivial situations in which parents expect children to assimilate and accommodate to normative social behaviors.

Worst of all, our calcified theory stories affect our clinical work, causing it to become fixed and formal. Imposing a story too strictly on clinical material

14   *Introduction I*

suffocates rather than opens and animates analytic experience. Haven't we all known well-meaning colleagues—not us, of course!—who are over-reliant on a trusted theory and turn strident about the truth of their convictions? For example, two members of my study group, adherents of a well-loved trauma story, recently declared that Skype therapy is absolutely contraindicated for an eating disordered patient. They expressed this conviction with such certainty and vehemence that the group—and I—accepted it without question. Only several hours later did it occur to me to ask, "Without knowing the intricacies of a particular dyad, how can they be so sure?" Clinical interaction should come first; that is, ongoing patient-therapist interaction—and the partners' responses to it—should form the basis for creating and revising our explanatory stories.

To conclude: many psychoanalytic theories have become, over time, reductive and closed. Because of the limitations in fixed theories, many contemporary analysts choose to mix and match theory stories in order to expand understanding and to draw from different perspectives as each seems relevant to a particular interaction. Currently, I use analytic theories instrumentally, not as instruments of truth but simply as they deepen the meanings of specific clinical situations. However, that we borrow and meld ideas from different models and language games makes it sometimes seem that we are constructing theoretical Towers of Babel and that the consequent clinical stories often lack internal consistency.

With respect to the clinical stories our patients tell about themselves, the shape, coherence, and complexity with which they endow their narratives illuminate a great deal about the person's human interactions: how they were experienced, organized, and dealt with over time. Patients come with vague to specific and detailed memories; they tell carefully structured or confused and disorganized narratives; and they reveal that their storied experience may weigh and bow their development or else sit lightly on their lives. When we listen with an open ear, our patients' stories are—or are potentially—much richer and nuanced and stranger than most of our theories. Then, how we respond to and interact with these stories not only sets the direction of treatment but also influences the resulting stories that we and our patients tell.

The book draws from my own clinical experience to present examples of the psychoanalytic stories that we and our patients tell, what they reveal about the storytellers, how they are used in the work of analysis, and, in turn, how they facilitate emotional and psychic change. After a few sample clinical stories, Chapters 1 and 2 will tell autobiographical tales about my introduction and indoctrination into the psychoanalytic world. Chapters 3 through 7 use clinical stories to enhance theoretical ideas about envy, free will, complexity theory, malignant loneliness, and bad faith. And Chapters 8 through 11 explore how different kinds of clinical interaction, reflective of the uniqueness of each therapeutic coupling, create very different intimate fictions.

References

Brandchaft, B., Doctor, S., & Sorter, D. (2010) *Toward an Emancipatory Psychoanalysis: Brandchaft's Intersubjective Vision.* New York: Routledge.

Bruner, J. (1991) The Narrative Construction of Reality, *Crit. Inq.*, 18:1–21.

Dunbar, R. I. M. (2004) Gossip in Evolutionary Perspective, *Rev. Gen. Psychol.*, 8 (2):100–110.

Goldin, D. (2019) Storylines. *Psychoanal. Self. Cxt.*, 14 (2):161–177.

Gottschall, J. (2012) *The Storytelling Animal: How Stories Make Us Human.* Boston: Houghton/Miflin.

Grosz, S. (2013) *The Examined Life: How We Lose and Find Ourselves.* New York and London: W.W. Norton Company.

Hsu, J. (2008) The Secrets of Storytelling: Why We Love a Good Yarn: Our Love for Telling Tales Reveals the Workings of the Mind. *Sci. Am. Mind.*, 19 (4):46–51.

Lachmann, F. M., & Lichtenberg, J. (1992). Model Scenes: Implications for Psychoanalytic Treatment. *J. Amer. Psychoanal. Assn.*, 40:117–137. 10.1177/000306519204000105.

Levenson, E. (1988). The Pursuit of the Particular. *Contemp. Psychoanal.*, 24:1–16.

Lichtenberg, J., Lachmann, F., & Fossaghe, J. (2017). *Narrative and Meaning: The Foundation of Mind, Creativity, and the Psychoanalytic Dialogue.* Oxen, NY: Routledge.

Lyons-Ruth (1999) The Two-Person Unconscious. *Psychoanal. Inq.*, 19 (4):576–617.

Main, M. (2000) The Organized Categories of Infant, Child, and Adult Attachment. *J. Amer. Psychoanal. Assn.*, 48 (4):1055–1095.

Ricouer, P. (1983, 1984, 1985) *Time and Narrative*, 3 vols., trans. K. Blamey and D. Pellauer. Chicago: University of Chicago Press.

Shaefer, R. (1994) *Retelling a Life: Narration and Dialogue in Psychoanalysis.* New York: Basic Books.

Spence, D. P. (1982) *Narrative Truth and Historical Truth: Meaning and Interpretation in Psychoanalysis.* London and New York: W.W. Norton and Company.

Spence, D. P. (1982) Narrative Truth and Theoretical Truth, *Psychoanal. Q.*, 51:43–69

Stern, D. (2004) *The Present Moment in Psychotherapy and Everyday Life.* New York: W.W. Norton.

Zak, P. J. (2015). Why Inspiring Stories Make Us React: The Neuroscience of Narrative. *Cerebrum*, 2015. Published Online.

Introduction II
Sample stories

Here are two brief illustrations of how narrative theory informs and is influenced by the stories my patients and I create. The first story tells of people who bring rigid and truncated stories about themselves, and the second is about a disorganized and chaotic storyteller.

Ella

Ella approaches 70 with distress, regret, and a pressured, closed story of bad treatment, poor choices, and personal failures. In our meetings her anxiety screams; she speaks loudly, rapidly, and intensely and performs a repeated litany of recriminations for what "coulda, woulda, and shoulda" happened in her life. Ella has two thematically related model scenes to which she frequently returns. At 5 she is left at Grand Central Station with a suitcase and some strangers, sent away from home for a whole summer at camp. When she is 17, her father drops her off at a rented single apartment where she is to live alone while attending college. Her parents ask for her house key and tell Ella she can no longer come home. "My mother hated me, and my father complied with her cruelty," she concludes, "They criticized everything I did, and I never learned how to make good choices. I've made a mess of everything." Everything, according to Ella, includes friendships, intimate relationships, and decisions about work and where to live and what to live in. She has clearly taken on the parental criticizing function, attacking herself relentlessly for things in the past. Sometimes she desperately cries "I have to change my life before it's too late"; but at other times she grieves that "It's too late; my life is hopeless." The future is a threatening blur. Besides empathic distress, her repetitive self-abuse awakens my impatient aggressive self. Her anxiety is catching, and I often want to shake Ella.

Yet, this is Ella's story. *Never mind that Ella educated herself, had a brilliant career as a teacher of disabled children, and then credentialed herself to be a child therapist. Never mind that she is an elegant, physically well-cared for woman, widely travelled, with a large but scattered network of friends and acquaintances.*

Ella is not alone. Robert, for example, is a perfectionist, who suffers from continuing performance anxiety about his work and an ongoing depression

Introduction II   17

that ranges from mild to severe and includes alexithymia. He tells a meager personal story, cannot access or name his emotions, and says his early family life was "probably O.K." He carries no imaginative pictures of the mother and father of his childhood and recalls only that his mother wasn't interested in him but liked to go to church, and his father did business homework and fix-it chores around the house. Robert remembers no family events beyond going to church and celebrating decorated Christmas mornings with educational toys and books and special food and treats. His current sense of his life mirrors his vague and paltry early memories. "My life feels so empty and gray; it's like I'm not really living. From week to week my days fade into nothing; it's all so repetitive and dull. And I don't know myself or how I feel about things. When I was a kid, I never had to smoke marijuana to kick back. I was a 'whatever' kid before the expression was born. Except for school and choir, nothing much mattered." For Robert the future is an extension of his gray present. With him I find myself wanting to get out my pom poms and be his cheerleader. His inertness makes me want to jump around.

This is Robert's story. *Never mind that he was an intellectual and musical prodigy and has had a recognized career as composer and performer. And never mind that he has a long-term marriage with a devoted and savvy woman, a marriage that has yielded two successful kids. His sense of past, present, and future are dim and lifeless.*

Nancy, too, has a thin and fixed narrative, one a bit like Ella's. Nancy also relates a backward-looking story of self-hatred, regret, and recriminations, except that she regulated anxiety for much of her life with an eating disorder. At times, she was obese and at other times bulimic. Her shame and hopelessness about her secret eating disorder/addiction and what she perceived as her disgusting body kept her withdrawn and socially alienated. For years she wore dark, loose-fitting men's clothing in order to hide and disguise her physical self from the world. Currently, she presents herself stiffly, holding her body tightly and choosing her words slowly and carefully. She speaks softly. In addition to shame about her addiction, Nancy tells me, she feels herself to be "the runt of a daunting litter." Her two older siblings are socially and intellectually brilliant while she experiences herself as mediocre in all things. According to her story, her body self-consciousness and shame kept her from social experiences that would have fed and enhanced her development. "I feel like I'm always way behind my siblings and my peers, and I'll never catch up." At 48, Nancy is respectful and admiring of her socially prominent and extroverted parents but tells me that her mother was and remains critical of how Nancy looks and presents herself to the world. As Nancy puts it, "She has no patience for shrinking violets, and I'm as shrinking a violet as they come." In response to her sadness, my inclination with Nancy is to be the gentle, encouraging, good mother she didn't have.

This is Nancy's story. *Never mind that she has been a "sober" eater for over ten years, is a pediatrician with a large practice and affectionate and appreciative patients, has maintained a successful marriage, and has developed a social world around breeding and showing Cavalier St. Charles spaniels.*

18   *Introduction II*

Dozens of other patient stories dance in my mind as I write about Ella, Robert, and Nancy's, but theirs are sufficiently instructive for the purposes of this introduction. The three possess many similarities. First, they each relate early neglect, abuse, and/or criticism and a failure of parental mentalization, empathy, and emotional resonance. Then, they all dwell on negative self-attributions that derive from the early deficient treatment. Finally, the stories they tell are not complex, detailed, or nuanced. They are small and closed stories, neglecting each person's positive experiences and achievements in the past and present, reducing the contexts of their productive lives to a few people, and depicting a vague or non-existent future. It seems that early deprivation inoculates a person both against registering life-affirming occurrences in the present and envisioning a realistic, positive future. Ella is mostly hopeless about the future; Robert doesn't even consider it; and Nancy plans short-term goals—hoping to do what she's doing now only better—but without any long-term future vision. The vagueness and/or negative tinge that all three lend to the future may account for the fact that two of the three are childless; choosing, as Nancy puts it, "not to bring a child into such an uncertain world."

I argue that a significant analytic task is to help such patients broaden and deepen and "complexify" their life stories. Unlike dwelling on usually negative, over-processed, and calcified stories, whatever promotes immediate and vibrant emotional experience—enacted and then reflected upon—furthers this goal. The process is analogous to what is foundational in good literature: creating life stories with layers and complexity and detail, *life stories that show rather than tell*. That is, our task is to help our patients find what is unique and specific in their human exchanges and to attend to and expand upon that. Sometimes the specificity is named, and sometimes it is acted out; but detailed inquiry—after such interpersonalists as Sullivan and Levinson —and the marking of shifting emotional moods, self-states, and enactments—after such relationists as Bromberg and Maroda—brings immediacy and life to deadened storied experience. Yes, emotional experience comes alive as patient and analyst interact in analytic space; the illusory, provisional, and exploratory nature of analytic space invites my patients and me to become increasingly open, specific, and human together.

In order to explain this statement, I'll present—in a very abbreviated form—my story of therapeutic change. It is mainly a developmental and attachment story about how minds grow and change as a result of rich interaction with other people over time. It is also a dynamic systems story, contextually framed and full of relational back and forth, action and reaction in continuous feedback loops. Recursive interaction is self-organizing, and in the analytic relationship interactions assume unique and complex patterns; idiosyncratic verbal and nonverbal patterns develop between the partners; rhythms and shapes emerge between partners over time. That is, self-organization creates for the dyad new, fairly stable, and unique expectations about the relationship—what Karlen Lyons-Ruth calls "enactive relational representations" (1999). Self-organization also alters old and static ways of looking at the world, creating instead—again through joint

Introduction II 19

attention—enriched old stories as well as new vibrant ones. Often the patterns of relationship and interaction that emerge in the dyad—as well as the resulting created stories—are different from and much richer than the patient's original experience of and expectations for relationship with other people. This is how stories grow and change.

People come to analytic therapy with well-established, unconscious patterns of expectations about relationships, varying degrees of dissociation, differing capacities for mentalization or intersubjectivity, unique emotional regulatory systems, and singular histories of behavioral responses to human interaction. Whether they stay in therapy depends on many factors, but two primary ones are how painful and unhappy these established patterns and experiences have been and how powerful are the patient's longing and motivation for a different kind of human interaction.

The new analytic relationship examines and deconstructs—emotionally and cognitively—old patterns of relational expectations and responses that were forged in the context of important early attachment relationships. By slowing down the narrative with emotionally alive and detailed inquiry, it questions a patient's closed stories. Traditional psychoanalysis mainly uses verbal interpretive strategies to explain and deconstruct old and faulty tales. Contemporary relational theory, however, also views therapeutic progress as occurring through non-verbal, out of awareness give and take, a back and forth process that stimulates associations, shifting self-states, and enactments. I value both the verbal and non-verbal in my work but understand that achieving verbal understanding lags behind registering and acting on non-verbal processes. This is a primary reason that contemporary analytic work is so challenging and takes so long.

So analytic work unfolds in a unique, co-created relational space in which dynamic changes occur. The space has as a hallmark feature two partners playing at or experimenting with being emotionally present, attuned, honest, and direct. In this safe but "not-quite-real" arena partners come to name affects, recover and integrate dissociated experience, and risk and practice new kinds of emotional interaction. Through practice, strategies that work relationally become part of new interactive patterns, and old, maladaptive strategies slowly begin to die away. The process involves attention to and articulation of subtle and shifting feeling states and perceptions and all their derivatives; it also involves risking new relational behaviors such as honestly confronting the other or expressing feelings of love and hate. In its unfolding, all the stuff of intimacy develops—private language and jokes, joint dramas, images, and stories. With intimacy, emergent feelings between the analytic partners deepen, thicken, and intensify; these feelings function as relational glue.

Think of a theatrical rehearsal stage on which actors discover surprising internal reservoirs of emotion and understanding in themselves and in their fellow actors. In interactions during rehearsals they also discover new ways of being together. As the actors practice over time, repetition causes affective

20 *Introduction II*

doors to open onto larger emotional possibilities, to more authentic ways of being together—more intimate and passionate ways—and to new relational expectations. In this rehearsal space old, constricting or clichéd relational configurations fade, modify, and/or die. In effect, the dramatic roles and performances become more complex and compelling and original. Old, constricted, and cliched stories lose their hold, replaced by new, enlivening narratives. The scripted story deepens and changes.

Here is a small example of the process of creating/uncovering/illuminating a larger story:

> *Ella comes to our session after a date with an eligible man. They have participated in a marathon bicycle ride, which necessitated Ella's spiffing up her old bike. At our last meeting she had been worried about navigating a long bike ride; yet, on entering our session, she tells me she made the ride with less difficulty than her partner.*
>
> *Beautifully put together in expensive sport clothes with a complementary silk scarf and matching socks, Ella looks like a million bucks; yet, she crumples on my couch in a defeated pile and launches rapidly into a familiar, pressured lament, "I can't talk with men. I had nothing to say to Alan at lunch after our ride. Probably he was bored and won't call me again. I'm o.k. with jerks, but Alan is a rich, retired guy who's healthy and likes music and travel and good times. These are the men I discard. All the great guys, who were successful and interested in me, I rejected. What's the matter with me? I'm afraid to get what I want; and so, when I'm close, I blow it. And here I am, alone, without any children. I could have adopted that baby girl, but I got cold feet—too afraid to make that kind of commitment. With a mother like mine, who hated being a mother and hated me, what can you expect? I'm just like her."*
>
> *I listen to Ella, amazed as always at her skill—no matter where she begins, no matter how far afield—at winding a circuitous way back to her familiar dark story of failure and hurt. "Ella, do you hear yourself? You started today telling me about a personal accomplishment—you rode fifteen miles through town on your bike. And where did you end up?"*
>
> *"What do you mean?"*
>
> *"You ended up with your horrible mother." I joke, "And I thought she was dead."*
>
> *Ella laughs. "I guess she's an undead. I'd like to bury her, but here she is."*
>
> *"You would be great throwing an Australian boomerang. Wherever you stand for the initial throw, however far you throw it, in whatever direction and with whatever force, it always seems to come back to the same place: your undead mother." Ella grins, and I say, "Why don't you tell me slowly about your date."*
>
> *"He was very nice and attentive. We got separated at one point on our ride, and Alan turned his bike around and found me in a crowd of bikers. It was clear he really was concerned and looking for me; he had to turn down an alley to find us. Then, he took me to a lovely restaurant, insisted on ordering and paying the check."*
>
> *"Tell me about the conversation."*
>
> *"He told me about his wife's death, and how lonely he was for several years.*

Then he retired and started traveling with a group of friends, and life got easier. He wanted to know if I was interested in some of their upcoming trips."

"How did you feel about his sharing personal pain?"

"I liked him. He seemed to care a lot about his wife; he told me about what a good artist she was and how he has kept her paintings around him at home."

"And it sounds as though he has some idea about you in his future."

"I didn't think about that. I only thought that I don't particularly want to see Iceland."

"Positive as always," I tease. "It also sounds as though you had a good time on your date."

Ella looks at me with surprise. "I did have a good time." She laughs.

This little vignette marks a small, incremental move to deconstruct the sad and boring and closed tale that Ella repeatedly tells about herself. It illustrates how, over time, she and I have developed sufficient trust in our mutual understandings and good will to engage in a joking banter that pierces the ossified surface of her story. The banter represents interactions in time, both verbal and non-verbal. The development of mutual rhythm; the repair of small ruptures; the negotiation of facial expressions, physical gestures, vocal exchanges, and differing attitudes; the conviction of genuine interest and good will—all of these create the mutual trust that allows for honest story-expanding jokes.

I also engage in a detailed inquiry, asking pointed questions that may enlarge Ella's closed and unexamined story. The critical reminder that her mother's ghostly presence spoils every story is important for Ella to register; and prompting some positive memories of her date and its meaning changes the tone and texture of not only the narrative, but also of Ella's mood. Thus, I'm advocating here that we borrow strategies from good literature and art: that we act as participant witnesses to looser and broader analytic theory and clinical stories; that we include in them an increased appreciation for change over time—which is the heart of narrative; and that we continually subject them to the rough and tumble details, surprise, and subversive power of freshly observed interactive experience. Such openness, ease, and fresh observations are not only hallmarks of good literature, but also the original ingredients of our best and most cherished intimate fictions.

With patients who tell disorganized or chaotic stories the process unfolds differently. Often these folks are so hyper-aroused that they hardly register and don't hold on to experience—except in the most diffuse emotional way. My initial goal with them is to slow down the narrative pace in order for us together to hear and feel emotional experience. I do this in two ways: first, by continually attending to shifts in affective experience occurring both in the narrated stories and in the therapeutic interaction; and, second, by providing continual mentalizing functions such as guessing and naming the patient's emotions while simultaneously revealing my own feelings and attitudes about the situations under scrutiny. Such emphasis on and sharing of affect often captures the patient's curiosity and quiets anxiety so that the narrative rhythms

22 *Introduction II*

may slow down. I also try to unravel story lines that seem tangled together, story lines sometimes so entwined and knotted as to obscure any sense at all about the separate stories and their respective intensities.

Take my patient Briana, whom I describe in Chapter 4. Her life is a frantic jumble of story fragments. Like bubbles in boiling water, her tales dance wildly with, merge into, and bounce off one another: her difficult marriage, her intrusive mother, her delinquent son, her unpredictable friendships, her daily failures and frustrations, her long-term failures and frustrations, and her conflicting and careening feelings about herself. Here's a typical opening greeting:

> *"UHH! … Sorry to be late … I got lost in Walmart … I broke the vacuum … and my son called from the Principal's office … He talked back to a teacher and is suspended … what will I do with him home for the rest of the week? … Are you mad at me? … I'm supposed to go to an auction with Linda but she's .mad at me … My mother said my shirt makes me look like Baby Huey, she says these things and doesn't care … Dan(her husband) doesn't help … He's in Costa Mesa doing business until Thursday … no help to me and the vacuum's broke … you know how I hate my house when it's dirty."*

What can one do with this verbal onslaught but identify the most salient feelings—to the best of one's ability—and then try to find a thread in this yarn ball of distress to unravel and explore?

At this point I move to slow down the process in order to soothe my own jangled nervous system as well as Briana's. I say something like, "Wow, Briana, you sure seem frustrated and angry with your important people. Let's take this apart and talk about these feelings. Why don't you tell me about the really mean thing your mom said? I feel rattled and upset just hearing it second hand from you." In naming and joining her affect and in selecting one important element to explore, I help Briana to relax a bit. If I'm lucky, thinking becomes possible, and we can then move to construct a more detailed and coherent story that illuminates the distress and anger that accompanied her into my office.

1 On my becoming an analyst

An overview of the contemporary analytic world

This story is about my patient Lara and me, placed in the context of my becoming a psychoanalyst. I hope the story not only traces my learning and growth process, but also illuminates the many worlds of psychoanalysis that I discovered in my training: the theoretical, clinical, and political worlds it inhabits. This is a rather long piece because in it I want to capture the maze of personal, cultural, theoretical, and associational paths that touch every psychoanalytic couple. These paths are dense, circuitous, and often lead to unexpected and surprising places.

Lara, a fascinating woman, trauma survivor, and long-term psychotherapy patient, agreed to be one of my control cases when I was in psychoanalytic training. I invited Lara to psychoanalysis because in our early therapy it was difficult for us to develop a working rhythm. Everything about Lara was rapid, darting, and hard for me to capture: her speech, her decisions, her mood shifts, etc. It was like trying to catch a grasshopper in a meadow full of grasshopper delights. Our once or twice weekly therapy did not allow sufficient time to hold her, to grasp each other, or to explore her inner world. I hoped things would change with the increased time and space that psychoanalysis provides. I felt lucky when she agreed to the analysis because Lara was a complex and challenging person from whom I expected to learn a lot. This turned out to be the case.

Shortly after the analysis began, I was invited to present Lara's and my work at a self psychology conference in Chicago. Robert Stolorow and Lewis Aron, two analytic luminaries, would respond to my paper. Estelle Shane, my supervisor, would moderate the panel. With Lara's approval and lots of trepidation, I accepted the invitation, and here is the case I shared:

Patient: Lara

Lara came to see me in distress about violence. She was in a destructive relationship with an alcoholic and compulsively unfaithful man. Her encounters with this man had become increasingly violent, violence in which she participated by baiting him and hitting him in their drunken rages.

Lara is a middle-aged beauty with patrician features, dark, well-cut hair, and hazel eyes. Her dress is either casual urban chic—good slacks and Armani

24 *On my becoming an analyst*

jackets with the sleeves rolled—or else raggedy blue jeans and boots, her "cowgirls-get-the-blues" look. She brings her big old dog to sessions, a loving yellow lab. A year ago Lara agreed to be an analytic control case and come to treatment four hours per week.

Lara grew up on an isolated farm with her intact family: parents, an older sister, and two younger siblings, a boy and a girl. Her father, charming and charismatic, was also an alcoholic womanizer. Many people from political, literary, and theatrical circles visited the farm. Lara says, "There were two different groups of people at our home: interesting artists and intellectuals and vicious alcoholics. The same people belonged to both groups depending on the amount of alcohol consumed." In the grip of alcoholic states the father and mother physically battered each other, violent encounters that Lara and her siblings witnessed. The father also beat the children in unregulated rages.

Her mother, the daughter of a socially prominent family, suffers from schizophrenia. Lara remembers her childhood mother as drunk, ineffective, violent, and not much involved in childrearing. Once, during Lara's adolescence the mother went on a rampage and trashed Lara's bedroom. Her father was kinder to her, and as a child Lara identified with her father's strength. When she was a teenager, the parents divorced. Mother now lives in a transient motel.

Lara's childhood was socially isolated and largely unsupervised. In addition to the domestic violence, she suffered from many early traumatic experiences. These include several sexual molestations—by her uncle, neighbor boys, and drunken family friends; an automobile accident that sent her—alone at 4 years old—to a hospital for several weeks; and a public school tenure in which her classmates, poor rural farm children, treated her as a social pariah. Lara wandered the farm to comfort herself and found an imaginary friend. Set into the stone wall bounding the farm was a medallion of a little deer. Lara imagined that the faun would come alive to play with her and protect her. She believes she saw it move and look at her on several occasions. This faun has been a kind of talisman for Lara in her life, a balm for her loneliness.

Lara left home early, left college early, and became a model and actress. She also became a jet setter, involving herself sexually with a roster of fast, famous, and powerful men. She participated in orgies. The history she describes is one of sexual exploitation, heavy drug and alcohol use, and occasional physical violence. Initially, she defined her life as moments of intense drama and of narrow escapes. Now she identifies her sexual experiences as "spaced-out," devoid of feeling, episodes of dissociation.

When Lara was in her mid-twenties, her younger brother committed suicide, an act she blames on her father's brutal treatment but for which she also carries deep grief and feelings of guilt.

At 28, Lara married a man known equally for artistic genius, destructive drug use, and reckless behavior. During the marriage he beat and sexually abused her. She fought back. Although divorced now, they still maintain close personal and business ties.

The treatment

During the first stage of our psychotherapy work, the transference was negative and testing, Lara often angry with and critical of me. How could I say so many stupid things? How shocked was I by graphic depictions of her sexual exploits? Could she seduce me with her tales? Sometimes! Could I stand her impulsive behavior, temper tantrums, and sometimes foul mouth? She would watch me, head cocked to the side with the smile of a naughty child, as she narrated some outrageous incident. She was surprised and touched when I commented at every opportunity on her strengths: her generosity, her senses of justice and loyalty and humor, her street smarts, her kindness to animals, and her ultimate self-restraint—the ways in which she played at its edges but never let herself fall into the abyss. In fact, our closest therapeutic moments have occurred when I have surprised her expectations; when instead of criticizing her, I have gotten beneath her narrative to find tender meanings.

Shortly into the psychotherapy, Lara tried to please me by becoming "a good girl." She would proudly report holding her temper or saying "No" to some powerful man. She even broke off her relationship with the alcoholic for a while. In return, she expected perfect therapeutic behavior from me, and was enraged when I came up short. She became even more sensitive to and critical of my every word, frequently accusing me of clumsiness and obtuseness in dealing with her. For example, with respect to her alcoholic lover, she felt I disapproved of the relationship and did not respect the depth of their mutual feelings. She scolded me for weeks "for not getting it right." I acknowledged that she read my concern about the relationship correctly.

When I presented her the offer of an analysis, she accepted immediately. (Parenthetically, Lara had left a classical analysis with a male analyst in early adulthood.) Later she wanted assurance that I would not become cold and clinical. She also insisted on my choosing a woman supervisor and liked my supervisor's name: Estelle. She called her Star. Lara argued that no man would comprehend her story. In her view, even if a woman supervisor missed something or was mistaken about something, at least a woman can admit a mistake and rectify an error.

Once Lara and I began analytic work, the clinical focus softened and mellowed. The difference between our psychotherapy and the analysis was like the difference between a spotlight or laser beam, on the one hand, and the wash of indirect ambient lighting, on the other. In the time-constrained weekly therapy, our attention had been sharp and concrete, concentrated on current life and relational events, on immediate problems in need of immediate solutions. Like a track hurdler, Lara talked fast and leapt from topic to topic. At the end of our weekly sessions, I often felt tired as after a race, my powers of concentration taxed and exhausted.

With increased time, Lara's pace slowed, and the contents of the hour changed. She began thinking more reflectively, formulating and making sense of dominant life patterns. Her attention and the clinical material became more

26 *On my becoming an analyst*

diffuse and the connections between topics more associative. She began to time-travel seamlessly between the present and past; she brought in more dreams; and painful sequestered memories emerged. And there were increasing silences between us, silences that were filled with emotion and reflections and that seemed to move the process between us along. The expansion of therapeutic space enabled Lara to elaborate her narrative of early deprivation, neglect, and abuse. Telling the story slowly allowed the emergence not only of long-buried incidents but also of long-buried sorrow. Particularly in relation to her dead brother, Lara has expressed profound grief.

Like Lara, I experienced diffuse attentional states as the analysis deepened. While these states stimulated imaginative associations, they affected my immediate memory. For example, as I reviewed each session, my recall was fuzzy. Then I realized that I had joined Lara in softening the therapeutic focus and, in doing so, had somewhat relaxed my rational faculties. The relaxation of focus afforded me a different experience of Lara, afforded me a chance to access her in the aesthetic/subjective/affective way that people like Marion Milner describe. Milner, for example, posits a two-stage aesthetic process that begins with being present with the object in attentive tranquility. In this state there is a continual oscillation between unconscious and associative activity relating to the object on one side, and more objective "surface mind" activity on the other. The second stage of the process involves state sharing with the other in an intersubjective dialogue in both verbal and non-verbal modes.

In such a state I attended to non-verbal as well as verbal emotional exchanges that took place between Lara and me. I also developed a deep caring for "Little Lara," the child as I imaged her: an eager and lonely little girl. For example, a vision took shape in my imagination of her roaming the family farm, her childhood home. In the vision she is about 4 years old, spunky, joyful, and curious, but also unsupervised and imperiled by the natural dangers of the rural terrain: hills, gullies, a running stream, and a storm culvert where, she told me, she sometimes used to hide. This image vibrates with some feelings I have about my own unsupervised childhood. It provided me with one of many points of emotional identification with Lara.

With respect to the non-verbal in the analytic relationship, then, contemporary inquiry has many interests. As in the above example of "Little Lara," it focuses on the analyst's personal images and associations, which a patient's presence may evoke. In addition, analytic interest is tuned to subtle changes in the physical features of the analytic interaction: in facial and vocal expression, in body posture and demeanor, and in the rhythm and tone of dialogue. Finally, contemporary analysts concern themselves with more overt, non-verbal actions and strategies called "enactments." Enactments represent the meeting of psychologically meaningful unconscious and unarticulated patterns in both patient and analyst. Both partners express these patterns behaviorally in the therapeutic relationship. Meaning-makers by inclination and training, analysts explore with patients the meanings, personal and relational, which underlay enactments.

On my becoming an analyst 27

An example of an enactment happened eight months into Lara's analysis. It was my first day back at work after a two-week vacation and fifteen minutes before our scheduled appointment. I was looking forward to seeing Lara, anticipating a happy reunion without considering any negative possibilities. This emphasis on the positive—with some might say a disavowal of the negative—is a characteristic, and sometimes problematic, pattern of mine. My front doorbell rang—my office adjoins my home. There stood Lara, looking forlorn and stricken. "You forgot me," she said in an accusatory but pitiful wail. Because I was glad to see Lara, and because her distressed demeanor seemed so out of place, for a second I thought she was joking. But I quickly saw she was genuinely upset, on the brink of moving from sadness and panic to rage. "I waited for you, and now I'm leaving. I can't talk to you now." She turned to go, her voice scaling in anger.

I paused a moment to catch my breath before pursuing her. I must have looked some combination of shocked, confused, and stricken myself because, when she turned back and saw me, Lara stopped, stared, and said with concern, "Are you O.K?" In response to her concern, I recovered sufficiently to recognize that Lara had mistakenly arrived early to our session. Thinking I had forgotten and abandoned her, she had become distressed and panicky. When I said something to acknowledge these feelings, she softened, her eyes tearing. We went into the office and teased out the meanings of the enactment.

The transaction indelibly reinforced my image of Lara as a little, abandoned, and emotionally disorganized child. Behind her angry withdrawal, I felt she had allowed me a glimpse of her early fragmented emotional life. The enactment also lent itself to a traditional transference interpretation—something to the effect that, based on early family experience, she expected me to desert her. The incident also revealed how flat-footed I can be when unforeseen circumstances upend my positive expectations.

Reviewing the enactment, however, I was most interested in how, together and wordlessly, we had negotiated our mismatched emotional states. Her sadness and my happy anticipation, her anger and my confusion, my distress and her concern, my empathy and her tears—these shifts expressed themselves in facial expressions, vocal intonations, and muscular and postural tension to a greater degree than they did in words. This was a non-verbal emotional dance, the choreography of which rested on habits of mutual observation and previously established trust and goodwill.

One way to speak of the dance is as an event happening on the level of procedural memory. In contrast to declarative memory, which has to do with symbolically mediated and verbally articulated recall, procedural memory relates to non-verbally mediated memory. Procedural memory, in effect, is embodied emotion expressed in action, emotion made manifest in sequences of behaviors occurring wordlessly and out of awareness.

Feeling pain is difficult for Lara, and she has a number of avoidant and protective strategies to distance herself from emotion. For example, she often cancels the session following an intense analytic hour. At times she wants a

28 *On my becoming an analyst*

phone session from her bed. Then, Lara brings her dog to analysis to guard her. Together we have observed that the animal does, in fact, regulate and modulate her feelings. If she is angry, distressed, or crying, the dog lumbers over and nuzzles her or licks her hand. Lara also relieves intense feeling by changing the subject. For example, she might abruptly shift from a painful memory to some superficial observation about my hair or clothing. I sometimes feel annoyed at the resulting choppiness in the flow of our sessions.

In addition to these strategies, Lara protects herself from painful emotion by isolating narrative content from feeling. To illustrate: Lara has horrible dreams in which demonic men pursue, threaten or sexually attack her. In different dreams these men assume different guises: "Machete Man," "Gangster Man," "Murderous Men of Color," menacing men, faceless or masked, and sexual predators, unknown and renowned, wielding all kinds of lethal weapons. In these dreams her places of refuge are compromised. They have broken door locks or fissures in the walls where the men can enter. When I appear in these dreams, I am far away, out of earshot or somewhere across a dangerous cat-walk, certainly beyond Lara's hope of help or rescue. Needless to say, my distance from and inaccessibility in relation to her has enormous transference implications for us. Early in our work Lara reported these terrible dreams to me matter-of-factly, sometimes with puzzlement, sometimes in a cheerful tone, sometimes even with a joke.

Now I'm going to describe several therapeutic incidents that will convey the ways in which Lara's issues emerged and were enacted in our analytic sessions. These incidents contain emotionally charged moments that upended Lara's relational expectations and perturbed the system between us. For me these are the kind of moments that offer the possibility of change and transformation:

1   Lara told me she had shown a picture of her mother to her friend Ann. "What a loser!" Ann commented. In that moment, Lara said she "wanted to kill Ann." A few minutes after relating this incident, Lara said she had meant to bring me the picture, but "… I forgot it." I suggested maybe there was a reason she had forgotten the picture. She was quiet and then agreed. She said she worried that I might also criticize her mother.

Lara continued to forget the picture. Then, after about two weeks, right in the middle of a session and <u>apropos</u> of nothing, Lara handed me a photograph. It took me a second to realize this was THE photo. "Another test," I thought. Lara was watching my face. The woman in the photograph had the vague look of a deteriorating schizophrenic. She stood stiffly and without expression, a slightly plump woman with a puffy face, swollen eyes, and facial skin sprinkled with small brown growths. Her hair was slightly disheveled, but her clothes were clean and the room spare and orderly. This is Lara's mother looking quiet and childlike, the lifelong fire of her mental illness having finally cooled.

On my becoming an analyst 29

Feeling sad for the two women, the one in the picture and the one in the room with me, I said that I appreciated Lara's bringing the photograph. It clarified for me how ill her mother must have been when Lara was a little girl. I also noted the effort her mother had put into fixing the room and dressing herself nicely. Lara's face lit up as she proudly pointed out the curtains in the room, which her mother had sewn. That was all. She took back the photo and changed the subject. At the next session she thanked me for recognizing her mother's suffering. "I figured you would," she said and then added, "Usually I can't stand Mother, but since our session I've actually felt some kindness toward her."

2   Last spring Lara described staying up all night watching a tornado disaster on T.V. She confessed that she took pleasure in seeing the body count rise. She was shy about telling me, worried that I would think her a "freak, perverse, horrible, and disgusting." She wasn't far off; my first reaction was of horror. She went on to say that she particularly liked it when fat "wonderbread" people died. The only thing that bothered her about the tornado was that innocent animals also suffered.

Remembering the farm children who had tormented her, I asked about "wonderbread" people. "You know," she said, "all blown up with air—no substance, stupid, no culture." She compared them to the terrible men she has loved. "They're like 'wonderbreads,' too, except for being sicker and more twisted, smarter and … much more interesting."

Then, Lara wondered about how I judged her perverse pleasure. She said, "If I were you, I'd think me horrible and disgusting." When I didn't respond, she looked me directly in the eye and asked point blank, "O.K., Joye, what do you think of me wanting the death toll to go higher?"

There is something wonderfully risky in how squarely, how authentically Lara puts herself into our relationship, in how directly she confronts me. This willingness to risk invites me also to risk, to enter her world more boldly than I might otherwise. And so, as in this instance, she pulls my imagination into her life, into her memories, feelings, and current experience. In order to understand what would cause her to celebrate human catastrophe, I imagine myself as little Lara, lonely, frightened, and hyperaroused—as Lara, the victim of neglectful and violent parents; as Lara, the butt of ridicule from the farm children who were her classmates; and as Lara, the object of sexual degradation.

I said to her, "I think you've been terribly disappointed with people, enormously hurt by them." She became silent and then teary. For several of the following sessions she alluded to what I had said and commented a few times, "That was right. People have hurt and disappointed me."

3   Lara still brings her bulky old dog to our sessions. One day he turned over a small table, shattering the glass top and knocking over a vase of flowers. The glass collapsed on itself in a neat pile of long shards. "Damn!" I first thought. Then, I caught sight of Lara. She had blanched and soon became

30   *On my becoming an analyst*

panicky and distressed, rushing around the room looking for something with which to soak up the spilled water and, all the while, apologizing: "I'm sorry, I'm sorry!" As her emotions heated, I noticed myself becoming cool and still. Surprised and curious, I watched her panic mount. Then I saw her bend down, about to pick up the sharp glass strips—heedless of the danger to her bare hands. While I didn't mind water on my Oriental rug, I really didn't want blood; and I didn't want Lara to hurt herself. So, at that point, I stepped in. In my best mother voice, I told her to sit down, assuring her that I had cleaned up much worse in my day. After that, she did settle onto the couch, bent, her head bowed, looking for all the world like a sullen child in the principal's office.

When I had finally disposed of the mess, an amazing thing happened. Lara's demeanor utterly changed. She pulled herself into an adult posture, raised her chin and assumed the same maternal voice I had just used with her: "It's O.K., Joye, you don't have to get so excited, you know. Settle down now, and chill out. You're overreacting, honey." Then her body relaxed, her shoulders fell, and her emotional state again visibly shifted. As though amused by what she had just said, her face softened, she laughed and said to me in her familiar joking way, "Pay attention, Joye, I want my appointment now, damn it!"

Confused by these changes, I asked her what had just happened. She replied, "I got scared and acted overexcited. I thought you'd be so mad at me." I realized that I had just witnessed an episode of dissociation and recovery. The episode was complete with alterations in Lara's facial expression, body posture, language style, and voice intonation.

Following this enactment and in subsequent sessions, Lara remembered many childhood instances of merciless and irrational punishment. Willful childish misbehavior, minor self-assertions, simple accidents, and acts of God—any of these earned beatings in Lara's family. Later, as an adult Lara continued to expect "without-rhyme-or-reason violence." In fact, for Lara physical pain is an integral part of intimate relationship and generally precedes resolution of conflict.

"How did you stand the pain?" I asked. Lara described first trying to avoid brutal treatment by "making nice"—that is, by being helpful and ingratiating. If that didn't work, she could numb herself so that she "didn't feel anything." She also fought back physically and verbally. Then, she added, "I always looked ahead—I knew when the fight ended, there would be peace." In light of all this, Lara and I reexamined the broken glass accident. We saw that she had enacted with me her whole dynamic of violence: the expectation that I would attack her, the panicky effort to placate me, and the willingness to injure herself in order to resolve the conflict. All of this had occurred in a procedural state, a state of dissociation.

4   As part of her business Lara receives first-run movies on video tape. In past years she has brought me some videos to see. This year she described

On my becoming an analyst   31

watching new movies on tape and repeatedly said in an off-handed way, "I'll bring [this or that film] for you to see." She didn't. Recently, when she again vowed to bring a movie, I commented, "You've mentioned bringing movies here several times, but you haven't." She stuttered nervously, "Oh..Oh, I'll bring some movies next time." When I asked if maybe she didn't want to bring movies, she thought for a minute and then answered that, indeed, she didn't want to, but she felt selfish admitting it.

Then, she started talking, excitedly and with rising anger, about all the people who exploited her, and not just with the movies. None of the exchanges in her life were reciprocal or fair. She began to catalogue—and this time sadness laced the anger—how often she has let herself be used and exploited and how seldom anybody has actually met her needs. I observed that she didn't want to feel that way about me. She wanted me to respect her boundaries and not to exploit her. She left the session happy, and since has referred frequently to my willingness to let her be a "selfish bitch."

5   I blew my nose in a session, and it began to bleed. I excused myself and went over to my desk until the nosebleed stopped. The session resumed. At the beginning of the next hour Lara said she felt angry and rattled off a number of small life events that had "pissed her off." I asked if she was also angry with me. Her face hardened. "I'm furious about the nosebleed," she said. It had taken away from her appointment time, and it was disgusting that I hadn't left and gone into the bathroom to bleed. She was very offended by my rudeness and lack of caring about her.

I was floored. I certainly never anticipated this, and I felt defensive. But I kept inquiring about her feelings. It seemed my handling of the nosebleed was a breach of boundaries. The sessions are for her, and I shouldn't burden her with my problems or imperfections. She felt embarrassed to tell me these things—they confirm what a "selfish bitch" she is—but I needed to know them.

I related these "nosebleed" feelings to the movie tapes. I said that analysis was the only place where she could express herself and claim her rights—even if they felt selfish and unreasonable, as they had to both of us in this instance. Any infringement on my being available for her made her angry. When I inquired about whether it worried her to see me bleed, she didn't answer and changed the subject.

Next day after the nosebleed confrontation, Lara recounted that she had had the most frightening experience of her life. She had dreamed her familiar "demonic man" dream, and this time it was her ex-husband who was sexually debasing her. The configuration of the dream was familiar but the emotional experience completely new. In the dream and then on waking a deep and wrenching sadness had overpowered her. She felt heartsick and cried for a long time in the analytic session. "What's happening to me?" she finally asked, and I answered, "You've connected normal feelings to your horrible dream. You're feeling your experience." For me this was a shining moment, the dissolution

32 *On my becoming an analyst*

of a lifetime of dissociated emotion. Of course, after the intensity of the session, Lara called to cancel the next appointment. Her voice message: "I need a vacation."

I know that Lara is a difficult person and by most standards a difficult patient. At times she infuriates me, and at times she exasperates me. Her impulsive acting out behavior—about which I've said only a bit—worries me. It also draws out a part of myself that I dislike: my judgmental and teachy self. In spite of all this, Lara is not a particularly hard patient for me. Here are some reasons why. I love and admire how immediate and real she is in her wildness and spunkiness. I love how she struggles to use in her life the reflective skills she is learning and practicing in our analysis. I love that Lara and I track each other affectively so that we are able to mend—in a fairly easy and continuous way—the recurring breaches in our relationship. And I love that over time Lara has come to trust that I read her pretty well. Finally, I am awed that, even without verbal cues, Lara reads me quite accurately in return. She will say things to me like, "I know what you're thinking. You're thinking,'Oh, no, Lara, you didn't do THAT!'" or "Joye, you look so cool, but your impatience with me is noisy today." And she also sometimes says, "I know you love me." She reads me quite right.

The conference

Waiting in the registration line for the Twenty-third Annual Self-Psychology Conference, I had my first inkling of choppy waves and seasickness ahead. I introduced myself to a pleasant Italian psychologist who recognized my name. "I read your case on the plane last night. I liked it and thought those guys had it all wrong," he said.

"Are the plenary presentations translated for foreign attendees?" I asked politely while simultaneously thinking, "Whaddaya mean, 'All wrong?' How 'All wrong?' Oh SH—! 'ALL WRONG??'" My stomach lurched, jiggled, hung for a beat in mid-air and then dropped precipitously. Crash! Seasickness.

At that moment I felt every bit the lowly and anxious analytic candidate while Lewis Aron and Robert Stolorow, the two case respondents, were prolific writers and noted theoreticians of contemporary psychoanalysis. Aron, from New York, represented the school of relational psychoanalysis, and Stolorow, from Los Angeles, the school of intersubjective systems theory. They were both at the top of their game, brilliant, ambitious, competitive, and rivalrous with each other. No false pride here: in their circles I was less than puny.

Why, then, had Lew Aron requested that I not see their responses to my case? Was it for the sake of surprise and spontaneity? Perhaps. Had they simply forgotten how anxious candidates become before their first public presentations? Probably. Yet, without knowing anything about Aron or Stolorow's motivation, I worried that this was a variation on the old Edward Albee games

On my becoming an analyst 33

"Get-the-Guest" and "Hump-the-Hostess": Pummel-the-Presenter! Staring into the eyes of the pleasant Italian, this was my fear.

I was not totally defenseless in Chicago. For one thing, I had a knot of friends at the conference. One of the wonderful things about psychoanalytic training is that one discovers grown-up people like oneself who, instead of taking up golf or bridge or pilates in middle age, choose to spend leisure time reading dense and turgid psychoanalytic prose. This oddity makes for close and devoted friendships. One of these friends, who was serving as a discussion leader for my case, clued me into the respondents' arguments. So much for skewed playing fields! In addition, I brought to Chicago two "stage fright" pills. As much as I am committed to the psychoanalytic reflective process for dealing with life's difficulties, chemical enhancement seemed like a good idea for Chicago. Actor patients had told me that beta-blocker medications, used only occasionally, can dramatically reduce such stage fright symptoms as sweaty palms, rapid heartbeat, and flushed cheeks. A psychiatrist friend had furnished the two pills, one for the performance and the second in case I lost the first.

The pills worked, and the presentation session turned out to be less fraught than anticipated. While the written contents of Stolorow and Aron's responses to my case seemed harsh, in the event the men were much more interested in besting each other than attacking me. My case was mostly a vehicle for each to promote his own theory. Estelle Shane as moderator clearly articulated their positions while, at the same time, representing mine quite positively and protectively. I think in an alternative life, she would have made a fantastic judge, a model of upbeat fairness and respect. In the end I was happy to have had the experience; and here now is an impressionistic sketch of the men, their theoretical positions and what they had to say to me.

***

For such a famous analyst, Bob Stolorow was soft-spoken and thoughtful but unprepossessing. Looking to be in his mid-fifties, his insouciant, laid-back manner—he came to the conference dressed in jeans and a denim work shirt—contradicted my more dominant sense of his keen intellectual intensity. He seemed serious both about his ideas and himself. With his slightly myopic stare, Stolorow looked like a man who has read too many books and thought too hard about them. After the Chicago conference, I studied intersubjectivity with him at ICP and had a chance to observe him a little. He speaks in a measured, rhythmical musical voice with plenty of pauses in it. These spaces in his speech seem to allow him room to consult some inner text. When done, he expresses himself, without notes, in dense sentences that magically cohere. Sometimes when he looks right at you, it's as though he is still reading, only now you're the text. You wonder—but can't quite tell—what he thinks of it. In our class I occasionally caught myself watching his eyes, checking to see if they were moving from left to right. Strangely, for someone who writes about intersubjective connection, Stolorow seemed to me opaque and difficult to

34 *On my becoming an analyst*

know. I'd wager that Stolorow, however loose and easy-going his dress and manner, doesn't relax and never stops thinking.

Aron, on the other hand, looked like a man of action. Physically compact and concentrated, he seemed all aggressive potential energy. In his writings he described himself as interested and engaged in therapeutic enactments. As an analyst he was active and sometimes combative with his patients. As he wrote to me after the conference, "I just enjoy a good fight and value mutual exchanges of aggression and survival." Pugnacious! Yet, because Aron doesn't take himself too seriously and is good natured and unusually open to new perspectives, these qualities helped to soften his aggressive stance. After the conference and over many years, he became my friend, and I grieve his recent loss.

Although they identified different origins for their ideas, both Stolorow and Aron shared many theoretical assumptions, assumptions that underlay a range of thinking known as "Big Tent" relational psychoanalysis. Relationality is a sensibility more than a set theory, a sensibility that views the analytic relationship through a two-person, constructivist and/or dynamic system lens and includes many perspectives that share some version of mutual influence and bi-directionality in the therapeutic dyad. These perspectives include contemporary relational self psychology, intersubjective systems theory, some interpersonalists, and relational psychoanalysis. The central idea here is that the analyst is as much a player in the analytic encounter as the patient; that she and the patient mutually affect each other and what happens in the consulting room. Every particularity and peculiarity of the analyst affect what happens in treatment. Such things as physical appearance, age and dress, voice quality and vocabulary, what clinical material she attends to, how she thinks, what she says, what limits she sets, her personal preferences, her very presence, in short—all of these factors make the old notions of analyst anonymity, of analyst as "blank screen," absurd. The work of psychoanalysis largely involves examining the many dimensions of and exchanges in the analytic relationship in order to recapture memories and explore emotional/relational patterns and meanings.

Attention to analyst subjectivity and contribution does not mean that analysis is symmetrical. The patient's interests and concerns are always central. But the analytic relationship is mutual—this sounds like a tautology—because in relational theory mutuality defines relationship. Indeed, for relational psychoanalysts, mutuality is key to all human interaction and development. Mind only develops in relation to other minds; mind only develops contextually and interpersonally.

In the American relational school, particularly as practiced in New York, analysts are quite open about being real and separate people. In the analytic encounter they frequently make explicit their own life experiences, thoughts and emotional attitudes—in hermeneutical terms, their "prejudices." These become a part of the analytic meeting. Relational analysts inquire about how patients perceive them—their analytic thoughts, interventions, and behavior.

And, at times, they disclose personal attitudes and ideas when they deem such disclosure relevant to analytic process. Reading some of the relational literature, and the central place in it for the analyst's feelings, classical analysts and traditional self-psychologists sometimes ask, "Whose treatment is this anyway? Is the analyst making too much noise here? Is she leaving the patient enough space in the analytic process? Is she being self-indulgent at the patient's expense?"

Stolorow and Aron also agree that psychoanalysis is not about a patient learning objective truths about herself from a rational and knowledgeable analyst. They dismiss the old Freudian concept of a perfectly rational analyst as an illusion. Rather, they believe that patient and analyst form a unit, and what emerges from that unit transcends the individuality of the two participants. Analyst and patient bring their "prejudices," their separate attitudes, life experiences, and presences to the encounter. There they construct together or, more accurately, create a meaningful story about the patient's world. A good analytic story is inclusive and feels authentic and plausible. It reflects the affective tone of the patient's world with the intermingling color and overtones of the analyst's presence in that world. Nevertheless, the story is not "true" in any objective sense.

The story is not true on several levels, two of which I'll mention here. First, we know from neuroscience that memory is deceptive and slippery. Memory is not a fixed, stored item in our brain as we have conventionally thought. We do not retrieve a memory as we might a piece of jewelry locked in a household safe. Instead, every memory represents an ingathering of traces of sensory data, traces that are scattered throughout the brain. What traces we choose and how they come together and combine—these depend, among other things, on the interpersonal context and the intensity of emotion at the time of retrieval. Our affective environment forms and informs our memories to a larger degree than common wisdom has taught. Memories are interpersonal constructions or creations, which rest on feelings and not objective facts.

The second level has to do with the complexities of both subjectivity and the meeting of subjectivities. Contemporary theorists note that just as patients are limited in their self-awareness, so, too, are analysts. Gone, sadly, is the old Freudian analytic omniscience. As fallible creatures, our perceptions of ourselves, of our patients, of our patients' perceptions of themselves, and of our patients' perceptions of us are all, unhappily, fallible. Yet, perceptions are all we have to go on. Therefore, we inquire of ourselves and of our patients about our differing perceptions. The stories we concoct from these inquiries represent a series of best mutual guesses, the guesses based on two emotionally engaged minds examining together and negotiating together in the here and now their shifting and disparate perceptions of the world. The created stories are necessarily unpredictable and unique. They, again, are not truth in any objective sense. The logical conclusion from these relational ideas is that each analytic couple is wholly original.

36 *On my becoming an analyst*

How does all of this look, how does it express itself in the psychoanalytic hour? Stolorow and Aron have different answers to this question, and their responses to my work with Lara reflect some of these differences.

Both Stolorow and Aron contend that I fail to make important interpretations about Lara's behavior towards me "in the transference." That term, "in the transference," refers to the patient's feelings, attitudes, expectations, and behaviors as they express themselves in the analytic relationship. Each man has a different view about what kind of interpretation I fail to make.

Stolorow thinks that I fail to confront Lara when she avoids painful affect—i.e., when she cancels therapy after emotionally wrenching sessions—and that I do not adequately interpret what he calls the "repetitive dimension" of the transference. This refers to the repetition in the analytic relationship of old feelings and expectations about relationship. For example, Lara dreams of an unbridgeable gulf which separates the two of us. Stolorow interprets this dream as reflecting Lara's hopelessness about the therapeutic tie. Based on experience with her schizophrenic mother, he believes, she despairs of creating a safe, sheltering and stable bond with me. He would say that this expectation of being alone, endangered, and unprotected is an "organizing principle" of Lara's psychological world. I agree with this view.

The fact that such organizing principles emerge in therapy is central to Stolorow's theory of therapeutic action. He argues that identifying these central relational constellations—in the context of an attuned analytic relationship—is at the heart of analytic change. Interpretation of and reflection on the organizing principles allow the analytic couple to make the principles conscious and therefore subject to emotional revision and/or resolution.

In his comments, Stolorow argues, like Freud, that interpretation is the primary instrument of therapeutic action. Unlike Freud, however, he underlines the importance of emotional attunement as integral to a good interpretation. He rails against the false dichotomy, rife, he believes, in dualistic psychoanalytic thinking, between a rational interpretation and affect attunement, suggesting that the impact of well-formulated interpretations "… lies not only in the insights they convey but also … in the extent to which they demonstrate the therapist's attunement to the patient's affective life."[1] He concludes, as in the following statement, that the mutative power of therapeutic action rests on verbal interpretive formulations, formulations which give the patient an "experience of being understood."[2] Notice the compressed Stolorow prose style and the way it illustrates all that reading and thinking I mentioned earlier:

> In the language of intersubjectivity theory, interpretive expansion of the patient's capacity for reflective awareness of old, repetitive organizing principles occurs concomitantly with the emotional impact of ongoing relational experiences with the therapist, and both are indissoluble components of a unitary therapeutic process that facilitates the establishment of alternative principles for organizing experience, whereby the

On my becoming an analyst 37

patient's experiential horizons can become widened, enriched, more flexible, and more complex.[3]

Aron thinks that sado-masochism is the dominant issue in Lara's clinical material, and that I should have continuously interpreted Lara's sadistic and masochistic interactions with me and mine with her. In contrast to Stolorow, Aron is as interested in behavioral enactments as he is in interpretation. The analytic consulting room becomes a space for the analytic couple to mix it up and duke it out. For example, even though the dog upended the table, Aron somehow sees the broken glass incident as an expression of Lara's sadistic behavior and my response as a masochistic enactment:

> I expect that what is talked about in analysis is simultaneously played out between patient and analyst in the analytic relationship, that what is talked about and what is enacted are isomorphic transformations of each other. So clinically, I would begin to wonder how I as analyst (or for that matter as supervisor or discussant) would get caught up in sado-masochistic scenarios … If a patient's life has been hell, if their childhood was hell, if their adult relationships have been hell, then I sure expect their analysis to be hell and I expect to have to burn there with them, as their tormenter, fellow-sufferer, witness, and rescuer.[4]

Aron presents here a notion about dealing with traumatized patients first proposed by Davies and Frawley (1991). It avers that work with abused people necessitates playing out and clarifying the many roles in the drama of abusive relationships: the victim, the perpetrator, the rescuer, the witness, etc.

Both men also criticize my non-interpretive interventions. The general sense is that they think I am much too nice and, perhaps, more than a touch naive. Stolorow, for example, guesses that I privilege "provision of positive new experiences" with the analyst over "investigation and interpretation of repetitive aspects of transference as the primary source of therapeutic action."[5] Judging from the context, for Stolorow positive new experience is not a good thing. It's probably something like supplying "provisions," a dirty word in psychoanalytic circles. To "supply provisions" means the analyst actually tries to satisfy a patient's developmental longings rather than simply investigating them. Such a goal is, of course, impossible to effect. Yet, even if I could "supply Lara with provisions," such an act would, in my view, preempt her psychological process.

Aron is clearer about my proclivities to "make nice." He urges for space in the analysis for me to "wear roles other than that of the good mother, good object, good analyst." He states, "… that the heart of the analytic relationship consists of Joye's deep identification with [a certain] aspect of Lara, namely, that they share a tendency to avoid brutal treatment by 'making nice'—that is by being helpful and ingratiating."[6] Elsewhere he says, "The difficulty in the analytic process is based on [Joye's] reluctance to identify with an aspect of the

38 On my becoming an analyst

patient, her sadism, because she dislikes that aspect of herself so very much."[7] I think Aron is right about this, and this observation has served me over the years.

Both Stolorow and Aron challenge Kohut's idea of empathy. Both men agree that in any psychoanalysis the analyst frequently "decenters" from the patient; that is, she shifts from empathy to an introspective look into her own subjective world. Stolorow believes the Kohutian concept of empathic immersion and the idea that such empathy can be neutral and objective "is saturated with [dualistic] philosophical assumptions inherited from Descartes." He suggests that one isolated mind, the analyst's, entering the subjective world of another isolated mind, the patient's, constitutes "a doctrine of immaculate perception ... and entails a denial of the inherently intersubjective nature of analytic understanding, to which the analyst's subjectivity makes an ongoing, unavertable contribution."[8] The analyst's introspection, "the historicity of his organizing principles" tempers the empathic stance; that is, the analyst's own subjective thoughts and feelings color and qualify the analyst's attempt at empathy. Stolorow says, "There can be no understanding without prejudice, no relationship without 'affective history' or transference."[9]

Aron's analyst is a central player in the analytic drama, her role varied and complex. She certainly does not limit herself solely to an empathic exploration of the patient's subjectivity. Some relational analysts actually view empathy as antithetical to "authenticity." They argue that the analyst's effort to subordinate her own subjectivity to that of the patient's is personally suspect and fraudulent. Aron doesn't go that far in his response to my case. Yet, because he implies that the analyst's subjectivity and preferences codetermine the nature of any given analysis, he states, "there cannot be any universal 'standard technique' or 'basic treatment model.'"[10]

My response

In thinking about my work as an analyst, I remember a story from my Jewish tradition. It describes the required conditions for priests who, on the holiest day of the year, enter the Holy of Holies, the most sacred space in the Tent of Meeting. In preparation, these priests must engage in purification rituals of body and spirit; they must cleanse themselves of everyday grime, of venal deeds, distracting thoughts, and social artifice. They must train and focus their attention on the sacred encounter. If they fail to do it right—as in the story of Aaron's sons—they get zapped by Divine Fire. As a child I tried to imagine what the really pure priests, the ones left standing, found in that holy and awesome space.

Not being very religious, I don't know much about holy space. The closest I come to such geography is in my intimate relationships, among them the carefully created intimate space of a long-term analysis. To be in this space the analytic partners also have to prepare, to come clean with each other humanly, to be their authentic selves: in Ghent's sense, they must "surrender" to the

On my becoming an analyst   39

relationship. Experiencing and examining the many and manifold meanings of such encounters are at the heart of the analytic pursuit. When the analyst slips up and does it wrong—when she turns away or backs off from the other's pain—there are hurtful and dangerous ruptures, sometimes even the threat of zapping the whole enterprise. The vulnerability of holy space is exquisite. The rewards are too: the privilege of knowing and being known in all the messy complexity of being human, including revelations of secrets and shame, treasure stores, and sacred strivings.

Let me say a bit more about my view of analytic space, borrowing from both infant research and attachment theories and relational ideas about the "analytic third." According to infant researchers and attachment theorists, mind develops and expands in rich intersubjective meetings; that is, through the coordination of interpersonal rhythms and other modes of non-verbal communication as well as through mentalized verbal interchanges. The resulting "dyadic expansion of consciousness" is one way to think about co-created analytic space.

The Boston Change Process Group adds a dynamic systems dimension to this notion of analytic change. If new analytic relationships examine and deconstruct old patterns of relational expectations and responses, patterns that were forged in the context of important early relationships, they do this through contextually framed mutual interaction. This interaction is full of relational back and forth, action and reaction in continuous feedback loops. Such recursive interaction is self-organizing, and in the analytic relationship repertoires of interactions expand and assume unique patterns. Idiosyncratic relational rhythms and shapes emerge over time. That is, self-organization creates for the dyad new, unique, more complex, and fairly stable expectations about the relationship. Self-organization also patterns behavioral responses consistent with those expectations. Often the patterns of relationship that emerge in the analytic space are very different from the patient's original experience and expectations of human interaction. And the co-created space, while reflecting both partners, becomes larger than the sum of its individual parts.

In describing the "analytic third," relational theorists Benjamin (2004) and Aron (2006) offer some related ideas about the process of analytic change. The idea of thirdness is a powerful, two-person expansion of Winnicott's idea of transitional or illusory space. Benjamin depicts the third as a space that emerges when each dyadic partner is able to recognize the other's mind.

> Elaborating this idea, we might say that the third is that to which we surrender, and thirdness is the intersubjective mental space that facilitates or results from surrender. In my thinking, the term *surrender* refers to a certain letting go of the self, and thus also implies the ability to take in the other's point of view or reality. Thus, surrender refers us to recognition—being able to sustain connectedness to the other's mind while accepting his separateness and difference. Surrender implies freedom from any intent to control or coerce.
>
> (Benjamin, 2004, p. 8)

40 *On my becoming an analyst*

Benjamin reminds us that the achievement of thirdness is not a stable state; rather, even under the best circumstances, we continually move in and out of intersubjective relatedness.

Aron sees the third as arising from co-created points of view that crack rigid, binary positions and open space for the therapeutic partners to consider new relationship perspectives. He argues that the third functions to transform relations of complementarity—collapsed empathy, emotional impasse, and mental stalemate—to relations of mutuality:

> An argument is made to the effect that intersubjectivity theory has direct implications for clinical practice, and that the notion of the third is particularly useful in understanding what happens in and in resolving clinical impasses and stalemates. Specifically, the author suggests that certain forms of self-disclosure are best understood as attempts to create a third point of reference, thus opening up psychic space for self-reflection and mentalization.
>
> (Aron, 2006, p. 349)

Aron particularly urges that the patient has access to the analyst's mind in order to "facilitate the gradual transformation from relations of complementarity to relations of mutuality." (Aron, 2006, p. 349).

People come to analytic therapy with well-established, unconscious patterns of expectations about relationships, varying capacities for mentalization or intersubjectivity, unique emotional regulatory systems, and singular histories of behavioral responses to human interaction. Whether they stay in therapy depends on many factors, but two primary ones are how painful and unhappy these established patterns and experiences have been and how powerful the longing and motivation are for a different kind of emotional interaction.

Traditional psychoanalysis mainly uses verbal interpretive strategies to explain and deconstruct old and faulty psychological organizations. Contemporary relational theory, however, views therapeutic progress as occurring primarily through non-verbal, out of awareness, emotional associations, states, and enactments. Verbal understanding lags behind the non-verbal processes, which is one reason why contemporary analytic work is so challenging and takes so long.

As stated before, the work unfolds in a co-created relational space. Dynamic changes occur in this space, which has as a hallmark feature two partners playing at or experimenting with being emotionally present, attuned, honest, and direct. There is a kind of illusory or "as if" quality to this private space—safe and "not-quite-real"—where partners come to name emotional experience and practice new kinds of emotional interaction. Through practice, strategies that work relationally become part of new interactive patterns, and old, maladaptive strategies slowly begin to die away. The process involves attention to subtle and shifting feeling states and perceptions and all their derivatives, and over time feelings between the analytic partners tend to deepen and intensify. Emergent feelings function as relational glue.

On my becoming an analyst 41

How do I conceptualize my meetings with Lara? In relation to Stolorow and Aron and in relation to other analytic ideas, where do I place myself as a contemporary psychoanalyst? I'll answer these questions in the process of answering the conference respondents, and then I'll add a short personal reflection.

First, Stolorow. I'll begin my response to Stolorow by speaking about myself as a relational self-psychologist. Kohut's ideas are meaningful to me as a person and analyst. His thinking about the interpersonal sources of human development, about the trajectory of growth in self-cohesion and expansiveness, is congenial to me. So, too, are his notions about empathy and self-object experience as keys not only to human psychological development but also to therapeutic action and process. Finally, Kohut's beliefs about the nature and place of aggression in human affairs conform to my clinical and life experience. His argument that aggression is primarily a reaction to and expression of interpersonal history suggests the possibility for healing in the analytic relationship. My clinical practice, then, uses many ideas from self-psychology.

I appreciate Stolorow's refinement and augmentation of many Kohutian ideas. His two-person, intersubjective emphasis, his understanding of the importance of psychological organizing activity, and his conception of affect attunement in the analytic relationship—all are notions that help me greatly in my work with patients. Simply put, I admire his contributions to psychoanalytic thinking, and I also think of myself as an intersubjectivist. In short, I like Stolorow's theoretical ideas and greatly respect his clinical inclinations.

Yet, I didn't like his response to my paper at the conference. It seemed that he hadn't read it carefully and/or taken it seriously. An example he gave of a misguided provision, one that came from his own clinical experience, seemed unrelated to anything in my paper. Unfortunately, I acted out my disappointment with his teaching by responding to him in kind, by treating him dismissively. I regret doing so, and he has never forgiven me.

So here I want to say to Stolorow respectfully and seriously that much of my work with Lara involves Stolorowian verbal exploration of her affective states and of our interactions. It also includes the articulation of organizing principles or patterns of relational expectation and the identification and interpretation of patterns in the repetitive pole of the transference. What Stolorow missed in his response to Lara's case was the nature of the incidents I chose to present. They mostly depict highly charged affective moments between Lara and me, moments of primitively-organized emotional states. At these moments Lara shifts from her customary attachment styles with me—usually engaged but, at times, avoidant—into more disorganized states. She becomes distressed and hyperaroused. Her emotional features resemble PTSD responses. Sometimes she panics, and sometimes she dissociates. A well-wrought interpretation at such a moment has about the same impact and healing value as that forcefully hurled, proverbial old "snowball in Hell."

When Lara is in such a highly charged state, I look for helpful responses, ones that work to contain and hold her distress. I want to help to soothe her,

42   *On my becoming an analyst*

to regulate her arousal, which is a selfobject function. Of course, I'm not always successful. But when I do succeed, it's generally because I have found a way to resonate with Lara's disorganized affect state and also to respond to some deep developmental longing. Sometimes I do nothing more than sit quietly and attentively watch her. I try to keep my facial and vocal expressions in the general range of her own in an effort to convey that I connect with her experience. Sometimes, I say something simple and tuned to an unrealized wish. My strategies have nothing to do with "making nice" or "supplying provision." They are, in a word, instrumental. They simply work better than anything else I have found to do.

I can anchor these strategies in contemporary psychoanalytic theory; but, in truth, they emerge, as any good theory emerges, from my life and from forty years of work as a psychologist. I can certainly cite infant researchers: for example, Daniel Stern (1985) and Beatrice Beebe (1994, 1998) for their enormously helpful ideas about multi-modal and cross-modal matching in dyadic interaction. Beebe's ideas about parental mid-range responsiveness (1998) and mutual affective coordination (1992) also support my reactions to Lara's disorganized emotional states. In addition, I am deeply influenced by the Boston Change Process Group's—particularly Lyons-Ruth's—understanding of the transformative power of new non-verbal ways of being with another

Yet, the great pleasure and challenge of analytic work for me begin with my own personal reactions. I most value those moments in which I am present and deeply engaged with another person. In those moments I learn what interactions work humanly, learn to distinguish between interventions which undermine process and those which advance development and healing. It is also in the context of such interpersonal moments that I can best use psychoanalytic theory: that I can draw from it and distinguish what harmonizes and what clashes with my experience.

At base, then, I am an empiricist—yet, an empiricist who loves theory and uses it instrumentally as I find it useful. I love theories that validate, illuminate, and expand on my clinical observations. If clinical experience is a simple form embedded in a marble block, then good theory provides the chisels and tools which help define the emergent form and reveal its details, its complexity of angles and expanses, and its lights and shadows.

I will continue now with some illuminating theory. Kohut describes two kinds of interpretations: "trailing edge" and "leading edge" interpretations. Trailing edge interpretations identify the dynamic and early-life determinates of a person's motivations and defenses. They frequently describe and explain the patient's pathology and neurotic constructions. Trailing edge interpretations are a familiar feature of our cultural climate. They are the staples of classical psychoanalysis as well as of old Hollywood shrink movies like "Snake Pit," "Bedlam," and "Spellbound." Leading edge interpretations speak to the person's developmental longings and strivings. Good interpretations usually include both leading and trailing edge qualities. When Lara is affectively aroused, however, if I say anything at all, I try to address two things:

On my becoming an analyst 43

her leading edge longings and her efforts to be an actor in her own life. Lara carries the pride as well as the guilt of a survivor. At the best of times, she has trouble hearing about her past suffering, an aspect of trailing edge interventions. When she is highly distressed and aroused, she has no tolerance for her own pain—for thinking, talking, or hearing about it.

I have many differences with Lew Aron's response, particularly what I consider his proposed "trailing edge" analysis of Lara and his tone. I'll begin, though, with an area of agreement. Aron presents a plausible story which has as its mono-thematic premise and focus Lara's sado-masochistic proclivities. I agree that sado-masochism is an apt term, although I don't much like it because of its classical drive theory associations. Yet, much in Lara's history and social behavior fits a sado-masochistic attribution. And, in our long relationship Lara and I have certainly explored this S-M configuration. As Lara puts it, "Ray Charles could see it."

Aron asserts, after Davies and Frawley (1991), that a valid treatment of adult survivors of sexual abuse requires both analyst and patient to enact all roles involved in the abusive drama: perpetrator, victim, witness, and rescuer. What's more, he insists, any analyst worth her salt—any authentic analyst, that is—could never remain cool in the face of a patient's provocative or sadistic strategies. The mother-in-me wonders if Dr. Aron has never seen parents remain cool in the face of a child's temper tantrum?

Yet, Aron's response was very helpful to me. His observation about my defensiveness, my shrinking from Lara's cruelty because I don't like the cruel parts of myself, seems right on. It clarified and caused me to rethink some of my choices. For example, did my emphasis on the positive aspects of Lara's functioning sometimes cause me to avoid confronting her destructive patterns in the world and in our relationship? Probably. And on reflection I agree that I am sometimes defensively "nice," not such a bad trait except when it blinds me to dynamic factors and impedes honest and helpful communication. Aron's observations have helped me to be more aware, direct, and perhaps tougher about Lara's aggressiveness—and subsequently to risk being more assertive with patients generally. Old organizations are very sticky, though, and as becomes clear in Chapter 8, the end of my relationship with Lara was angry and wrenching and, sadly, a repetitive enactment of her lifetime of sado-masochistic experience. Had my defensive structure been different, maybe I would have been more prepared and helpful at that time.

My trouble with Aron is less with content and more with tone and presentation style: the fairly rigid way in which he presents the abusive drama. His depiction feels fixed and mechanistic and reminds me how, through overuse and routine, wonderful living ideas sometimes become hackneyed and turn to *schtick*. I acknowledge that Lara's sado-masochistic organization played out with my own, but it did so in surprising and unpredictable moments, rarely taking center stage in our relationship, and feeling more nuanced than Aron's schematic presentation suggested.

44 *On my becoming an analyst*

Oddly, Aron seemed not to realize that his categorical statements, delivered in a tone of authoritative certainty, clashes with basic tenets of relational psychoanalysis. Relational analysts, after all, believe that theories and techniques are merely reflections of individual analysts and of their interactions with a limited number of individual patients. Such interpersonally derived ideas are not the absolute truth about anything. Relational thinkers also believe that each working analytic couple is a unique joint creation. Presumably, what works in one dyad might not in another. However eccentric and strangely tinged a given couple may seem, it nevertheless has its own private integrity, one that may be beyond the ken of even the smartest and most experienced outside observer. Simply put, there is a high "unknowability quotient" in the relationship of others; nobody has the corner on truth; and theories are best held lightly in an open palm.

In any case, if Aron were working with Lara—if she stayed in treatment with him, that is—they would likely create a story that has sado-masochism as its focus. I can also imagine them getting into some scrappy enactments. We certainly know that expectations are predictive: what we expect to happen or to find, we usually create/discover. Furthermore, Lara is an accomplished street fighter, quick to angry, disorganizing outbursts. In fact, many dissociated episodes in her life involve such violent eruptions. For Lara, the memories of these eruptions are like pools of shame. I expect that diving into and swimming in those pools with her analyst would likely retraumatize her. Provoked in this way, I also imagine she would abort the treatment. However, I could be wrong. In any case, Lara and I together created a very different story with a different emphasis. Ours includes sado-masochism but places it in the narrative exposition, not in the foreground or unfolding of the action. Before I describe our story, however, I want to discuss several of Aron's assumptions.

Aron's first assumption is that when working with traumatized patients, "It is not enough to be a good or a new object; one must be an old, a bad or a traumatic object, as well." As Shane put it and I concur:

> I myself would disagree that in work with a traumatized patient, one has to assume the role of the bad or traumatic object, or that such a view of the analyst must inevitably emerge. It may pervade the patient's experience of the analyst ... but it is not always the case, and just to assume the emergence of that transference configuration runs the risk of iatrogenically provoking it.[11]

"Iatrogenic" originally referred to medical treatment which creates more disease. In current psychoanalytic parlance, it means problems manufactured in the analytic dyad. To expand briefly on Dr. Shane's statement: I wonder if Aron's emphasis on enactments and role-playing may not also constitute an evasion of the pain of trauma, an escape into action as a means of avoiding its anguish.

The second assumption has to do with the place of aggression and destructiveness in a person's life. This discussion is at least as old as the Biblical story of Adam and Eve and Original Sin and as the theological Problem of Evil. Leaving aside philosophical musings about such inexplicably evil people as Iago and Hitler, I would like to present two contrasting psychoanalytic streams of thought about aggression. Aron suggests that aggression is a primary force and must be "ruthlessly" confronted in analysis. He shares this assumption with classical and many object relational analysts. I, on the other hand—along with attachment theorists Bowlby (1969, 1973, 1980, 1985) and Main (1995, 1996) and self-psychologists Kohut (1971, 1977, 1984), Shane et al. (1997), and Lachmann (2000) understand aggression not as a primary drive but as a complex response to a number of factors. These factors include frustration from trauma, neglect, separation, and insecure attachment as they interact with such influences as parental, social, and cultural models and possible neurological anomalies.

Lachmann adds to the argument the idea that the absence in early life of any contingent responsiveness may produce the conditions for extreme violence. No "contingent responsiveness" means that parents and caretakers—and, perhaps, the culture—have failed to respond to the child's very being, failed to recognize or provide for the child's needs, failed to provide soothing for her pain or regulation for her physical and emotional arousal. At the same time, these same caretakers have prevented "the organization of the other [motivational systems] such as attachment, exploration, and sensual and sexual pleasure."[12] The child who receives such treatment dies psychologically. Lachmann notes that common to all serial killers is "some variant of deadness,"[13] lifelessness, and lack of affectivity. Violence for them may serve an arousing and enlivening function, an antidote to existential nothingness. Finally, Lachmann speaks of the central role of shame in the motivation toward violence. He reports studies that show humiliation and disrespect and the loss of pride and self-respect as antecedent to many anti-social acts. Many contemporary analysts, me included, view aggression, then, as essentially reactive and a derivative of some combination of constitutional predispositions and painful lived experiences.

These differing understandings about violence express differing belief systems about human nature and have implications for analytic treatment. For example, if all patients are born with a reservoir of rage, then the regulation of aggression—its control, containment, and sublimation—becomes a primary treatment goal. This certainly was true for Freud and for Melanie Klein. Self-psychologists and intersubjective theorists do not subscribe to the "reservoir of rage" concept. Therefore, the evaluation of a patient's aggression, its intensity and meaning for the person, becomes the therapeutic goal. Attaining the goal requires an understanding and exploration of the sources of that aggression.

For my patient Lara, neglect and shame are bedrock, foundational to her hostility. Incidents and interactions that feel insulting or disrespectful can cue her rage reactions. I understand this about her and try—mostly with success—to avoid comments, which she might construe as disrespectful. The times when I have inadvertently shamed her, Lara has certainly let me know.

46   *On my becoming an analyst*

Besides, I genuinely respect Lara and am a responsible partner in our relationship, with minor lapses, of course. These factors account, I believe, for the absence of significant anger between us.

I have a final quibble with Aron. I believe his conception of Lara's case is too static, too anchored in a single trailing edge formulation. Healthy, established analytic relationships are always moving and changing in a forward direction. We know from non-linear dynamic systems theory: Cilliers (1998), Edelman (1992, 2000), Thelen and Smith (1994), Weisel-Barth (2006), Coburn (2013) for example, that the analytic dyad constitutes a complex system, a system that obeys the principles of organization for complex systems generally. These principles are all about change and expansiveness: they track changes in a system's organization, in its discontinuities, and in its reorganizations. Development is embedded in a complex context—including the influence of a respectful, attentive analyst—and it is keenly sensitive to that context. Even small changes in existing contexts—complexity theorists call them "perturbations"—may trigger the emergence of new and larger contexts. These, in turn, produce new system organizations and sometimes radical transformations. With all this emphasis on movement and change, Aron's critique seems rather cramped and anemic, far too focused on the fixed there-and-then rather than on the dynamic here-and-now and the exciting what-may-be.

Before concluding this paper, I want briefly to return to the Chicago narrative. At the plenary panel after Stolorow and Aron spoke, Dr. Shane summarized their statements. Then because time was short, I could say only a few words. I directed them to Lew Aron, and what I said was a quick version of what I have just written. I felt clear and centered during and after my response. After the presentation, elated and feeling very full of many things, I headed for the Ladies Room. There I had the most surprising and affecting encounter, my own "now moment." The assembled women—and after sitting for almost three hours at the plenary session, there was a swarm of them waiting in line—turned toward me in what seemed like a single movement. Then, practically in unison, they gave me a rousing and affirming "YESSS!" Somehow, it seems, I had spoken for them. I think they were cheering, in part, a feminine version of David surviving the Giant. By some unintentional accident, Estelle Shane and I, on one side, and Stolorow and Aron, on the other, had inadvertently aligned ourselves across complicated gender lines.

Later, many women approached and thanked me for "getting it," and a few men accused me of blindness to Lara's innate aggression. For example, with respect to the incident of the picture of Lara's mother, several men chided me for not recognizing and confronting the hostility in Lara's testing of me. On the other hand, Marian Tolpin, a well-known self-psychologist, of blessed memory, said of the incident, "Of course, the girl wants to love her mother and doesn't know how. You gave her a way to appreciate her mother. Those men just don't get it."

Such encounters caused me to reflect about gender issues in Lara's case. Without wanting to slide into a sexist swamp, I nevertheless recognize a

On my becoming an analyst 47

feminine spirit hovering over and informing my work with Lara. To begin with, everyone involved with the case was female: Lara, Estelle Shane, me, and the invisible muse in this enterprise, my analyst Janet Hadda.

What, then, are the features that stamp this case as particularly feminine? The answer, I think, is two-fold: content issues and therapeutic approach, both of which have a feminine flavor. With respect to the feminine content issues, from the outset, sprinkling our sessions were the familiar topics of female small talk—opinions about clothes, hair, plastic surgery, other women, and the eternally imperfect female body—the small talk out of which women's relationships spring. Also, early on, I watched and felt Lara sizing me up as a woman, non-verbally of course, although I heard the unspoken questions. How does this shrink decorate her office and herself? What kind of taste does she have? What's her history with men? How does she take care of herself? How's she holding up in the age department? Much later in our relationship, Lara laughed as she admitted that I had, indeed, heard these unarticulated questions correctly. Without reducing their complexity, I believe these deliberations functioned in part to help her decide if she could identify with me, trust me and ultimately create with me a reparative bond of a maternal/feminine nature. In my view, absence of maternal—and also paternal—nurturing seems the primary injury, the seat of deepest longing, and the main arena for therapeutic enactment and focus in my work with Lara.

Weaving through all our sessions are the themes of Lara's history as a woman with men, her need to tell the story, and her longing to be empathically comprehended. Her history reflects a continuing effort to assert herself with powerful men in a man's world and the ensuing frustration and rage at failing. Despite brutal and exploitative treatment by male figures—beginning early with her father—she has used her beauty, brains, brassiness, and sexuality in a lifelong struggle to equalize power and establish a place for herself in their world. To that end, she has played many and varied roles: tomboy, sex kitten, femme-fatale, spitfire, and vixen. Unfortunately, she has repeatedly chosen the same kind of man, demonic and brutal, and, consequently, has repeatedly suffered the same pattern of frustration and failure. The fact that, after childhood, Lara became a co-creator of these dark, repetitive relationships does not diminish their pain.

Lara's story, while extreme in its brutality, is part of a larger feminist story, a story to which her analyst and her analyst's consultants are no strangers. While not always as violent as Lara's encounters, sexism—its cruel inequalities and injustices—takes many forms, wears many guises, and inhabits many worlds, including the worlds of marriage, academia, and, yes, even psychoanalysis. Shared suffering deepens understanding and creates compassionate community. I think this particular compassion—feminine compassion—has been a crucial feature in my relationship with Lara.

As important as the content issues is the analytic approach in this case. I have aimed to create with Lara a holding environment in which she might feel safe and free with another person, probably for the first time in her life. To accomplish this aim requires non-verbal attention and engagement that is responsive to Lara's affect states as mediated through my own subjectivity.

48 *On my becoming an analyst*

I express this attention and engagement with Lara in physical ways, using such gestures as assenting head nods, continuous visual scrutiny, facial expressions that match Lara's emotions, and body extensiveness—i.e., leaning into her at heightened moments. Vocally, I notice myself making frequent non-linguistic responsive sounds. Clicks, sighs, and many "Hm's," "Tsk's" and "Uh huh's" pepper our interactions. This non-verbal approach, validated by ideas from Winnicott, attachment theory, and early childhood research, clearly has a feminine/maternal character, regardless of the analyst's gender.

Gerhardt, in an essay on gender differences in psychoanalytic process, speaks of such gestures as "acknowledgment tokens." She remarks on the softening of boundaries, which such markers promote:

> such use bespeaks a mode of relatedness in which the separation of the therapist and patient is less well defined. It is as if in using these markers the therapist is in the "experiencing-self" mode of engagement with the patient, in which she sustains a relatively more *interdependent* way of being, and thus experiences her own reverie as a product of the intersubjective situation.[14]

This approach is as notable for what is background as for what takes center stage in the analysis. Conflict and confrontation in the analysis, for example, have been minimal—and, as acknowledged above, maybe too minimal. That aggression has not been central is surprising given Lara's stormy relational history. In our work, there has also been little attention paid to some usual therapeutic agenda items, and I refer here to serious and important items like forging an intimate relationship if the patient is single. One day in supervision, for example, Dr. Shane asked me if I thought Lara would ever be able to sustain a relationship with a man. I was surprised at the question and surprised at my surprise. While I realized that I had a quick response to the question—"I'm not sure, but probably not"—I also realized I hadn't ever thought about the question. During all the years, my work with Lara has focused on creating with her the trustworthy therapeutic space—a place to breathe easy and just "be" with another human being—and the difficulties of doing this. I believe this is the important analytic task; yet, it does keep us cocooned, in a space analogous to one occupied by a mother and child at an early developmental stage. We deal with issues of adult life, of course, but they are not at the heart of our work together.

What remains to write about my patient Lara and about my wanderings in the fields of contemporary psychoanalysis? Certainly, I have indicated that Lara and I have created a story together. It is a story of a constitutionally strong person who, though seriously wounded, survived a neglectful, abusive, and traumatic childhood. Entrained with the childhood pain, her adult relational patterns—which mirror the early traumatic configurations—have left her with problems of esteem, self-regulation, and entitlement. Gifted with health, intelligence, and beauty, until recently she has short-changed herself in personal transactions. After several years in treatment, she still struggles with feelings of worthlessness and failure. Her emotional fuse still trips easily. She works herself to exhaustion. She still takes care of her ex-husband and sick friends and probably gives too generously and indiscriminately of her time and money. She rescues stray animals; and at the end of the day, she still finds herself in debt.

Yet, Lara would say her life is much improved from our first meeting. She hasn't engaged in a destructive sexual relationship in years; and self-interest now, at least, figures into her life plans. Lara no longer feels all alone and credits our relationship for making a great difference in her life.

Why? Contemporary theories of mind and psychological development yield suggestive answers. While studying infant developmental research particularly, I had a transforming insight about psychological growth.

> Development does not begin in loneliness but in connection with other minds. Everything important in psychological growth happens outside what we have traditionally called the psyche. Even though, like Freud, I always thought it happened inside—a bounded psyche or whatever—I see now that everything important in psychological life, in the development of mind, happens in the shared space that I create with another person. While some of us elaborate and refine our interactive experience in solitude, it is the real, lived interactive experience that sets all psychic growth in motion. And I would add this corollary: In addition, feeling suffuses and infuses every important event and process in psychological development.

Notes

1 Stolorow (2000), p. 2.
2 ibid., p. 3.
3 ibid., p. 3.
4 Aron (2000), pp. 2–3.
5 Stolorow, op. cit. p. 5.
6 Aron, op. cit. p. 10.
7 ibid., p. 11.
8 Stolorow (op. cit.), p. 9.
9 ibid., p. 10.
10 Aron (op. cit.), p. 13
11 Shane (2000), p. 7.
12 Lachmann (2000), p. 143.
13 ibid., p. 143
14 Gerhardt and Beyerle (1997), p. 405.

References

Aron, L. (1996) *A Meeting of Minds*. Hillsdale, NJ: Analytic Press.
Aron L. (1999) Clinical Choices and the Relational Matrix. *Psychoanal. Dialog.*, 9 (1):1–30.
Aron, L. (2000) The Role of the Relationship in the Therapeutic Process. Paper Presented at The 23rd Annual International Conference on the Psychology of the Self. Chicago, Illinois.

50 *On my becoming an analyst*

Atwood, G. E. & Stolorow, R. D. (1984) *Structures of Subjectivity: Explorations in Psychoanalytic Phenomenology*. Hillsdale, NJ: The Analytic Press.

Bacal, H. A. (1998) *Optimal Responsiveness: How Therapists Heal Their Patients*. New York: Jason Aronson.

Balint, M. (1968/1999) *The Basic Fault: Therapeutic Aspects of Regression*. Evanston, IL: Northwestern University Press.

Beebe, B. (1998) A Procedural Theory of Therapeutic Action: Commentary on the Symposium, Interventions the Affect Change in Psychotherapy. *Infant Mental Health J.*, 19 (3):333–339.

Beebe, B. (2000) Co-Constructing Mother-Infant Distress: The Microsynchrony of Maternal Impingement and Infant Avoidance in the Face-to-Face Encounter. *Psychoanal. Inquiry*, 20 (3):421–440.

Beebe, B. & Jaffe, J. (1992) The Dyadic Regulation of Mother-Infant Coordination. *Infant Behav. Dev.*, 15:113.

Beebe, B. & Lachmann, F. (1994) Representation and Internalization in Infancy: Three Principles of Salience. *Psychoanal. Psychol.*, 11 (2):125–165.

Beebe, B. & Lachmann, F. (1998) Co-Constructing Inner and Relational Processes: Self- and Mutual Regulation in Infant Research and Adult Treatment. *Psychoanal. Psychol.*, 15 (4):480–516.

Benjamin, J. (2004). Beyond Doer and Done to: An Intersubjective View of Thirdness. *The Psychoanal. Quart.*, 73 (1), 5–46. 10.1002/j.2167-4086.2004.tb00151.x.

Bollas, C. (1978) The Transformational Object. *Int. J. Psychoanal.*, 60:97–107.

Bollas, C. (1987) *The Shadow of the Object: Psychoanalysis of the Unthought Known*. London: Free Press.

Bowlby, J. (1969) *Attachment and Loss*, Vol. 1. New York: Basic Books.

Bowlby, J. (1973) *Attachment and Loss*, Vol. 2. New York: Basic Books.

Bowlby, J. (1980) *Attachment and Loss*, Vol. 3. New York: Basic Books.

Bowlby, J. (1985) *A Secure Base*. New York: Basic Books.

Brandshaft, B. (1994) *Structures of Pathological Accommodation and Change in Psychoanalysis*. Unpublished Manuscript.

Breger, L. (2000) *Freud: Darkness in the Midst of Vision*. New York: John Wiley & Sons, Inc.

Bromberg, P. M. (1998) *Standing in the Spaces: Essays on Process, Trauma and Dissociation*. Hillsdale, NJ: The Analytic Press.

Brothers, L. (1997) *Friday's Footprint: How Society Shapes the Human Mind*. New York, Oxford: Oxford University Press.

Bruschweiler-Stern, N., Reflections on the Process of Psychotherapeutic Change as Applied to Medical Situations. *Infant Mental Health J.*, 19 (3):320–324.

Cilliers, P. (1998) *Complexity and Postmodernism*. London and New York: Routledge.

Coburn, W. (2013). *Psychoanalytic Complexity*. London: Routledge.

Damasio, A. (1999) *The Feeling of What Happens: Body and Emotion in the Making of Consciousness*. New York: Harcourt Brace & Co.

Davies, J. M. & Frawley, M. G. (1991/1999) Dissociative Processes and Transference-Countertransference Paradigms in the Psychoanalytically Oriented Treatment of Adult Survivors of Childhood Sexual Abuse. In S. A. Mitchell & L. Aron (eds.) *Relational Psychoanalysis: The Emergence of a Tradition*. Hillsdale, NJ: Analytic Press.

Edelman, G. (1992) *Bright Air, Brilliant Fire*. New York: Basic Books.

Edelman, G. & Tononi, G. (2000) *A Universe of Consciousness: How Matter Becomes Imagination*. New York: Basic Books.

Fonagy, P., Steele, M., Steele, H., Moran, G. S., & Higgit, A. C. (1991) The Capacity for Understanding Mental States: The Reflective Self in Parent and Child and Its Significance for Security and Attachment. *Infant Mental Health J.*, 12 (3):201–218.

Fonagy, P. & Target, M. (1997) Attachment and Reflective Function: Their Role in Self-Regulation. *Dev. Psychopathol.*, 9 (4):679–700.

Gerhardt, J. & Beyerle, S. (1997) What if Socrates Had Been a Woman? The Therapist's Use of Acknowledgment Tokens as Nonreflective Means of Intersubjective Involvement. *Contemp. Psychoanal.*, 33 (3):367–410.

Knoblauch, S. H. (2000) *The Musical Edge of Therapeutic Dialogue.* Hillsdale, NJ: Analytic Press.

Kohut, H. (1971) *The Analysis of the Self.* New York: International Universities Press, Inc.

Kohut, H. (1977) *The Restoration of the Self.* New York: International Universities Press, Inc.

Kohut, H. (1984) *How Does Analysis Cure?* Chicago: University of Chicago Press.

Lachmann, F. (1999) Music and Psychoanalysis, *Program for the 22nd Annual Conference on the Psychology of the Self.* Toronto, Canada.

Lachmann, F. (2000) *Transforming Aggression: Psychotherapy with the Difficult-to-Treat Patient.* Northvale, NY: Jason Aronson.

Lachmann, F. & Beebe, B. (1997) Three Principles of Salience in the Organization of the Patient-Analyst Interaction. *Psychoanal. Psychol.*, 13 (1):1–22.

Lyons-Ruth, K. (1998) Implicit Relational Knowing: Its Role in Development and Psychoanalytic Treatment. *Infant Mental Health J.*, 19 (3):282–289.

Main, M. (1995) Atttachment: Overview, with Implications for Clinical Work. In S. Goldberg, R. Muir & J. Kerr (eds.), *Attachment Theory: Social, Developmental and Clinical Perspectives* (pp. 407–474). Hillsdale, NJ: Analytic Press.

Mitchell, S. A. (1993) *Hope and Dread in Psychoanalysis.* New York: Basic Books.

Mitchell, S. A. (2000) *Relationality.* Hillsdale, NJ: Analytic Press.

Mitchell, S. A. & Aron, L. (1999) *Relational Psychoanalysis: The Emergence of a Tradition.* Hillsdale, NJ: Analytic Press.

Nahum, J. D. (1998) Case Illustration: Moving Along and, Is Change Gradual or Sudden?, *Infant Mental Health J.*, 19 (3):315–319.

Ogden, T. H. (1994/1999) The Analytic Third: Working with Intersubjective Clinical Facts. In *Relational Psychoanalysis: The Emergence of a Tradition.* Hillsdale, NJ: Analytic Press.

Orange, D. M. (1995) *Emotional Understanding.* New York: The Guilford Press.

Orange, D. M., Atwood, G. E., & Stolorow, R. D. (1997) *Working Intersubjectively: Contextualism in Psychoanalytic Practice.* Hillsdale, NJ: The Analytic Press.

Schore, A. N. (1994) *Affect Regulation and the Origin of the Self: The Neurobiology of Emotional Development.* Hillsdale, NJ: Erlbaum.

Schore, A. N. (1997) Early Organization of the Nonlinear Right Brain and Development of a Predispostition fo Psychiatric Disorders. *Dev. Psychopathol.*, 9:595–631.

Shane, E. (2000) Moderator's Commentary for Panel II at the 23rd Annual Conference on the Psychology of the Self. Chicago, Illinois.

Shane, M., Shane, E., & Gales, M. (1997) *Intimate Attachments: Toward a New Self Psychology.* New York: The Guilford Press.

Siegel, D. (2000) *The Developing Mind: Toward a Neurobiology of Interpersonal Experience.* New York, London: The Guilford Press.

Siegel, D. (2001) Toward an Interpersonal Neurobiology of the Developing Mind: Attachment Relationships, Mindsight, and Neural Integration. *Infant Mental Health J.*, 22 (1–2):67–94.

52 *On my becoming an analyst*

Stern, D. (1985) *The Interpersonal World of the Child*. New York: Basic Books.

Stern, D. (1998) Non Interpretive Mechanisms of Psychoanalytic Therapy: The "Something More" than Interpretation. *Int. J. Psychoanal.*, 79:903.

Stern, D. (1998) The Process of Therapeutic Change Involving Implicit Knowledge: Some Implications of Developmental Observations for Adult Psychotherapy. *Infant Mental Health J.*, 19 (3):300–308.

Stern, D. B. (1997) *Unformulated Experience: From Dissociation to Imagination in Psychoanalysis*. Hillsdale, NJ: Analytic Press.

Stolorow, R. D. (2000) On the Impossibility of Immaculate Perception: There Is No Relationship Without Interpretation, and There Is No Interpretation without Relationship. Paper Presented at *the 23rd Annual Conference on the Psychology of the Self*. Chicago, Illinois.

Stolorow, R. D. & Atwood, G. E. (1979) *Faces in a Cloud: Subjectivity in Personality Theory*. Northvale, NJ: Jason Aronson.

Stolorow, R. D. & Atwood, G. E. (1992) *Contexts of Being: The Intersubjective Foundation of Psychological Life*. Hillsdale, NJ: Analytic Press.

Stolorow, R. D., Brandschaft, B., & Atwood, G. E. (1987) *Psychoanalytic Treatment: An Intersubjective Approach*. Hillsdale, NJ: Analytic Press.

Thelen, E. & Smith, L. (1994) *A Dynamic Systems Approach to the Development of Cognition and Action*. Cambridge: A Bradford Book, The MIT Press.

Travarthen, C. (1993) The Self Born in Intersubjectivity: The Psychology of an Infant Communicating. In U. Neisser (ed.) *The Perceived Self: Ecological and Interpersonal Sources of Self-Knowledge* (pp. 121–173). New York: Cambridge University Press.

Tronick, E. Z. (1998) Dyadically Expanded States of Consciousness and the Process of Therapeutic Change. *Infant Mental Health J.*, 19 (3):290–299.

Van der Kolk, B. A., McFarlane, A. C., & Weisaeth, L., eds. (1996) *Traumatic Stress: The Effects of Overwhelming Experience on Mind, Body and Society*. New York: The Guilford Press.

Varela, F., Thompson, E., & Rosch, E. (2000) *The Embodied Mind: Cognitive Science and Human Experience*. Cambridge: The MIT Press.

Weisel-Barth, J. (2006) Thinking and Writing about Complexity Theory in the Clinical Setting. *Int. J. Self Psychol.*, 1 (4), 365–388.

Winnicott, D. W. (1971/1989) *Playing and Reality*. London: Tavistock.

Winnicott, D. W. (1975) *Through Pediatrics to Psychoanalysis*. New York: Basic Books.

2 On analytic certainty and delinquent dissembling

The case of Sharon

Recently, I've given some invited talks at psychoanalytic institutes around the country and have found with dismay that old analytic certitude is alive and well. I thought it had died. The certitude extends from knowing what psychoanalysis is to knowing its correct procedure and proper outcome and then—in response to my talks—to knowing what I've done wrong. I particularly hate that last certitude about what I've done wrong.

Here's an example: after I had described an intimate therapeutic exchange, a senior analyst at a Midwestern institute rose and with a booming voice announced, "But your interpretation didn't begin with what happened between the two of you in the previous session! Why not?" Her volume and tone accused, tried, and convicted me of something bad—on the spot, publicly and with great contempt! By not referring to the previous therapy session, I had evidently violated one of her procedural analytic shibboleths; and in doing so I had aroused her defensive ire.

The analyst's righteous certainty at first took me aback. Rigid adherence to theory seems passé to me: dynamic systems thinking suggests convincingly that the maps of psychoanalytic theory are only abstract and pale guides to the complex and layered terrains of the human mind and heart. But, then, the woman's accusation sent me back in time to my early professional training at Thalians Mental Health Center in Los Angeles, circa the early 1970s, where I learned about many uses of theory beyond its simple function as organizer of intellectual data. There at Thalians theory, in a particular dogmatic form, often served as a weapon in political and personal struggles. And I remembered Sharon, my first patient at Thalians, and how our relationship began in a theoretically dogmatic climate.

Thalians, now defunct and shuttered, was then a part of the prestigious Cedars-Sinai Hospital complex. It was the domain of prominent Beverly Hills and West Los Angeles ego psychologists just as that particular school was beginning its descent from economic and cultural hegemony. The powers-that-were had a great deal to protect, and they partly did it by knowing more—and with more certainty and authority—than anybody else.

Thalians was housed in a spanking new modern building—now shuttered—and staffed by an eminent guard of psychoanalysts. My initial

54   *On analytic certainty and delinquent dissembling*

encounter with the building should have been the tip off. The entrance stairs sprawled toward the street in a twisted, askew fashion. They moved on an angle that didn't match the angle of the accompanying stair railing so that entering and leaving the building felt both treacherous and disorienting. Arriving on my first day, I briefly imagined a troubled person trying to negotiate this disturbing staircase. But I was twenty-something, eager, earnest, and a master of disavowal, and so I cast the image out of mind and was thrilled to enter the building.

Inside I encountered a twisted, askew, and confusing world on many levels: political, theoretical, and personal. Power struggles and jockeying for control occurred between people and departments up and down the rigid professional hierarchy. The ego-psychologists, all physicians, occupied the upper echelons of the hierarchy and directed the traditional treatment and training programs: long-term inpatient and analytic outpatient and child departments. The power structure was so stratified that—for probably proprietary reasons—the senior analysts excluded psychologist and social work interns from the inpatient hospital entirely.

At the bottom of the hierarchy were newer departments with newer mental health models such as a short-term crisis clinic, a community outreach program, and a therapeutic nursery school based on a family systems model. For government funding purposes and for the designation "community mental health center" these departments were mandated. Not surprising, women headed and/or staffed these programs in large numbers while only men ran the more traditional treatment programs. The senior analysts regarded the upstart departments with suspicion and disdain. Like the women who ran them, the new models had no standing or prestige in the scheme of things.

Similar to toxic particulates, power tensions polluted the air at Thalians; they soiled most encounters, and nobody could avoid breathing them in. Yet, as a lowly psychology intern, I couldn't figure out whether the hatreds, the in-group/out-group rivalries, and the theoretical disputes were principled, personal, or merely a reflection of the struggle for dominance among a company of ambitious and rapacious people.

From a forty years' distance many of my memories of Thalians are comic. For instance, I remember one analyst throwing a temper tantrum and storming out of a lecture on Winnicott's "Hate in the Countertransference." Exiting, he tearfully accused the lecturer, Roger Grey,[1] of "murdering psychoanalysis." Winnicott's depiction of the analyst's subjectivity—with negative affect to boot—must have threatened the man's theoretical certainly and propelled his distressed departure.

Another time, when a young man threatened to blow up the building, all the senior psychoanalysts and psychologists fled, leaving the young man in the care of Ellen, a measly social worker. Ellen, while at the bottom of the professional pecking order, was a terrific therapist. She directed the Crisis Clinic, whose charge was to provide responsive, short term, acute mental health services focused on concrete life contexts. Because these goals conflicted with the classic psychoanalytic commitment to long-term, transference-based treatment, the power elite regarded this department and Ellen as unwanted stepchildren; distaste ran from simple suspicion to downright contempt. I tried to imagine what the august ego psychologists would have to say about the measly social worker's successful intervention with the threatening young man, who, thankfully, was unarmed. I remember she said something like, "You must have good reasons for wanting to scare people, but if I were your mother, I'd spank you." The young man melted and started to cry.

Scapegoating each other's interns was one way the senior analysts waged war against each other. Soon after arriving, I began to worry about being somebody's cannon fodder; and when I was assigned Sharon as my first private patient, I found myself in crossfire territory. Let me set the scene. My placement supervisor, Louise, and the director of clinical training, Zev, were hateful rivals—were there any other kind at Thalians? Zev especially resented that, through some glitch in the organizational flow chart, Louise supervised psychology interns. I imagined him plotting ways not only to destroy her, but her interns as well.

This brings us to the treatment protocol for Sharon: June, a post-doctoral psychologist, would supervise my therapeutic work with Sharon; and Zev, the director of training, would supervise June's supervision of me. This protocol potentially put me in harm's way. On first pass, I liked June well enough, but Zev would be scrutinizing and criticizing my work by proxy—that is, through June. As a result, he could potentially get at my boss Louise, injuring her by skewering me. As devious as this sounds, such machinations were daily occurrences at Thalians, and as luck would have it, I now stood directly in Zev's crosshairs.

Enter my patient Sharon, a pretty, plump young girl with freckles on her nose and a terrified look in her eyes. Sharon, newly discharged from a month-long stay in the inpatient ward after a suicide attempt, was 20 years old but looked to be about 15. Oh, and she was mute, hadn't uttered a word during the whole month in hospital. Anxious, inexperienced, and with all my ego psychology theory having suddenly evaporated, I wondered, "What the hell do I do with this?"

At my preparatory supervision session, in the best Freudian tradition, June instructed me to remain silent with Sharon until she spontaneously began to speak. My withholding the provision of speech would create the conditions for Sharon to move forward. This made no experiential sense to me and simply sounded like a mean and depriving approach. However, good, compliant girl that I was, I tried to justify the recommended silent treatment by notions of "therapeutic neutrality" and "therapist as blank slate."

I wince remembering this, although clearly and absurdly I was trying to become a good ego psychologist. In those days when the claims of real, lived experience clashed with the dictates of received theory, one was supposed to surrender to the theory. Given the power and influence of the analytic community and my deep wish to belong, I struggled with this conundrum

56 *On analytic certainty and delinquent dissembling*

until, eventually, I found it too hard to torture my feelings and experience and manacle them in a constraining theory. I finally gave up trying. In hindsight, the prevailing culture at Thalians seems more like that of a sanctimonious religious seminary or cult than of a treatment center for mental distress.

My silence with Sharon lasted until I sat facing the mute, frightened girl for the first time. She seemed terrified, trapped and very young—like one of the shrinking "loom and dodge" babies that Beebe and Lachmann (2002, pp. 111–115) describe. With her body and hands clenched, her spine jammed against the back of the chair, shoulders hunched forward, and eyes wide and vigilant, Sharon had physically positioned herself for an anticipated assault, maybe even for violence.

I began to talk quietly. Who knew I had so much to say? Over weeks I talked about training to be a psychologist, what I liked about it and what was hard. I asked Sharon whether she had something that she loved to do or wanted to learn. She sat watchfully silent. I told her about growing up in Los Angeles in time-filling detail: where I went to school, who my friends were, what we did and where we went for fun, and all the trouble we found or created for ourselves. What was her story, I wondered? Did she have places she liked to go? She didn't answer. I described as a child climbing on the concrete animals at the La Brea Tar Pits—the saber-tooth tiger was my favorite—and losing my mother at Ohrbach's, the great discount department store. I told Sharon how I cried, imagining my mother falling into a sale bin in the center aisle of the store and being smothered under bulky women's sweaters. I asked Sharon about her family and friends; she didn't respond. I talked about liberal politics and inquired about her political preferences. I ranted against the Viet Nam War and wondered what she thought. I talked about books I liked and movies I hated; I told her about my favorite music—this being the great age of rock and roll and fantastic musicians. What music did she like to hear? Several weeks into our meetings when I came to the part about knowing some musicians personally, Sharon began to talk back. "I like Carole King," were her first words. Fortunately, so did I.

Thus, began our fifteen-year therapeutic relationship. After Thalians, Sharon followed me to my beginning practice as a psychological assistant and then remained with me as I built a professional life. I learned from her about personal and familial trauma and searing pain and loneliness; I learned that a person can grow to 20 without ever having another person attend to or care about her feelings or her mind. She also taught me about some of the defensive things a person might do to protect herself from human hostility and indifference.

Early on, Sharon followed me puppy-dog like, an abused and neglected second-generation Holocaust child, hungry for any kind of attention. At first, I mostly worked with her from an attentive and attuned mirroring stance. Then came a long period of anxious testing. Shaky and jittery, she introduced into our relationship tentative self-disclosures and small confrontations with attenuated anger. All the while she scanned me closely, fearfully poised to retreat if I became too dangerous.

On analytic certainty and delinquent dissembling   57

Yet, she also hung in with me. In my failures of attunement, my failures to "get her"—sometimes I responded too quickly or defensively—she behaved like a patient parent with a backward child. With effort she risked confronting my awkwardness and blunders and showed me how hard some patients work—how much teaching they have to do—in order to make a therapy go. During this time, she also began to make anxious forays into the larger world of work, education, and friendship relationships. A few years into our therapy, Sharon told me how lonely and cold her Thalians inpatient experience had been. And she said that if I hadn't talked so damned much, if I hadn't tried so hard—and clumsily—to reach and touch her, she would have silently left therapy. By that time, I knew this without her words.

Meanwhile back at Thalians, I had my supervision to survive for nine whole months—an extended stretch of real time, all symbolic associations aside. How to manage it? Could I risk trusting June? Should I confess to her about speaking to Sharon? I guessed not; June seemed so sure about the utility of analytic abstention. Thankfully, I could trust Ellen, the "measly," aforementioned social worker, who was such a good therapist. In consultation she wholeheartedly supported my lying about my work with Sharon for as long as necessary.

Needless to say, the supervision with June was initially tense and excruciating. In retrospect, I realize that she and I were enacting our difficulty with all the silence, the silence in Sharon's therapy specifically and in classical analytic theory generally. I am a lousy liar; therefore, with June I was nowhere near as loquacious as with Sharon. I mumbled about the difficulty of remaining silent in the face of the girl's obvious fear, and I tested the possibility of my initiating conversation in the therapy sessions. June was impassive, practicing the very rule of silence that she was preaching. In turn, I had trouble finding anything to say. When we did talk, it was mostly about theory and how, in doubt, one can always rely on it. I felt huge relief when Sharon finally began talking, and I could stop lying in supervision; yet, with all my stuttering and dissembling and June's silence and stiffness, we never found a useful therapeutic footing. While not ultimately hurtful, this was a sad waste of a learning opportunity.

A funny yarn in retrospect, my sojourn at Thalians nevertheless catches a serious and sad strain that runs through the history of psychoanalysis since Freud. Kirsner's (2002) book *Unfree Associations* captures much of my experience at Thalians. It describes the analytic heritage of personality cults, institutional authoritarianism, and the ongoing competition for power and prestige often fought under the guise of theory and ideology. Kirsner also deplores the historical and current lack of objectivity in psychoanalytic standards for theoretical "truth claims," clinical practices, and teaching procedures at many institutes; and he critiques the group pressure—sometimes organized around ideology, sometimes around a charismatic leader, and sometimes around both—that impedes free intellectual exploration and dialogue. Dishonesty and delinquency are natural byproducts of such a system.

58   *On analytic certainty and delinquent dissembling*

Unfortunately, in the history of psychoanalysis dishonest behavior like mine is a common response to authoritarian tyranny. Stories told by senior members at my own institute, the Institute of Contemporary Psychoanalysis in Los Angeles, are filled with memories of conscious and unconscious deceptions. Refugees from other Los Angeles institutes, a group of these senior analysts founded ICP almost thirty years ago. They were fleeing their institutional homes because of oppressive theoretical orthodoxies, communal schisms, and vicious personal battles, frequently fought using ideology as the weapon of choice. The founders' vision for ICP was of an intellectually pluralistic community, unaffiliated with the American Psychoanalytic Association, democratically run, and open to equality of opportunity and the free expression of ideas.

Several early members of ICP remember their training at affiliate institutes of the American Psychoanalytic Association and often acknowledge lying in order to fulfill certain rigid candidacy requirements. "Yes, my patient was on the couch."/"We actually met face to face." "Yes, we dealt with her penis envy and castration complex."/"We didn't." "Of course, we tackled and conquered his Oedipal complex."/"Fat chance!" "I was open and honest with my training analyst."/"Had I been truthful, I would never be an analyst now."

Shocking and shameful—and funny—as these confessions are, they are also commonplace. And, it seems that dissembling operates at more subtle levels as well. A reluctance or failure to question authority, to challenge dogma, to rock a boat, or to honor one's own inner voice—these are the self-deceptions and self-betrayals, deriving from group pressure, economic interest, and political ambition, that have dogged analytic organizations since the advent in 1906 of Freud's Wednesday Society.

To grasp the depth of the authoritarian strain in psychoanalysis and its relation to power, we only have to recall its history. For example, the Committee, founded in 1912 by a group of Freud's faithful followers, was a secret group that functioned with Freud's support until 1936 to preserve the theoretical purity of psychoanalysis and to quash conflict. It sought to root out heresies, stifle debate among members, and impose censorship in analytic publications. Then, Freud's excommunications of, among others, Adler, Jung, Rank, and Ferenczi for theoretical heresy provide more instances of the authoritarian climate that suffused psychoanalysis, supported censorship, and informed institutional decisions. Finally, a later example of this dysfunctional dynamic is the personal/ideological warfare between Anna Freud and Melanie Klein. Their theoretical and personal animus splintered the British analytic world into three parts in the 1930s. The third part, the Middle Group, was apparently made up of analysts, who had little heart for vicious antagonism and aggression.

The question now is how persistent is this legacy of authoritarianism and delinquency in psychoanalysis? As I began this piece, I suggested that authoritarian thought and behavior are alive in varying degrees at institutes I have visited, sometimes in pockets and sometimes in dominant forms. At my own institute ICP—in spite of a continuing commitment to pluralism and open exploration—it also functions in abbreviated ways.

For example, at my institute personal enmities have at times created theoretical schisms and communal divisiveness. Hurt and angry feelings have played out—at least, in part—in the defensive hardening of theoretical and clinical differences and in the generating of competing language games. Sometimes rivals have published combative articles and sought to recruit followers for confirming support. At public meetings, opposing theoretical and clinical positions have occasionally interfered with open dialogue about ideas and practice. And in candidate classes one dominant clique can sometimes limit exploration and/or stifle conversation. What results is a diminution of complexity and openness in exploring ideas: a flattening of conversation to the loyal and safe and familiar instead of toward a thickening and deepening of thought, the process of dialogic enlargement from which springs the surprising and new.

In closing this little essay on the impact of authoritarian certainty on the field of psychoanalysis and on me, I notice my own reluctance to address its occurrence at my own institute. This hesitation constitutes a personal delinquency, an enactment of the dynamic that this paper highlights. I feel cowardly for not wanting to risk rocking my institutional boat or to incur anger and perhaps ostracism. This is shameful and painful for me to acknowledge. Yet, my reluctance underlines how deeply embedded I am in the history, tradition, and practices of psychoanalysis and how adhesive even outworn and discredited practices can be. It's not just that old psychic and behavioral organizations "die hard," but perhaps they never quite die at all.

Note

1 I will use disguised names here.

References

Beebe, B. & Lachmann, F. (2002) *Infant Research and Adult Treatment: Co-Constructing Interactions*. Hillsdale, NJ: Analytic Press, p. 280.

Kirsner, D. (2000) *Unfree Associations*.

3 Analyst envy in working with an artist

Four scenes

In the circus there are trapeze acrobats, and there are catchers. The catchers are the guys who swing by their knees and pace their rhythm of flight in perfect time to catch the flying trapeze artists. They create a living system with the artists, their aerial ballet a graceful synergy. When the acrobat–artists soar, I'm dazzled, hot cheeked and breathless. The arching torsos and spinning bodies are like transforming cannonballs. Now they're exploding spheres, and now suddenly they're projectiles with tapering hands seeking home and safety in the catcher's grasp. I admire the catchers, but I adore the artists and their heedless courage. I imagine myself the character in the old song about the grace and ease of the young man on the flying trapeze. Working with my patient Richard, however, I was the catcher, a fairly good, if sometimes uncertain, catcher, swinging upside down, sometimes unsure of my rhythm but straining to capture my wild artist patient, to protect him from dangerous gyrations and an emotional freefall. I also strained to catch and contain Richard's creative volleys, which scattered everywhere like blasts of buckshot.

Acrobats and catchers are complementary to each other. Mirrors of each other really, they possess many of the same gifts and developed skills. And they speak silently to each other, from body to body and from cell to cell in space. But each has taken a different dominant role. The acrobats pursue a bold, extensive performing role while the catchers adapt and attune themselves to helping the artists do successful work. The roles sometimes contrast, sometimes interlock: the king and the handmaiden, the extrovert and the introvert, the daring and the cautious, the shrieking peacock and the cooing pigeon. The best acrobats also possess catcher skills: that is, they are highly attuned to the patterns and placement of their catchers. I often felt that Richard and I, as different as we appeared, had a great deal in common and many similar gifts. Yet, he had taken the artist's path, and I had become a catcher. Having left a writing career in my twenties, I recognized that Richard represented my road not taken; and, consequently, I was aware of bringing envy as well as curiosity and admiration to our work. The envy sometimes obscured my vision of Richard as the glare of klieg lights, spotlighting the circus acrobats, may temporarily blind the catcher. On the other hand, I believe my envy also served a curative role in my work with Richard, both for him and for me.

Analyst envy in working with an artist 61

Envy has had a bad rap in psychoanalysis. Melanie Klein, who captured the concept and cornered the market on it, emphasized envy in its most malignant forms. Few discussions of envy in the literature have challenged the terms of her conversation. Klein's concept of envy is two staged. First, there is the emotion of envy, either conscious or unconscious, which arises from identifying the other as possessing some enticing quality—some goodness—that is absent in the self. Second, there follow envious strategies and efforts to spoil or destroy the other. Envy, which derives from the death instinct, then, is a wholly destructive emotion.

When an envious person encounters valuable aspects or special gifts in another, he is unable to acknowledge those aspect or gifts. There is a paradox in this situation: the same faculty that allows the person to appreciate the good qualities of the other is, at once, the source of terrible pain and rage. The person feels depleted by the other's qualities, and the resulting senses of emptiness and inferiority generate fury and hatred. I think Trump's hatred of Obama is an example of this kind of envy, what the Kleinians call "malignant envy."

Kleinians and neo-Kleinians agree with this definition and with the fact that the emotion of envy is morally and psychologically unredeemable, totally lacking in any secondary gains:

> [U]nlike other entrees on that list of seven deadlies, unlike gluttony or lust or pride or righteous anger, the sin of envy does not offer even the temporary illusion of short-term pleasure … It ushers in an anguish, fury, self-hatred and shame … [C}ertain forms of envy carry not merely shame and empty longing at someone else's advantage, but also deeply destructive wishes.
>
> (Harris, 2002, p. 298)

> Envy begins early in psychic development and is initially characterized by destructive primal hatred … We can conceive of this primal emotion as a blend of hatred and greed which leads to cannibalistic and murderous impulses ….
>
> (Shengold, 1994, pp. 615, 618)

There have been only a few beginning revisions of Klein. For example, Benjamin reinterprets castration anxiety and penis envy as possible spurs for the young girl to identify with the father and, by extension, with the father's independence and access to the wider world (Benjamin, 1988). Hers is a novel suggestion that some forms of envy may have potential value. Then, Fosshage posits that envy exists on a continuum, and malignant envy is only an extreme instance of the affect (Fosshage, 1998, p. 50).

Finally, and most significantly, Ruderman describes her own—the analyst's—envy in the countertransference. In her case she associated her envy to grief about her own lost or absent opportunities for gratification. She

62 *Analyst envy in working with an artist*

writes, "Envy has its productive and constructive uses; when understood and appropriately managed, it can lead not only to admiration and awe, but to motivation to emulate the envied" (Ruderman, 2002, p. 499). My envy of Richard and its functioning in our relationship well illustrate this last idea.

So, to sum up the discussion: First, Klein's proprietary possession of the term "envy" and her defining it as entirely malignant have mostly kept analytic theorists from thinking seriously about any other forms or functions of envy. Then, discussion of envy has traditionally kept a one-person focus, that is, a focus on the patient's envy. I suppose because psychoanalysis has frowned on intense countertransference feelings; and because envy is nothing if not an intense negative and shame-filled emotion, analysts have either avoided noticing it or avoided including it in descriptions of their own affective responses.

There is clear blindness in such a position. With the myriad of brilliant people, of beautiful, cultured, creative, socially prominent, and wealthy patients, whom our couches have cushioned during the past century, the almost total absence of reported countertransference envy is quite surprising. Ridiculous really! When I found Ruderman's article about the analyst's envy, I felt the same relieved recognition that I felt when first reading Winnicott's "Hate in the Countertransference" (Winnicott, 1965). The dynamic relational thinking of contemporary psychoanalysis finally allows for dark, complex, and shameful emotions, such as envy, on the part of the analyst.

Besides describing my work with Richard here—an appreciative tribute, really—this talk is an attempt to reassess the uses of envy in the cotransference. Here I emphasize my own envious feelings toward my creatively accomplished patient. As I use the term, envy refers to a covetous feeling in relation to something another person has or does. The focus of envy is not on the other person *per se*, but on the enticing experience or object, which the person enacts or possesses. Think of the Ten Commandments which emphasizes the objects of envy: "Thou shalt not covet thy neighbour's house, thou shalt not covet thy neighbour's wife, nor his manservant, nor his maidservant, nor his ox, nor his ass, nor any thing that is thy neighbour's."

Yet, beyond coveting one's neighbor's ox or ass or, indeed, his sexual partners, fancy houses, buff body, or petroleum reserves, envy may also express itself psychologically as intense desire to possess some gift or state or trait or accomplishment of the other. This was the case for me with Richard: I envied his artistic creativity. The experience of envy may lead to feelings of rage or hate toward the possessor of the enticing object or state, but not necessarily. It may also lead to or parallel the related feeling of jealousy. Jealousy does, indeed, focus negatively and resentfully on the other person, taking the form of "I want to be him." But, again, that is not necessarily how envy plays out in analysis, and certainly in this case I didn't want to be Richard.

Envy, indeed, may have productive uses. In the analytic relationship these uses may benefit both the envied and envious partner. For Richard my envy, while not verbally expressed, was alive between us and certainly affected him implicitly. From one perspective, it probably served to humanize me, making

Analyst envy in working with an artist   63

me something less than perfect. For Richard, who dealt in his life and in our analysis with deep feelings of unworthiness, deficiency, and guilt, my being imperfect may have leveled our playing field a bit. It may have contributed to his feeling safe and trusting with me.

I also suspect that my envy worked for him in a way similar to Kohut's mirroring selfobject function. Envy, after all, presumes admiration and recognition. Richard could hardly have failed to register my amazement and delight with the wit and freedom of his imagination or with his manual facility as he created art objects in our sessions. I expect that my envy, expressed in my valuing the time he spent in artistic engagement, contributed to his forgiving himself for nurturing and protecting his artist self. My envy, in fact, contributed to creating the unique color—"spring green" comes to mind—and values of the analysis, the celebration of Richard's courage to be his creative self. In this light, being "green with envy" gains additional meaning. The expression does not carry the accustomed connotation of a condition of moral distress, but rather a new one: renewed growth. I am sure that another analyst, holding more conventional attitudes and values, might have created with Richard a very different experience.

The theoretical part of this presentation is complete, and now a bit of autobiography seems necessary. My feelings of envy toward Richard coincided with my own mother's physical and mental decline. During the years I worked with Richard, my mother changed from a charismatic, creative, funny, and difficult woman to a docile, demented, much-diminished version of herself. Finally, she disappeared. As an adult, I admired, loved, and also hated my mother, yet never came close to resolving with her our complicated relationship. Accompanying my grief over her physical and mental deterioration and regret about our unfinished possibilities was a stinging reminder of my own mortality. In this context witnessing Richard's amazing creative fecundity intensified my grief and produced urgent feelings about lost life chances, opportunities evaded, and boats missed. My envy of Richard, in fact, has been a motivational spur, contributing to my return to writing as, at least, a part-time day job.

Although Richard rejected his conventional mother, I tried—mostly successfully—to fulfill my mother's conventional expectations of me: home, husband, children, career, with all of them remunerative, if you please. At the same time, I have remained a frustrated midnight writer. Therefore, my envious feelings are not surprising as I watch Richard, who, burdened with guilt and ambivalence but ultimately free of convention, continuously plots ways to live out and savor his visions. If I have been stingy with my imagination, he is profligate. Except for allowing it to help me in my work, I save my imagination, like dessert after a balanced dinner, for when all my chores and tasks are done. I am clean and neat and fiercely responsible. Richard, on the other hand, is a slob and in worldly matters fiercely irresponsible.

In fact, in our first year together after his wife left him—taking his daughter—for a new man and an artsy life in Santa Fe, Richard barricaded himself in squalor. Literally! Filled garbage bags, piles of old papers and magazines, half-empty boxes from many household moves, discarded furniture

64 *Analyst envy in working with an artist*

and appliances, and a urine-soaked couch used by desultory cats who lived without a litter box—all these he piled in an arc surrounding a single, small pristine room. Here he slept, ate, watched T.V., composed music and created art on an elaborate computer set-up with multiple components and intricate wiring. Early in our work Richard also wore one outfit at a time, the same outfit, in all seasons, day and night, until it shredded and flaked. It consisted of black cotton pants, a black button-down shirt, and a black leather jacket. He even sometimes showered in this get up—*sans* jacket—at once accomplishing the tasks of laundering himself and his clothes. Certainly, nobody would want to traverse the putrid perimeter of Richard's inner sanctum and self, and this is just as he wanted it. There was a protective method in his muck and mire. I understood this liberating and defensive maneuver.

* * *

Model Scenes About Barricades in Richard's Life:

1 *About his mother Richard tells me, "Imagine a Donna Reed type, dusting the house with her feather duster, dusting, dusting—dusting everything up to and including the trophy case. Now she really gets into it. It turns out that gal can also polish, and the trophy case gleams! She reaches right into the cabinet and grabs the trophy. She scrutinizes it, turning it upside down and sideways, until it wants to blush. Now she's ready to polish it—with plenty of her own spit. After that she rubs it to a sparkle until it feels skinless." Richard continues, "She should have gone to work. Instead I was her hobby. I am her trophy and trophy case."*

2 *And of his father: "In the basement my mother arranged a rumpus room for my father and my brother and me. She made sure there were plenty of art supplies for Craig and me, and my father had his computer toys there, too. He used about a third of the room to build a space for himself and his toys. He set off his space with a chain link fence and locked gate, apart from my brother and me. We could see him through the fence playing with his equipment, and we could look at the equipment through the fence when he wasn't there. But we could never get into his space. My father."*

* * *

About two months into our work

Richard says, "I saw Dr. N. The effexor seems to be working. What a relief to not feel again. I don't have to check and recheck the house or cut myself anymore. (On two different occasions in the first weeks of our meeting, Richard sliced his arms in tiny measured rows.) Mr. Spock is back, but I'm scared. Maybe I'll lose my creative edge on the medicine."

"Mr. Spock?" I ask. Right now I'm thinking about how often Richard refers to old T.V. shows and movies. Although I know Mr. Spock is from *Star Trek*, I never followed that show or many of the others to which Richard

Analyst envy in working with an artist 65

alludes. I am flat-footed, a pop culture dud. Richard's savvy pricks my pride at not being with it and savvy myself. How will I be able to keep up with his cast of pop culture icons? *"Bag it, Joye. Just keep honest,"* I think to myself, *"and ask questions when you don't understand."*

"From *Star Trek*. He's my guy, all logic and words and control. Not sexual. My ambition has always been to be Mr. Spock getting a blow job. I'm sure he'd feel the sensation and be curious about it, but he'd never be out of control. In one show he had to have sex to procreate. It made him sick. The most upsetting Spock story happened when he followed a girl who was banished back in time. The time was a period before Vulcan logic, and Mr. Spock goes there—back in time—after the girl, falls in love, eats meat, smiles, and becomes territorial. He was just a man before logic. Sad. I hated it."

"Apparently Mr. Spock's troubles were with the girl and sex and human feelings."

"That's about right; at least, for me. I'd like to be Mr. Spock, but I end up feeling more like Desi. Remember Lucy and Desi? Lucy is a kind of a hair-brained woman, loud and dissatisfied. She always has a scheme. But in her marriage she requires 'permission' from her husband to do anything beyond cleaning the toilet. So she has to resort to delinquency: always sneaking, being dishonest, and designing silly schemes in which Desi catches her five minutes before the show ends. She is exasperating! And Desi, he's always exasperated. But he must like it. After all his Latin screaming, he makes up with her. He must get a hard on from being exasperated. That's my idea of Hell. That's me and Diane."

"So, relationships with women seem pretty irrational, and you long for dispassionate logic."

"It's safer. But sex gets in the way. Sex is an eel, dangerous, slippery, electric. Why would I allow myself to get shocked again? And then you are some woman's slave, and she squeezes the life out of you. Dr. N. says I may have less sex drive with the effexor. That's fine with me."

"I think I know what you mean, but explain."

"You know my brain melted when Diane and I began having sex, and that wrecked my life. I couldn't just enjoy it but had to get married. Before long I had a baby I didn't want and responsibilities that have ruined me. And then the sex stopped, but the baby and responsibilities go right on. The bowl of my life became a colander. My marriage is a colander; my bank account is a colander; my art could become a colander if I am not careful."

I think, "My art is the colander in my life. How amazing that Richard has been able to protect his artist's vessel, to keep it intact!" I tell him this last part without the self-disclosure and, hopefully, without conveying too much envy. This is the first tipping point for me. How do I hold the tension between my admiration for Richard's fertile imagination, my envy, and my professional charge to help him deal with his crisis of loss? I turn to a tried and true strategy, inviting Richard to talk about me. I say, "Your relationships with women—your mother and Diane—have felt so irrational and entrapping that maybe you worry that I'll be like them? Maybe I'm also a hairbrained, dishonest, and untrustworthy woman."

66 *Analyst envy in working with an artist*

"Oh, no. You're a doctor, not a woman." He pauses, looks down and smiles shyly. "Well, even if you are a woman, most of the time you feel like a rational person. That's unwomanly. Can I change the subject? Last night on T.V. I watched *Postcards from the Edge*, about Debbie Reynolds and Carrie Fisher. What I want is an Uncle Harry."

"Who's Uncle Harry?"

"He's the older guy, the lawyer who talks to Carrie, very sober and experienced, someone who knows how the world works."

"Changing the subject, indeed!" I think to myself, but I say, "You'd like a fatherly figure like Uncle Harry in your life, somebody who knows the ropes, somebody who could be a model of a competent man for you. Was there anybody like that for you?"

"My father was useless. It's a good thing he loved computers and could make a living, because otherwise he was helpless at life. And my mother—all feelings, ridiculous! She could look perfect and poised. She took care of the house fine. But just let something important happen, and she'd cave; she'd fall into an emotional fire pit and ignite: red and orange flames for hair. Once I was in the car with her—I was about 7—and my mother hit a boy on a bike. Really, she just sideswiped and grazed him, but he fell off his bike. She fell apart, started wailing and shrieking and flailing her arms. So did the woman in the car next to ours. Two cats in heat! It's a good thing that bystanders called an ambulance and got the kid to the hospital. After that my brother and I used to sing this ditty about my mother: 'When in worry/When in doubt/Run in circles/Scream and shout.' But back to your question: she was so awed by my gifts that she didn't teach me anything."

"Your mother's panicky outbursts—all that shrieking—must have scared you off feelings. You seem a bit contemptuous of women's feelings in particular. And this makes my work harder. You probably can't imagine that as a woman I could be an Uncle Harry for you. If you could, I think I could help you develop some Uncle Harry skills of your own."

"I'd rather have you be my Data Storage."

"Oh Brother!" I think, "What the f ...?" I inquire, "Data storage?"

"My life is in your head. That's it. I put data in your head."

"And the value of putting the data in my head?"

"Yah! And the more stuff I can put in there ..." He falls silent.

"There seems to be value in giving me all this data—putting it in my head."

"You'll know me and be able to help me more."

We sit in silence; I wait; then Richard says, "You'll remember things for me."

"Hmm, and the value of that?"

"I forget things—in my moodiness. I don't want to repeat my old mistakes. I've made some doozies. You can remember for me."

"So I can be a kind of thinking and memory machine for you, without moodiness or strong, disorienting feelings."

"Exactly." *I get that Richard's fantasy is that I will become his own Mr. Spock, a great, rational container. How imaginative and sad and impossible a fantasy!* I tell him that I am the wrong phenotype for Mr. Spock, and he laughs. As we sit

Analyst envy in working with an artist   67

quietly, looking at each other, I notice that Richard has relaxed in the hour. When he is anxious, as he was early on, the muscles in his face strain right down to his pores. It's as if they are pressing the pores to expel some rank emotional toxins. There is even a stink to Richard's anxiety. Now I am struck by his square-jawed, Dudley Doright, ordinary American good looks—complete with freckles on his snubbed nose and a clear blue-eyed gaze. With his muscular frame, the brawn just beginning to soften into fat, he could be an aging former football player. How discrepant these looks are with Richard's eccentric behaviors, fierce intelligence, and creative imagination!

The silence continues for a while until Richard says, "I have a confession to make. I've been doing young boy porn on the Internet. Last night after I spoke to Diane, and she told me what a lousy dad I am, I went to Barnes and Noble and bought a book I've been reading there. It's on cherubs—you know, like Cupid with his bow and arrows. Mostly there are photos of chubby baby-like boys, naked or covered in wisps of gauze. But one photograph really grabbed me. The boy is about 11 years old. He's dressed as a cherub—the gauze and arrows and laurel wreath, all the details—but he's no fat baby cherub. He's beautiful and sexy and stares directly at you like Goya's Maja or Ingres' Odalisque. His black eyes are hooded, and he's clearly conscious of his nakedness and its effect on you. The picture is very compelling. I've been thinking of it all day. I'd like to bring it here for you to see."

It's the end of the hour. I'm suddenly hot and thirsty. I swallow dryly; my heart is hammering. I don't yet know what the cherubs mean or what to make of them. I have no thinking time, and all that occurs is *"Yikes! Richard—all of his moves and twists and turns and somersaults are making my hot head spin."* Naturally, I have more to learn, so I suggest to Richard, "Well, why don't you bring the book here next time." After he leaves, I notice my hands are damp and clammy, not the best of conditions for a catcher.

* * *

Some Model Scenes about Creativity:

1   *Richard's paternal grandmother was a wild gal, an artist and runaway wife and mother, who became a Christian Science missionary in the Yucatan. She wore flowing, colorful caftans and turbans, the clothes and the person radiating the humidity and spikiness of the tropics. "She looked like a pale Carmen Miranda," Richard says, plucking his allusions for her, as he does generally, from T.V., movie, and advertising figures. Richard's father, nervous and Asperger's like, hated visiting his mother in Mexico. He detested being dragged to sultry, stifling revival meetings under filthy tents. "Just imagine Don Knotts meets Carmen Miranda." On the other hand, Richard loved his grandmother's expressive creativity, her spicy, pungent, banana-flavored cooking, and her dour Christianity. She told him, and he believes, "Life is an illusion, only a waiting room for the real thing. God is the only reality, and the pain of living is the avenue to that reality. You may as well color and embellish the waiting room as you suffer, because this world has no*

68   *Analyst envy in working with an artist*

intrinsic meaning. In meditation and art you may even move past the pain a bit. But remember even so, death is the desired door."

2   *Richard, at 6, is already a committed artist, creating animated figures by drawing graduated pictures on the blank corners of small paper tablets. When the pages are rifled, the figures move. These are called fly books. It is morning, and Richard is drawing action figures in a tablet as the school bus arrives. His mother frantically urges Richard to leave his drawing in order to catch the bus. The little boy is paralyzed, caught between mother's panic about missing the bus, on the one hand, and his wish to be left alone with his drawing, on the other. He frets and sweats and freezes. Then he begins to cry. Mother has a temper tantrum.*

3   *Richard creates an abstract, multi-media art piece for his college graduation project. His original music and art combine in a startling installation that garners praise from the whole community at his prestigious art institute. At the graduation ceremonies, his mother is horrified at the wild art and cacophonous music. She throws a hissy fit. "I didn't pay good money for you to make garbage like this."*

* * *

About a year and a half into our therapy: two scenes

The frequency and regularity of our analytic sessions and my focused, serious attention help to settle Richard's terrible anxiety and regulate his moods: his insomnia, compulsive behaviors, obsessive thoughts, and suicidal ideas recede. My goals with him initially are to help him resolve the crisis of loss, encourage functional behavior, and begin to explore his relational world in the context of our analytic pairing.

In grieving the loss of his family, Richard continues to use lifelong schizoid defenses—long work hours and solitary creative explorations in music and art—to regulate his volatile emotional life. Although in the tumult and disorder of loss, Richard seems desperate for an emotional connection to me, he is avoidantly attached to his other important people. Therefore, his artistic activities afford him outlets for affective expression without the danger of human interaction or ties. In addition, he uses our therapy relationship intensely but gingerly. While he sees me four times a week and leaves many messages daily on my voice mail, he shies away from transference inquiries, preferring to keep me "the doctor as repository of his mind." Yet, because I catch him—am emotionally tuned to him, can follow his imaginative flights, can comprehend his art and music, and make observations about his internal world that interest him—Richard is very respectful. A new and growing trust seems to persuade him that I can hold him safely. He is especially surprised when I understand something he considers subtle or arcane.

* * *

I happily anticipate seeing Richard after a ten-day winter break. I've missed our visits and wonder whether he'll bring a prop along. Richard has recently

Analyst envy in working with an artist   69

taken to doing activities in session or bringing "show and tell" items. He sometimes draws self-state pictures on a sketchpad or he may bring a tape recording of his computer music. I receive and enjoy his artist self like a beaming first grade teacher. His originality often evokes envious feelings. Yet, I also worry that my enjoyment may detract from our work. I do not want to confirm Richard's conviction that people see only his talent and do not recognize him as a person. Because he does not trust that others can comprehend or relate to his complicated feelings about life—a distrust he often describes and laments in our therapy—he presents himself publicly as a simple, affable guy. This defensive presentation, of course, guarantees that he will not be seen. Consequently, his distrust and behavioral dissembling have left him feeling lonely and sorrowful.

Richard arrives with a large stuffed paper bag. He does not refer to it, and I do not know its contents; but Richard's slumped shoulders and pained expression suggest that the bag is burdensome and heavy. He begins to spin a jerky and jumpy narrative, starting with a sarcastic remark about my holiday break and a direct gaze that I read as a rebuke. As the narrative slips and slides and lurches along, I feel myself to be an out of synch catcher, searching for some fixed angle from which to watch and anticipate where Richard's story will land. I find myself feeling frantic for some way to grab hold of him.

"I took Jenny (his daughter) to buy a Mac for Christmas and also bought one for myself. When I told Diane about mine, I felt kind of ashamed."

"Ashamed?"

"I shouldn't have bought anything so extravagant for myself. Diane and I both know that she spent all our money on junk and then ran up credit card debt as big as Half Dome, but I still feel guilty. From guilt I promised Jenny we could talk by e-mail every day. Did I mean it? Will I remember? She got busted for smoking, and I told her, 'It hurts me to imagine you smoking.' I feel so far away when these things happen. But then I leave. When I turn right at Highway 25 and head south to Albuquerque, I get a migraine or I throw up. But afterwards I feel relieved. Last night I dreamed that I was Achilles, visiting my family in Elysium. In the dream Jenny did not know she was dead. Only Achilles knows. In his loneliness and profound grief, he knows this."

As Richard expresses these complicated feelings about his family, he draws on his sketchpad, all the while looking directly at me with only a few cursory glances at the pad. I watch from my peripheral vision as he scribbles something near the outer boundaries of the pad. He then turns the pad a few degrees and scribbles something more. He continues slowly to turn the pad and draw until he has made a full circle. Then he begins the circle again, this time making his scribbles closer to the center of the pad. This continues; there are many concentric circles before Richard is done. I am fascinated and find it difficult to follow Richard's narrative, keep eye contact with him, and track his hand movements and turning sketchpad all at the same time.

"Richard, you are a jumble of mixed and conflicted feelings today. There seems to be anger at me about our break and painful ambivalence about being a responsible family man. Or I should say that you are torn about your

70 *Analyst envy in working with an artist*

responsibilities, torn between being responsible to your family and to your art. I know that for a long time you've wanted a more sophisticated computer for composing your music; yet, at the same time you tell me that you're ashamed of giving it to yourself. And though you're mad at Diane for squandering the family's resources on junk and for judging you—at least, in your imagination—you still feel you deserve nothing. The only thing that's not jumbled is your love for Jenny. With all your conflicted feelings, your care and desire for her are perfectly clear. Your desire and love and your sadness and worry about separating from her show on your face."

"Wrong, that's conflicted, too. My desire has many stipulations. I want to be alone as long as I want, and then I want all the people I desire to be there, especially Jenny. Very self-centered, but that's want I want. M.C. Escher's son described how his father withdrew into his work—how he disappeared into it. I am this father. When I finally got home, I needed to read the cherub book."

"That book soothes you."

On the couch Richard reclines his body, and his muscles calm. His head propped on a pillow and his body in repose, he stares at me, looking like an odalisque himself. His voice turns creamy. "Well, the boys are beautiful—smooth and round and childish. They're just pleasant, playful and affectionate. They're not threatening—innocent, I guess you'd say. Did I ever tell you about Tommy? No, of course I haven't. I never told anyone."

"Who is Tommy?"

"Tommy was the boy next door. The joke is he could have been the girl next door. He was a few years older, and we built a fort in his garage. We played with each other sexually for years. He was cool, just affectionate and interested, and so was I. I loved Tommy, but then he got older and just dropped me. He was nice and all that; but once he was 12 or 13, he acted as though nothing had ever happened between us. Our parents never found out or anything, but he'd be embarrassed when he'd run into me. I know he's married now, and I hope he's happy. But..but."

"Hmm. So, Tommy was your important love relationship."

"He didn't mess with me."

"When he dropped you, it seems that you felt crushed. Now I understand the cherubs. They remind you of that childhood friendship. It sounds so natural and right and unambivalent."

Richard's head is now bent; his eyes avoid my gaze. After a moment, he turns his sketchpad to face me. I look and am astonished. From small geometrical shapes, some shaded, some elaborated, some filled with squiggly lines, each figure drawn with detail and arranged in complex relationship to each other, he has fashioned a perfect and symmetrical mandala—almost without looking!

From just a second before when I was feeling sad and heavy along with Richard, I am suddenly light. As I look at the mandala, this conjunction of inspiration and craft, I marvel at the miracle and mystery of creativity; I'm filled with joy. Richard's technical proficiency and spatial imagination are

Analyst envy in working with an artist 71

awesome, and his ability to organize a confused mess of feelings artistically amazes me. I realize that Richard has invited me into his intimate creative space and given me a glimpse of his artistic process. I feel privileged and suppose he has done this in thanks for my understanding. Envy joins my delight; and the instant is hot.

I chuckle and grin. "Wow" I say, "How'd you do that?"

"I feel it in my fingers." He smiles back, and then we start to laugh. It starts slowly with mutual giggling, at first, and then it rises in graduating surges to crests of laughter. The sound vibrations echo in our bellies. Richard continues to laugh until tears run. We are acknowledging the messiness of life and the consolations of art and relationship. The session ends, and Richard leaves with his mysterious stuffed paper bag. I find out later that the bag contains months of unpaid bills.

After this session I think about many things. I think about how lucky Richard is to have his artistic gifts, how they enable him to regulate unbearable feelings. I think of the intimacy involved in his sharing his private process with me. I also think not only about my pleasure in the "moment of meeting," but also about my envy. I pinpoint the place where admiration shifted to envy in that moment of surprise and shock when Richard turned his mandala toward me. "I can never do anything so miraculous," I say to myself with how many mixed feelings. I wonder whether Richard knows my feelings; I suspect he does and speculate on the possible effects of his knowing.

* * *

Richard's analysis occurred many years ago when I was in psychoanalytic training. He consented to be one of my control cases, and halfway through the training analysis, I changed supervisors. My new supervisor urges me to explore some active therapeutic strategies for eliciting emotional interactions between Richard and me. This supervisor suggests that I inquire persistently about Richard's affective responses to his own narrative and to our exchanges. As I proceed to do this, I feel that my verbal interventions are intrusive and contrived, a marked change from the quiet, receptive, and mirroring stance that has worked well for us up to this point. In any case these strategies certainly perturb the analytic encounter. For example, when I inquire one too many times about his feelings, Richard says to me, "I know! This is the diminishing Kleenex trick. You guess a feeling, and I grab the Kleenex train for crytown. But, whoa girl, it doesn't work with me. I don't feel a bit like crying." Or he simply jokes, "Uh, oh, here comes the Kleenex caper."

Because the new strategy turns out to be clumsy and clunky in this relationship, I drop it in short order. Soon I find myself again laughing easily along with Richard. Laughter seems to invade our sessions now even when there is plenty of misery manning the barricades. We both feel relieved when I return to the receptive therapeutic pattern and rhythm that has seemed right and authentic to us. It turns out that sometimes the most instructive supervision is one that fails. This one violated the synergy between Richard and me and felt wrong to both of us. Thus, my last control case supervision was

72   *Analyst envy in working with an artist*

enormously helpful. It illuminated for me how presumptuous even well-meaning suggestions can be when those suggestions fail to recognize the existing design and system of a functioning analytic couple.

This brings me to some thoughts on my analytic approach in working with Richard. As an analyst I bring to sessions a large assortment of psychoanalytic theories—ideas drawn from contemporary self-psychology, American relational thinking, attachment theory, and early infant research, all in the context of a dynamic systems process model. I also bring along practiced strategies of observation and interpretation. My analytic self is an integrated and genuine aspect of who I am humanly; after forty years of practice, it fits like comfy clothing. Thus, with Richard I certainly inquired about many things that he said; and I made interpretations relating both to the model scenes I have described as well as to the process between us.

Yet, with Richard—when I think about it—I am aware that our relationship depended mostly on the implicit exchanges and procedural patterns we developed together. These were expressed in affectively matched and complementary facial expressions and bodily posture. We were good at reading each other's winks, eye-rolls, and shrugs. Our procedural patterns were also expressed in our lightness of tone, humor, and laughter. Richard's fancy soared, and I did my best to catch its flights. Identifying the non-verbal and the metaphoric in our relationship—the procedural and associational patterns and their meanings—became my most important way to understand Richard. And I believe that my ability to join him on these levels—his experience of being met and recognized—accounts for some of the life changes he made.

* * *

I'm making "poison tumbleweed." Upset and agitated, anxiously awaiting a visit from his estranged wife and an encounter with her about finances, Richard is spinning out imaginary conversations.

"Poison Tumbleweed?"

"I'm gathering sticky evidence. Some of it doesn't fit together; but it's all very sticky, so it adheres. I catalogue and magnify the evidence and then roll it all together. It's full of air and takes on volume as it rolls along." He includes in the "poison tumbleweed" many problems and much pain in his life, including the growing debt balance for our analysis.

I tell him, "I'm glad you remember and care about our bill."

That evening he leaves me a message saying, "I'm very angry at the world, and nobody is safe. Even victims of my forgetfulness are targets of my rage." The next morning there is a second message, one that demonstrates his growing tolerance both for feeling and reflective functioning:

> I had a dream last night in which I was beating Dr. Ben Casey over the head with a hammer. He was trying to get me to do something I did not want to do. Now, Joye, the symbolism is too disturbingly close ... You're the only doctor I know. Unfortunately, I have it in for all women, and

Analyst envy in working with an artist 73

you fall into that category. For me there are two types of women in the world: women who leave me totally alone, and women who want to use me for their own purposes.

In the session that follows Richard talks heatedly about all the ways he wants to continue to be "on strike," free of the burdens of adult responsibility. He wants to live in a filthy house, never having to clean it "in case" visitors come. He wants no visitors. Nor does he ever want to pay bills—including mine. He doesn't want to be a father.

What I long for is to be mothered … I need cuddling, to hear somebody else's heartbeat, to be back in the womb. Usually you're feeding me. I hate when you snatch the bottle away. Monday night I had the feeling you think I ought to get my own bottle. Nervy bitch.

I'm enjoying Richard's riff on being an infant. I'm glad for his flowing anger and feel as though we're back on the trapeze together about to execute some fancy tumbles and twists. By now his life issues have landed squarely in our relationship, so I invite him to continue. I ask, "You said the doctor in the dream wanted you to do something you didn't want to do. How have I expressed that?" Richard answers:

Recently you want me to tell you about my feelings in words. That jars me. I tell you about my feelings in music. You know how to listen—that feeds me. I draw you pictures, and you know how to see them—that feeds me. But you're happy that I'm paying my bills. That really makes me angry. I think you want me to get motivated in my life. I don't want to be motivated. Then, all summer long I just repeated, 'I can't pay my bills,' and you would say, 'Time's up.' 'I can't pay my bills.' 'Time's up.' I hated the 'Time's up' part, but I liked that you let me repeat myself. I won't go off strike until I'm good and ready.

He continues, "I was upset the other night with the dream of beating you, but I was mad that you want me to live as a responsible adult. If I do that, I'll only be exploited again. More will be sucked from me."

I say, "Boy, I see that we have made plenty of poison tumbleweed together. You feel I've been messing with you over how you express yourself in our sessions, about how you conduct your life, about how responsible you ought to be, even about whether you pay my bill or not. You're plain pissed that I've come on like a demanding mother. I guess you want me to provide the care and attention of a loving mother without demands or judgments."

Richard does not respond to me but goes on, "You want me to have faith in rules. That's what mothers want. You are a mother, the worst kind—except when you're not. Women are either vampires or mothers. Oh! I don't know what I'm saying." He adds that he just wants to be naughty. "Not paying you is naughty."

74 *Analyst envy in working with an artist*

"It enrages you that I want you to be responsible."
"You take the bottle away, and I feel yanked. Sure I'm angry."

* * *

The premature ending

The company where Richard has built a wonderful artistic career—the only place he had ever wanted to work and the place where he earned accolades and a fine living—first announces several successive "downsizing" layoffs and, finally, shuts down its local art department entirely. This process occurs over the last two years of our four-year analysis. Although Richard survives the many layoff cuts, he has to endure the contagious agony of collapsing company morale, all the collective anxiety and distress over threatened unemployment and job dislocation.

Richard might have gone into a panicky tailspin, as did many of his colleagues. He didn't. Instead, he buttressed his defenses, developing new computer skills for both his art and his music. His new technical accomplishments enabled him to create an innovative computer-generated musical and visual presentation. The presentation, in turn, gained him a prestigious job offer in another city. The job would also move him closer to his child. So overall, during this period of professional reorganization, Richard successfully uses our relationship to contain his anxiety, explore his fears, and express his feelings, particularly a lifetime of jammed angry ones.

For my part during this period, I think a lot about my road not taken: how in early adulthood I had abandoned a writing career amid fears of creative and economic poverty and worry that I would be unable to nurture a marriage and children, on the one side, and creative work, on the other. I watch in awe the powerful inner creative resources at work in Richard—and his ultimate confidence in his imaginative gifts. I appreciate how they lend structure, support, and direction to his life, the way in which they enable him to regulate and contain otherwise chaotic feelings. Watching him battle the collapse of his professional life, I doubt that I possess these particular creative resources in sufficient sustaining strength and quantity. Traveling with Richard through his testing period, I realize in a new way that my own life strength has developed mainly through human interactions and close relationships. My family, friendship, professional, and community connections provide the scaffolding for my psychic life. My turning, my choice to become a psychologist and analyst rather than a writer, has been a good and mostly satisfying road for me. Yes … Yet … but … how envious of Richard I often feel!

During this time Richard makes other important moves in his life, moves which furnish additional background for our final session. For the first year and a half after his marital breakup, he deliberately ignored bill-paying obligations. His finances were in a mess with growing credit card debt, frequently interrupted phone and electrical services, and endless harassment from bill collectors. We agreed that the financial tangle served many purposes, punishment and protection

Analyst envy in working with an artist 75

being the primary ones. Staying debt ridden not only confirmed his conviction that he is a failure as a husband, father and man, but it also provided him with a defense against his estranged wife's money demands. Shortly after the "mandala" session, he begins to bring bags of bills to session where he sorts them and pays a few of the most pressing ones. I suggest that when he is ready to organize his finances, he might consult a credit counselor. Richard is angry at me for pressuring him to be responsible. Yet, several months later and several weeks after his company's first layoff notice, Richard announces that he has devised a plan with such a counselor to retire all his debts within a year's time. I didn't even know he had consulted the counselor! By our termination, Richard is debt-free.

Keeping his house dirty and in disarray was another way that Richard barricaded himself against invasion from his ex-wife and other potential intruders. He and I also identified punishment and protection meanings in this disordered living situation. Then, in the last year, he begins a slow clean-up operation. Over several months Richard moves cats outside the house and sets them up in his garage, an arrangement that even includes buying a litter box. He also carts his cat-toilet couch to the dump. Throwing out his collection of overflowing garbage bags, moving the living room boxes into the garage, and shampooing the carpet—these are other tasks he tackles in the year before moving away. "Only five rooms to go," he announces after making the living room actually livable. I ask why he thinks he can begin cleaning now. "I'm beginning to feel that I have a right to breathe." He adds that, while not sure he could say "No" to his wife if she wanted to move back with him, he is now less worried that she will want to. And, if she does, he has the analysis to support his saying "No."

Richard does say "No" to Kathleen, his on-again, off-again woman friend, who has played a "come hither-go away" game with him. They go to dinner, and she invites him to her house to watch a movie. Richard describes the experience: "She has a little couch in her den that faces the T.V. directly, and a straight back chair over in the corner. Kathleen settles onto the couch, curling up kitten-like, and covers herself with a blanket. She's bloody cozy while I'm standing in the middle of the room watching. I sit down on the chair that requires me to twist my neck to see the T.V. I'm so twisted I'm fucking Linda Blair in *The Exorcist*. Kathleen doesn't want to see me; she doesn't want to touch me; and she doesn't care if I'm comfortable—just like all the women in my life. All she cares about is a cushy place for herself."

"You're feeling furious."

"Nope, not this time. I just got up, grabbed my jacket, and told her she was a selfish c—t. I left feeling great. You know, while I was sitting there, I thought of this room. My couch here is just as comfortable as your rocking chair. I like that you look right at me and pay attention to me. Maybe I'm getting used to this."

* * *

"Here's a fitting dream I had last night." Richard begins our last session. "There's this funny computer lady who laughs a lot." *"I guess I'll always be data storage," I think.* "She's having an eleven-month pregnancy and then the world's longest labor. She gives birth to a slow child. He sleeps and dreams a lot, nurses for hours, and doesn't want to walk when the time comes. She seems to like that he is so slow. The baby has a toy, a flying Winged Victory. The animal has eyes all over it like a potato, and the baby spends hours rocking on it."

"Your dream knows that I like who you are."

"You know how I get depressed and exhausted when I drive back from Santa Fe? I feel dead and in the dead zone driving down the I-40 after seeing Jenny, and then I come home groggy and sleep the sleep of the dead? Well, this weekend I felt the same deadness going the other way. Now I feel dead leaving our therapy. I'm not ready. This isn't the way it's supposed to end. I can't win for losing."

"Our work together has become central to your life."

"This room is the only human place where I can ever settle down. Time has no domain in this room. I used to check the clock. Not anymore."

"We've made a real relationship here. As your dream says, it's been a long gestation and a wonderful birth. The Winged Victory is your precious, perceptive artistic soul. In the dream you get to enjoy the ride."

"I'm worried about working so near to Jenny. There's no moral responsibility in creating. I'm so selfish and cranky in my artistic flights. Then I want to be fed, babied, and sexed. Except for the sex part, that's what I get to do here. It's not too attractive, and it's awful for kids."

"Richard I hope someday you won't feel such shame about your basic nature. We both know that you have vital and pressing needs to make art; that you need time and room for your artist self. And the artist requires that you mainly fly solo."

"It's fitting that I have lived in a bombed out house and made it look like ancient ruins—derelict temples, mausoleums, broken, cracked, empty cities. Living in the remaining evidence of people vanished—and all their artifacts. Sometimes there's a lone animal there. The relics are connected to my mind—so ironic that I'm immersed in cutting-edged technology all in the service of funky analogs of childhood. I want to record imperfect childhood instruments: autoharps, accordions, harmonicas, potato whistles, and ukuleles. I want human sounds."

"But Richard, there is so much humanity buried in your ruins. You've put it in your art. Your art is so human and funny. I also understand that's why you hold onto so much old kitschy junk. It's funny and human. I think our work is like this. We've been retrieving old human feelings here."

"You know I'm still angry at the company. I think, 'These guys have to die.' I think of waiting a few years until people have forgotten that I ever worked there and then pulling off the perfect murders. Even if I don't use your Kleenex, I do feel rageful. Yes, I might still have to kill them. They created the Black Plague at work—terror and rape—until I felt like prowling the halls with a shotgun. Their stupid insurance didn't even pay for our therapy. But I am fully covered for feet problems—in case I have to pound the pavement again."

Richard and I continue to sit quietly, returning to our by now small and familiar argument about his artistic selfishness: "Yes I am." "No you're not—well, maybe a little you are." Now the argument is only a soft musical accompaniment to our rhythmic psychic give and take. We are together on the trapeze, in synch, me holding him as we swing back and forth. I am sad that he is leaving before we have perfected all our tricks. Then, I let go of him, and he is airborne, gliding headlong into a graceful aerial pirouette. My trajectory pulls me away from Richard, and so I do not see but trust that he lights precisely on the trapeze platform. I hope he will make it safely down the rope ladder and out into the big world.

Conclusion and epilogue

The earth has made a few turns since Richard set forth, and circuitous life paths have led Richard and me back to our analytic work a few times. But the story about envy and its constructive uses has hopefully been sufficiently told here. I have tried to show how a fairly benign form of envy that emerged for me with Richard resulted in psychic support and validation for him and a shift in personal identifications and new motivational directions for me.

RICHARD'S MANDALA

78 *Analyst envy in working with an artist*

References

Barth, L. (2007) *Psychic Determinism and Free Will: The Irresistible/Irresolvable Paradox.* Unpublished manuscript.

Beebe, B. & Lachmann, F. M. (2003) *Infant Research and Adult Treatment: Co-Constructing Interactions.* Hillsdale, NJ: The Analytic Press.

Benjamin, J. (1988) *The Bonds of Love: Psychoanalysis, Feminism, and the Problem of Domination.* London: Virago.

Brandschaft, B. (1994) Structures of Pathological Accommodation and Change in Analysis. Presented at the *Association for Psychoanalytic Self Psychology*, October, New York City.

Buber, M. (1923) *I and Thou*, trans. W. Kaufmanm. New York: Scribner's, 1970.

Cavell, M. (2003) Freedom and Forgiveness. *Internat. J. Psycho-Anal.*, 84:515–531.

Coburn, W. J. (1999) An Instrument of Possibilities. A Discussion of Dorothy M. Levinson and George E. Atwood's "A Life of One's Own." *Prog. Self Psychol.*, 84:183–190.

Fosshage, J. L. (1998). On Aggression: Its Forms and Functions. *Psychoanal. Inq.*, 18 (1):45–54. 10.1080/07351699809534169.

Harris, A. (2002) Mothers, Monsters, Metors. *Stud. Gender Sexual.*, 3 (3):281–295.

Ruderman, E. G. (2002). As Time Goes By: Life Experiences and Their Effects on Analytic Technique. *Psychanal. Inq.*, 22 (4):495–509. 10.1080/07351692209348999.

Shengold, L. (1994). Envy and Malignant Envy. *Psychoanal. Quart.*, 63:615–640. 10.1080/21674086.1994.11927430.

Winnicott, D.W. (1965). Hate in the Countertransference. *Int. J. Psycho-Anal.*, 30:69–74.

4 Thinking and writing about complexity theory in the clinical setting

Psychoanalysis has increasingly embraced complexity or non-linear dynamic systems theory as a model of development and change. Not only is it a broadly inclusive model, able to contain diverse schools of contemporary psychoanalytic thinking such as self-psychology, attachment theory, infant research, intersubjectivity, and relational ideas, but, in addition, it can also account for contradiction and paradox, for the occurrence of the surprising, the puzzling, and the strange in many areas of human inquiry. Thus, it's a change model that can contain the unfolding human twists and turns and contradictions in both the analytic relationship and narrative fiction. Along with excitement about the theory, there are early efforts to describe analytic experience within the context of a complexity model (Arnetoli, 2002; Aron, 1996; Beebe, 2004; Beebe and Lachmann, 2003; Cilliers, 1998; Coburn, 2002; Harrison, 2003; Orange et al., 1997; Shane et al., 1997; Stern, 1985, 2004). This essay, which examines complexity theory as it applies to the analytic relationship, is an attempt both to understand and join these new efforts.

I begin with these questions: What is complexity theory? How does adopting complexity theory as a model of development and change affect one's clinical sensibility? How does complexity theory look and feel in the clinical setting? And how can our clinical writing capture and convey the context-sensitive, non-linear, and fluid nature of complexity thinking? Using a clinical story from my work with Sally, I will try to illustrate some specific ways a complexity or dynamic systems sensibility transforms one's thinking about clinical material and how it informs diagnosis and therapeutic strategies. I will also highlight some of the problems that a complexity sensibility poses for the writer of case reports.

Complexity theory, a short course

Before examining the clinical story, I will present some basic premises of complexity theory as I understand and use them in my clinical work.

Complexity theory is a process model of change. Although it applies to many content areas—e.g., meteorology, mathematics, biology, brain research, sociological modeling—the general model limits itself to description of

80 *Thinking and writing about complexity theory*

process. As a descriptive model, it is content- and value-free. General complexity theory posits that living systems are active and open, always changing in relation to energy exchanges with the environment. Multiple parts of a complex system are in continuous interaction with each other and with the external world, taking in energy, using and transforming that energy into information, and feeding back this information into the environment. All experience is contextual and happens within open, multi-faceted, and multi-layered contextual networks.

Complex systems are self-organizing. Systems change and develop coherence through cooperative interaction. Self-organization occurs within and between systems. What does this look like? The human brain, for example, organizes itself into increasingly ordered and interwoven subsystems of neural networks (Edelman, 1987). Within the brain, hierarchical patterns of neuronal organization emerge from the cooperative joining of neural groups, the joining a response to stimulation from the external environment and from the body. These neuronal groups yoke themselves into nets that are related thematically and/or functionally. Complexity theory, then, describes a universe which tends toward patterned connection.

Gerald Edelman offers an ingenious metaphor to illuminate the idea of self-organization. He imagines a "weird" string quartet, one with no conductor, no verbal communication, and no score. He assumes only two conditions for this string quartet: first, a "value" in the quartet directed toward making music and, second, the ability of each player to play his instrument:

> each player responds by improvisation to ideas and cues of his or her own, as well as to all kinds of sensory cues in the environment. Since there is no score, each player would provide his or her own characteristic tunes, but initially these various tunes would not be coordinated with those of the other players. Now imagine that the bodies of the players are connected to each other by myriad fine threads so that their actions and movements are rapidly conveyed back and forth through signals of changing thread tensions that act simultaneously to time each player's actions. Signals that instantaneously connect the four players would lead to a correlation of their sounds; thus, new more cohesive, and more integrated sounds would emerge out of the otherwise independent efforts of each player. This correlative process would also alter the next action of each player, and by these means the process would be repeated but with new emergent tunes that were even more correlated … and such integration would lead to a kind of mutually coherent music that each one acting alone could not produce.
>
> (Edelman, 1987, p. 49)

System changes occur in discontinuous, jerky, and unpredictable ways. Small system changes may produce large and surprising consequences. At times systems may be in perpetual reorganization. At other times, they settle into relative

Thinking and writing about complexity theory 81

equilibrium or stability, called attractor states. Depending on the depth of these attractor states, greater or lesser pressures—or in dynamic systems parlance "perturbations"—are necessary to disturb the system into new organization. In *Oedipus Rex*, Oedipus provides an example of a fixed attractor state. In answering the Sphinx's Riddle, he chronicles a fixed sequence of infant motor development. Babies, he tells us, move invariably from sleeping on their stomachs to crawling to standing to walking. In recent years as a response to sudden infant death syndrome, however, babies no longer sleep on their stomachs, and parents now observe that many babies never crawl on the way to walking. Rather, as a result of sleeping on their backs from birth, some infants now move directly from sitting to standing and then to walking. The change in sleeping positions functioned as a perturbation to a deep attractor state, changing contingencies and altering the old developmental sequence that included crawling. Thus, an old universal "truth" about locomotive development crumbles, and an understanding that development is variable and context sensitive replaces it. Sorry, Oedipus, this is complexity theory in action.

The election of Donald Trump illustrates how perturbations function in complex systems. Factors such as the president's coarseness and selfishness; his ignorance of history, Constitutional government, and foreign affairs; his media savvy; the submission of Republicans to his bullying tactics; all the resulting strategic decisions and their numberless repercussions; and accidents—all of these have influenced the unfolding of events in the United States in unpredictably unhappy and transforming ways. Complexity theory suggests that while the situation may appear chaotic in the present moment, organization is, in fact, occurring. From a phenomenological perspective, complex systems may appear at times frozen in deep attractor states while at other times they may seem totally chaotic. Chaos, however, invites new organization. New organization, in turn, may just as likely appear divisive and destructive as look stable and coherent. Yet, beyond phenomenology, it is clear that developing complex systems can never move backward or return to states of simplicity or innocence. The idea of regression is an illusion. Rather, from the perspective of dynamic complexity thinking, a movement, a tendency toward activity and ordered intricacy, seems to be in the nature of things, in the nature of destructive forces as well as in the nature of deepening intimate relationship.

Complex dynamic systems are "recursive" and "degenerate" (Edelman, 1987). These are Edelman's technical terms for two properties of complex systems. "Recursive" means that complex systems refer back to, use, and affect previous configurations as well as draw from new, environmental energy sources. "Reentry" is another term that Edelman uses for the recursive processes in complex systems. Memory, for example, is a recursive system. We understand from neuroscience that a memory represents an ingathering of sensory traces distributed throughout the brain. The construction of a memory, what traces are selected and gathered, depends on the affective context in which the memory occurs. Therefore, memories are really situational creations, creations that continuously change according to the

82 *Thinking and writing about complexity theory*

emotional environment in which they are fashioned. Edelman's second term "degenerate" means that complex systems employ many redundant paths in attaining a single goal. The injured brain illustrates a degenerate complex system. It demonstrates in recovery after a stroke, for example, that multiple neural pathways may result in producing the same brain function.

Complexity theory as a sensibility and its function in analytic process

Human relationships, including the analytic relationship, are the most complex of all dynamic systems. Yet, they follow the rules of complex systems generally. In the following discussion I hope to show how the analytic relationship concretely embodies general dynamic systems principles. I also hope to illustrate how a complexity sensibility enlarges an analyst's appreciation and attention for multiplicity and simultaneity in the analytic space. It also makes the analyst's job immense.

Returning to music as a metaphor, I would liken the classical analyst's task to that of a sophisticated musicologist. The analyst listens to a patient's music and analyzes the influences and structure of that music as well as the patient's musicianship. He also makes sure that his own musical preferences and biases do not interfere with his analysis of the patient's music. Contemporary psychoanalysis expands the analyst's role. Still the musicologist, the analyst realizes that he is also, simultaneously, a performing musician. Not only does he listen in his sophisticated way to his patient's music and style, he also listens to his own music and style as well as to the musical give and take between the patient and himself. Finally, he must consider and articulate all the ways in which the resulting duet does or does not harmonize.

A complexity sensibility creates a boundless, impossible job for the analyst. The duet now becomes a concerto with two featured players and an orchestra as well as the orchestra hall. Each featured player contributes his own particular music to the whole, music that, in turn, is continuously influenced and changed by all the other orchestral parts. The hall provides resonance and echo to the whole assembly. While the patient and her music are still the focus of the enterprise, the analyst must now take into account this myriad of other musical factors and all their countless interactions, interpenetrations, and permutations. While the task is ultimately impossible—there is too much material for one person to comprehend—the analyst nevertheless perseveres. To do this, he must use his subjectivity to break up the job and limit his focus, all the while granting that such partitioning trades accurate rendering of the whole for increased understanding of some parts. Complexity theory in action!

Let us look now at the analytic relationship through the lens of dynamic complexity theory. First, as with all complex systems, the analytic couple exists in an open contextual network with multidirectional exchanges of energy sources and information within and between partners and with the environment. Each partner's mindbrainbody interacts with its environment and with

Thinking and writing about complexity theory 83

the partner's mindbrainbody. In the clinical setting "With self" and "Between Self and Other" happen simultaneously. If bi- and multi-directional influences are the rule of relational experience, the interpenetration of minds or inter-subjectivity is the given condition of all relationship. A complexity sensibility, then, leads an analyst to the awareness of both the perpetual oscillation of experiences of self and other and the porosity of physical, mental, and affective boundaries. Such a sensibility confirms many of the observations of infant development researchers and the intuitions of intersubjectivity theory as Stolorow, Atwood and Orange express them.

The analytic relationship is also self-organizing. Between people, tighter and tighter system coordination—that is, the expansion and elaboration of the points of meeting within and between systems—constitutes relational devel-opment. In the complex system that is the analytic relationship, how does this happen? What determinants promote such increasing levels of organization and coherence? As we have seen, the dynamic systems model suggests a "value" toward interaction, relational connection, and intersubjectivity. Building on this value, we may view system interactions moving to integrate correspondences and complements between partners—to create experiences of intersubjective recognition—as well as to negotiate and repair rips and rup-tures in the process of perpetual reorganization.

Because we know that new experience arises and takes shape from multiple interpenetrating systems, much analytic attention is focused on consciously and verbally capturing some of these salient systems. Such attention must encompass explicit and implicit systems; it must take into account both the patient's and the analyst's history and environment as well as their non-verbal and non-verbal symbolic communications, their mutual enactments, and their organized verbal exchanges. In the past several decades, relational analysts, attachment theorists and infant researchers have described and elaborated some of the mechanics of this process (e.g., Aron, 1996; Beebe and Lachmann, 2003; Bucci, 2002; Gergely and Watson, 1996; Lyons-Ruth, 1999; Mitchell, 2000; Sroufe, 2000; Stern, 1985, 2004).

Interaction, repetition, and overhaul—the continuous interaction, repeti-tion, and redesigning of themes—then, constitute the condition of the com-plex analytic system. As a result of all this interaction, unpredictable patterns emerge within and between the partners over time. Because interacting parts of a relational system will likely undergo successive levels of coordinated effort before organization and coherence emerge, building an analytic relationship requires considerable time and practice.

The perturbation of rigid organizing experience also furnishes opportunity for therapeutic change. While patients and analysts bring their respective historical patterns of relating to the analytic encounter, the analytic meeting also provides opportunity for new relational events to loosen and alter these old patterns. For example, the influence of a respectful, attentive analyst "getting" the patient, responding with fresh and authentic thoughts and feelings, helps to create a new

84 *Thinking and writing about complexity theory*

relational context for both partners. Even small changes in such a context may trigger new and expanded life contexts. These, in turn, produce new system organizations along with sometimes small and sometimes radical personal and relational perturbation to rigid emotional attractor states.

The recursive or "reentrant" and degenerate nature of complex systems also puts a new spin on ideas of co-transference. New and old experiences as well as separate subjectivities converge in any given present moment so that clear delineation of temporal experience as well as spatial relationships in the couple blurs. These ideas suggest that in specific moments one cannot know whether one is dealing with new regulatory configurations or old ones or where in the system—or analytic couple—the sources of therapeutic action lay. One way to describe the condition is to say that therapeutic action is "evenly distributed" across the system (Coburn, 2002).

Yes, in specific moments one can neither know exactly where one is in time—the present is in the future, and the past exists in both the present and the future—or space—is one a separate speck in a disconnected and alienated universe or deeply connected to and part of a cosmic whole; as better poets suggest, wider than the sky and containing multitudes?

So, as we have observed, a complex understanding of any single moment in any interpersonal encounter, including an analytic meeting, must include each person's complete history of experience, environment, and subjectivity as well as the analytic couple's history, environment, and current intersubjective state (Coburn, 2002). While such consciousness expands the scope, material, and possibilities of the analytic relationship, it can also feel daunting. Clearly, as we have also noted, the infinite number of interacting variables involved in all this—the metaphor of an intricate web is apt here—makes complete under-standing impossible.

The impossibility of completely understanding such a moment is increased by the fact that moments flee, and every passing moment brings not only some change in the neuronal architecture of the brain but also in the state of a given dyadic encounter. Change is relentless: new connections are made; old neu-ronal connections weaken and die; memory and emotional response are continuously engaged in the process of change (Damasio, 1999; Edelman, 1987; Siegel, 1999). It follows that intersubjectivity is always in flux, and our access to complete history is necessarily limited.

Two other factors serve to limit our awareness of both the external and intersubjective environments. First, in order to make feeling and thinking possible, perceptual screens filter out much of the overwhelming volume of internal and external stimulation. Of necessity, we are blind to most of the sensory and affective stimuli that surround us. And, then, much if not most of our affective and behavioral life occurs procedurally, in the realm of the im-plicit, and, therefore, is outside of our conscious and lexical awareness.

In addition to creating screens, we survive the overwhelming condition of chaos, the condition of having infinite and unbearable stimulation constantly bombarding us, by placing frames on our experience. Frames delimit the scope of our attention and make it possible to organize perceptions and thoughts. The retrospective frame, for example, allows patterns of meaning to emerge from the chaos of present moments. Complexity theorists put it this way: experience, while chaotic at the local level, assumes aesthetic and cognitive pattern and organization retrospectively.

Theories, vignettes, model scenes, "now moments"—all of these are types of frames. They allow us to create the twin illusions, the necessary fictions, of coherence and of comprehensiveness. At least for a moment, life seems ordered and complete. Like the ancient artists who fashioned the heavenly constellations, frames organize flashes of light so that patterns emerge in a sky of infinite and random twinkling, a sky a jumble with stars. Expressed another way, frames provide us with small islands of cognitive and affective peace in seas of chaos. These islands allow us a place to stand, solid ground from which to face the confusing and terrifying vitality of our life surround. Yet, even while we fashion the islands, we know that they are heuristic creations and do not afford us absolute truth about anything.

Some frames are better than others. Good frames delimit relatively organized and coherent slices of life. A good theoretical frame, for example, creates a complete and persuasive story, one that contains breadth and depth of meaning. It is like a good cross-sectional CAT Scan picture, which, while depicting only a single slice of a given brain, may nevertheless contain a wealth of significant information about that brain's structure.

Sensitivity to complexity creates—more accurately, demands—intellectual humility. Like the blind men who each described one limited, sensory aspect of the same elephant, our theories and organizations are, at best, piecemeal and, therefore, only partially accurate. We must hold them provisionally because we do not know if our subjective formulations are pertinent; if they are partially pertinent; or whether they, in fact, entirely miss the elephant.

Limited intellectually, we are thrown back on our more foundational ways of knowing: our emotional perceptions and responses (Damasio, 1999). Complexity theory as applied to the clinical encounter gives parity, if not privilege, to affective experience. This includes attention to non-verbal ways of knowing: sensations, aesthetic perceptions, associative linkages, and all the fittedness, contingent responsiveness, rhythmic correspondences, and cross-modal matching that infant research enumerates. In addition, Daniel Stern argues that examining small momentary units of intersubjective experience, examining especially the emotional charge in these momentary units, may yield more powerful information about relational/therapeutic change than broad narratives of therapeutic process (Stern, 2004).

The case of Sally

With this cursory overview of dynamic complexity theory, I turn now to a clinical vignette from my work with Sally. I hope the vignette will provide a canvas for illustrating some aspects of complexity thinking:

86 *Thinking and writing about complexity theory*

It's a bad sign when I dread an appointment. But here it is, dread rumbling inside like a storm warning. It is Thursday, a cool early evening in fall. Anticipating winter, the sky is already growing dark as Sally arrives for her 6:30 appointment. I feel a shiver and wish to be done working and inside my warm, bright house. Instead, I rub my hands together and hug my arms in preparation for another likely icy session with Sally. It has been rough going for a few months, a negative, angry transference in full tilt, ever since I returned from my three-week summer vacation. Sally had come for twice weekly therapy for only six weeks before I took this vacation; but during that time she had struck a sympathetic chord in me, touched me, and challenged me to help her. She seemed to have made a beginning connection to me as well.

Sally had come to therapy for two main reasons. The first reason: she was in a failing relationship with a married man who did not love her. This liaison typified Sally's relational history. The second more general reason for therapy: she wanted to know why she feels so dead in her life. Hard working and professionally accomplished, successful by social and economic measures, she feels nothing except alien, disappointed, and empty. The mother of high achieving adult children, whom she likes well enough, she claims to feel no particular love for them. One child recently married; and while Sally orchestrated the wedding, she felt nothing particular at the occasion, except perhaps a moment of displeasure at not being adequately acknowledged in the wedding toasts.

During the first few weeks of therapy, her lover of several years terminated their relationship. Sally spent several sessions grieving, her tears expressing an array of feelings: sadness, loneliness, emptiness, but noticeably, no anger. At that time she thanked me for understanding her and for the few simple interpretations I made. Then, over a single weekend, she shut down her feelings. She told me at our Monday meeting that she no longer felt anything about the loss. She has never again mentioned her ex-lover.

Sally embodies stark contradictions. She shows capacity for both fiery feeling and frigid withdrawal. While she claims to "feel nothing," I read in her intelligent face and deep eyes sadness and longing. Sally has one of those "rubber faces" with large eyes and a wide mouth, an elastic face that expands and contracts, crinkles and stretches to encompass a wide range of emotional experience. Her voice, too, is full of feeling. Even in a straightforward narration, it has a pleading quality. Her sentences end on raised notes, their music like a continuous stream of questions. And her strong pull on me for focused attention and cognitive understanding seems to belie her claim to "feel nothing." However, after certain empathic responses on my part, responses in which I amplified Sally's feelings with my own, she made clear that she neither likes nor wants that kind of empathy from me. It was shared emotional resonance that upset her. The experience of emotional resonance, in fact, makes her angry.

Empathy and emotional resonance come easily for me with Sally. Her story is wrenching; it moves me, and I am unable to conceal my strong, empathic feelings. I find it disappointing and frustrating that Sally rejects the empathy that flows so naturally from me. At 3, Sally's policeman father, whom she idealized then and now, was killed in the line of duty. She presents a model scene of the event. On the day he died, she remembers running after him, grabbing at his long legs, begging him to stay at home with her. Despite her premonition of catastrophe, Sally was helpless to stop her father. At 4, her

Thinking and writing about complexity theory 87

neglectful mother placed Sally in foster care and moved to Europe for five years. At 10, the mother remarried and removed Sally from her foster family to a small, rural town. There, children excluded her from their social groupings. She made few friends and had nobody to protect her from or buffer the hurtful interactions with her raging and critical mother. Graced with artistic and intellectual abilities, she immersed herself in art and school and somehow "survived" childhood. She became fiercely self-regulating. College and young and middle adulthood were marked by hard work, rich achievement, and impoverished relationships.

Sally cancels the first session after I return from vacation and tells me first thing at our reunion meeting, "The spell is broken. I missed you the first week you were gone. Then I shut down. I'm feeling o.k. now and am not sure I want to continue therapy." I answer, "My leaving must have felt miserably familiar and so disruptive that you shut down to the whole process." "Yeah, so what?" she says. "Ouch!" I recoil in surprise. I am suddenly confronting a different and pugnacious Sally. The therapy space feels transformed into a boxing ring with each of us thrust into her own corner.

After that, Sally begins each session with a statement that the therapy isn't working or isn't what she wants or isn't what she needs. Usually she reports not wanting to come and doubting my competence. Several times her criticism grows quite pointed: "Who the hell are you to think you can help me?" To all of this I mainly just listen or comment that she finds it hard to believe that I—or anybody—can help her.

She then tells me that life has become meaningless, and she is thinking of suicide. She has a clear and workable plan. I respond to Sally's strategies in an emotional haze, some confused mixture of hurt, anger, hopelessness, and, especially, worry and dread. Worry! I feel demoralized, but at the same time I am also motivated somehow to save Sally. "Oh, Suicide!" I keep thinking, "Please no suicide!" There's nothing like a quiet, matter-of-fact suicide threat to mobilize one's attention, energies and grandiosity. And so I feel determined to help Sally comprehend and resolve her hostility and destructiveness. I wonder how I can find the lost chord with her, an opening to resume the rhythm and melody we had begun fashioning together before my vacation?

At each session after she attacks our work, Sally resists dealing with any negative feelings toward me. To my inquiries, she answers, "This therapy is about me, not you," and abruptly changes the subject. She turns to some event at work, some phone conversation with a friend, or some picture she is painting and proceeds to engage me in active listening and interpretive response. With only small inquiries from me, memories emerge and connections get made. It is simultaneously crazy-making and easy for me to feel a therapeutic bond with her, to follow her emotional path, and to feel momentarily that we might enlarge our exploration into her life. While I know I am inside an angry and unstable system, by the end of each session I somehow deceive myself that we have attained a truce.

So far there is no carryover from one meeting to the next. Which brings us back to that chilly Thursday evening. I wait for Sally, anxiously anticipating and dreading the ritual of anger. Family dissension and a raging mother in my own childhood have led me to avoid angry encounters in my adult personal life and to struggle with them as an analyst. Therefore, I dislike the patterned antagonism that begins each session with Sally yet am unclear how to modify it. I feel a wave of hopelessness.

88   *Thinking and writing about complexity theory*

Sally arrives with a frowning, pursed mouth and narrowed eyes. She glowers at me and sits tautly at the edge of the couch, tensed and wary like a cat about to pounce. I'm reminded of the lion-tamer contests in the old Ringling Brothers' Circus. "I don't see the point of this. All I do is tell you stories. What good does it do for me to entertain you?" She lunges, and I imagine myself raising a chair for protection with one arm and brandishing a whip for aggression with the other like the animal trainers of my childhood. "Sally, I think there's good reason for you to be in treatment. No one should go through life feeling as angry and as lonely as you. At least, that's my view."

"So how are you going to fix it?"

I answer lamely, "Well, I'm a person, and I want to … I mean I'm here to get to know you, to make a relationship with you." My thinking apparatus is sputtering.

"You're a doctor, not my friend, not a real person in my life. This therapy is about me, not about you. The relationship bit is a lot of hooey."

About now I have the foggy feeling, the one that has become familiar to me in the past months. I find it hard to think, my brain shuddering and shaking as after a one-two blow to the head. While I feel almost down for the count, I nevertheless try to think. I talk to myself: "This must be some distant echo of Sally's mother's voice, a history in the present moment of Sally's life with her mother's voice: not only her imitation and practice of that voice, but all the ways she has used it, transformed it and made it hers in her life of relationships. We know that victims often assume the tactics of their persecutors. But what in the world can I say to this annihilating bitch? Do I possess any resources, any psychic hooks besides my own anger to attach me to Sally's nastiness?"

I hate that I am losing it, hate the foggy feeling and hate the fact that I have just called Sally a bad name. Clearly, I am very mad at her. These feelings also signal that I am deeply involved in some non-verbal enactment with Sally. I take a deep breath and let my mind wander. "Worthless," "stupid," "incompetent"—these are the words I find in the dark place to which my wandering takes me. They are ancient personal labels, despised personal labels, labels with which I have wrestled. I study them a moment. "All right," I think, "Go for it."

"Sally," I say, "I hate feeling worthless, stupid, and incompetent. I work so hard and want to do a good job. And so I hate feeling like a failure. You tell me I'm not good enough and just don't measure up. I feel awful. I know you also work hard to do a good job and to feel competent. I wonder if you also know this feeling of not being good enough? Maybe in being so critical with me, you're conveying to me and helping me to experience what it's like—what it's like down in the guts—to feel worthless and stupid."

Sally's features mellow; her shoulders soften and fall; she settles back on the couch into stillness. After some period of silence during which her face moves from thoughtful to sad, she remembers her mother's verbal criticism and physical punishment, her mother's cruel responses to everything from instances of minor failure to moments of accomplishment that were not quite sufficient. "I was never good enough, could never get it right." Sally looks soft and on the verge of tears as the session ends, and I feel something has begun to knit between us.

On Monday morning I pick up a message from Sally, "I've thought about our work all weekend and don't want to continue. Please don't call me or try to change my mind."

Discussion

In discussing Sally, I want to ask three questions in an effort to relate complexity theory to our encounter. First, how can a complexity sensibility add color and depth to our understanding of this analytic relationship? Then, how can such a sensibility help make sense of Sally's story, particularly make sense of her leaving treatment? And, third, what are some problems in embodying such a sensibility in our written case presentations? In this section I'll address these questions. A wonderful feature of complexity theory is that it allows broad room for speculation, allows us to play with several explanations while knowing that we cannot be sure of any. Hence, granting that uncertainty and indeterminacy remain in the foreground, here are some plausible speculations.

To describe complexity theory in action, I'll start with two givens in the case. The first given is that Sally and I shared the "value" of meeting to make a relationship. Open systems, once they are exposed to each other, tend toward interactive organization. Human beings hanker for connection. In spite of her history of solitude and in spite of her protective strategies of angry provocation and emotional withdrawal to keep distance, Sally nevertheless pursued a relationship with me. She came diligently to our sessions, arriving anxious and early, and she brought energy and passion to all of our encounters. Even when her angry pounding was the most intense, I still felt it functioned more in the service of breaking the barriers between us than in erecting them.

The second given borrows from Edelman's metaphor of the "myriad of fine threads." His metaphor suggests an inborn predisposition for intersubjectivity complete with a rudimentary communication network operating within and between complex systems. From the first, I felt such a system growing between Sally and me. In Edelman's view—and the view of many infant researchers as well—this communication network provides a metaphor for imagining an expanded view both of the self-system and the system between self and other. That is, this image of an intricate communication network elaborates the idea of self. It describes a self that subjectively registers verbal, non-verbal symbolic, and non-verbal experience. As Estelle Shane puts it,

> expanding the concept of self from a phenomenological, subjective experience to an experience that encompasses on an explanatory level the totality of maindbrainbody as a nonlinear dynamic system ... includes subjective, nonsubjective, and nonconscious experience; and communication between this expanded view of the self-other system is significantly affected by bodily-based and procedural expression.
>
> (Carleton and Shane, 2004)

The human capacity for intersubjectivity, then, prepares minds for relationship and also provides the mechanisms for cultivating connections with other minds. With these two givens, we may speculate on the early factors that promoted the development and organization of relationship between Sally and

90 Thinking and writing about complexity theory

me. I'll mention a few of the factors that occur to me, but at the same time I want to underline that there were other connecting factors—probably an incalculable number of other factors which were out of my awareness.

On meeting, Sally and I began sizing each other up. Consciously and procedurally—in our minds and in our bodies—we compared and contrasted our similarities and differences, trying to determine the grounds for relationship. We had many similarities, and according to Hebb's Theorem, an important notion from complexity theory applied to neuroscience, "Neurons that fire together wire together" (Hebb, 1949). Women of about the same age and education, we were both mothers and professional people, who had shared the same cultural history. We both grew up with left-wing politics, the women's movement, and the wonderful music of the sixties and seventies. We both held countercultural social attitudes and had similar takes on current politics. We both loved the life of the mind. I admired Sally's intelligence and sophistication, her developed aesthetic eye and gifts. I also felt enormous respect for her resilience. Although I never verbally articulated my history or opinions or any of my feelings about her attributes or accomplishments, Sally seemed to read the nonverbal signals that indicated my recognition and assent. As I listened attentively to Sally, we began knitting a thickening net of threads between us.

For her part Sally liked my perceptiveness and my décor. She identified and admired the folk art in my office, art that stimulated her memories of travel and artistic experiences and caused her to imagine how I related to the art and its origins. Then, she began to savor the quiet of our hours together, remarking several times that she felt calm after seeing me. How many nonverbal factors contributed to the calm I, of course, do not know; but a complexity sensibility considers as much of the non-verbal and atmospheric context as possible. I imagine the secluded surroundings as well as the color, lighting, and comfortable furnishings in my office contributed to the mood. I also expect that we had found a good enough rhythm of body and facial responsiveness and vocal turn-taking to keep our connective threads multiplying and weaving together.

Finally, in the beginning, Sally liked my empathic listening skills and ability to zero in on relevant clinical issues. When she brought me her grief and distress over her ruptured love affair, she expressed appreciation for my understanding comments. Her romantic breakup represented our first important relational test, and my passing that test cemented and augmented our early tie (Weiss and Sampson, 1998). Taking in and acknowledging my emotional understanding marked a new experience for Sally. Complexity theory might describe this event as a perturbation to our system, thereby loosening and altering Sally's fixed relational expectations and deepening the connection between us. Such perturbations can lead to shifts and dislocations, openings and rearrangements, and sometimes radical reorganizations of emotional experience. In the early weeks of our meeting, then, we may surmise that the many points of meeting between Sally and me began to distribute themselves evenly across the complex system of our developing relationship.

Thinking and writing about complexity theory 91

From a complexity sensibility we might next evaluate the state of the analytic relationship at the point of its rupture. I suggest that the system was not sufficiently organized at the point of my summer vacation to absorb such a major disruption as my leaving; that it was not strong, coherent, or cohesive enough to counter the impact of a major perturbation. This formulation stands free of any specific content, and from it two possibilities suggest themselves. The first possibility is that after the rupture happened, I could have stood on my head or performed handsprings to no avail because all efforts toward repairing the breach were simply inadequate to offset the damage done. The nascent web of complex connections between Sally and me had been irreparably torn. The second possibility is that the system was capable of repair; that over time and continuing interaction, the system could right itself. These possibilities remind us that complexity theory is not a content theory of optimism or progress; rather, it is a process theory of change and development. Complex systems can as easily organize themselves for failure and implosion—look at the frequency of divorce and war, for example—as they can organize for cooperative and coordinated connection.

Complexity theory also allows us to consider multiple theoretical frames in this case, frames that cover and explain large portions of the clinical material. No frame, however, encases all the data, and most lack a thorough contextual sensibility. Nevertheless, here are a few theories. First, a consideration of Sally as a trauma survivor adds content to the complexity model outlined above. Let me explain: given that Sally had suffered multiple abandonment trauma early in life, my leaving for a three-week vacation early in our work may have represented a repetitive and retraumatizing experience. Our promising analytic system was simply not developed enough at the point of my summer break to absorb an experience of abandonment; our connections to each other were delicate and had not developed sufficient strength and elasticity to withstand the flood of feeling that such an experience likely unleashed. The fact that Sally had begun to soften her rigid defenses probably made my leaving even more devastating for her. After a lifetime of distrust and self-protection, she had begun to move tentatively toward me, and then I left her flat. I can only imagine her feelings of "being had!" If my absence had, indeed, triggered the overwhelming return of betrayal and abandonment anxiety, then the failure of the therapy may rest on external, repetitive factors, unwittingly triggered by my behavior and likely beyond repair.

Winnicottian theory might see our rupture differently. It might view Sally's leaving as a result of my failure to survive her rage after the disruption, my failure to be a safe enough object for her use. In protecting myself from her anger, did I intervene on the negative transference prematurely? Did she experience my intervention as an inability to tolerate her anger?

Also, from an attachment perspective, Sally demonstrates sometimes dismissive and sometimes disorganized attachment styles. Such attachment styles speak to difficulty in acknowledging and integrating affect into one's life. Such styles often join extreme emotional constraint, the intense defensive effort to

92 *Thinking and writing about complexity theory*

keep feelings at bay, on the one hand, with irritability, aggressiveness, or confusion when emotions threaten to overwhelm, on the other. Understanding Sally's attachment styles, I wonder if I came on too strong with her. From my own desire for connection, did I threaten her emotional defenses, push too early for emotional response from her, and thereby send her running for safety?

Finally, from the frame of contemporary infant research findings, Sally and I may have failed to establish and maintain an optimal balance between our respective self-regulatory activities and our mutual interactive regulation. Knowing that Sally has historically relied on herself to regulate emotional distress, I may have worked more successfully with her had I been initially less active with her. This possibility suggests that our system had not yet attained a synchronous rhythm—that we had not yet gotten our mutual dance steps down—even though coordinated efforts clearly had been in process before the vacation disruption. There are, of course, many other theoretical frames that might plausibly fit the clinical material; yet these examples suffice to make the argument that from a dynamic complexity sensibility, all of these theories, while suggestive and useful, are nevertheless provisional and instrumental. None of them represent truth or reality. In fact, from the perspective of complexity theory, the ideas of absolute truth and essential reality are illusory.

How does my complexity sensibility deal with these diverse theoretical possibilities? Simply put, it allows me to consider and employ them all, to consider all of these theories as they seem situationally useful. I, of course, determine usefulness subjectively and realize that none of the theories I use represents absolute truth about anything. I am grateful for non-linear dynamic systems because it provides me with an overarching sensibility—an inclusive, integrated, powerful, and persuasive sensibility—that encompasses the complications and contradictions, the uncertainty and surprise, which I observe in human interactions.

Just as the theories held by analyst and patient in a complex analytic system influence the texture of their relationship, so, too, does the environmental context. From a complexity perspective, features of the environment may crucially influence or alter the development of the dyad. While mostly beyond immediate awareness, elements of this environmental context include all the sensory stimuli that surround the system. Smells, sounds, temperature, the aesthetics of the analyst's neighborhood, of her office, and of the analyst herself—all of these inform in subtle and not so subtle ways the developing system. I'll examine only one environmental factor in my work with Sally. She and I met at twilight after long workdays for both of us. In summer the light is golden, but in fall during the hour we met, the lowering light outside my large glass windows negatively affects the ambient light in my office. At that hour, everything inside looks dimmer and duller than at any other time of the day. I have noticed over the years that this changing light lowers my arousal level and mood, and it is possible that the dusky light also cast an emotional gloom over our sessions. Thinking about a subtle contextual factor such as light as possibly contributing to the therapeutic rupture underlines the myriad subtle contextual factors—many beyond our ken—that influence every moment of analytic contact.

Non-verbal features of the relationship are also part of the context and history of our mutual system. These are difficult to access because, like environmental elements, they are elusive, largely outside of awareness. Such features include dimensions such as body posture and orientation, the matching of gaze and facial expressions and vocal rhythms and pitch, and patterns of verbal turn-taking. After my vacation, for example, Sally positioned her body at about a forty-five-degree angle away from me, her left shoulder facing me. Similarly, she generally kept her head and gaze averted from directly encountering me. She also spoke in a much louder and emphatic voice than my own, and I found myself striving to raise my voice to approximate her range. These observations suggest that Sally and I were out of non-verbal synchrony or harmony. According to complexity theory, I could have expected, had Sally and I continued to meet and the rupture healed, that our non-verbal behaviors would have become increasingly coordinated.

Any explanation of Sally's leaving must include consideration of my subjective responses. This is one reason that I wrote the vignette from my subjective point of view. Another reason is that, from a dynamic systems perspective, there is no other way I could have written it except from a phenomenological perspective. I can only know my relationship with Sally as my subjective worlds of experience intersect with her subjective worlds. My knowing—the ways in which I organize relational experience—is subjective but "systemically derived" (Orange et al., 1997).

Embodying this notion in case presentations is challenging because it requires new ways of describing intersubjective process. How does one capture in writing the countless contextual elements—and the interactions of these elements—that affect such process? Certainly, one must avoid knowing diagnoses and one-person formulations and descriptions of therapeutic action. In the case of Sally, for example, I have attempted to describe how the issue of aggression expresses itself intersubjectively. As I stated above, I believe my historic difficulty with aggression was a likely contributor to the rupture with Sally. Because I am sometimes numb to anger, my own and that of other people, my response to anger often ranges from none to too little too late. In this case, of course, I was well aware of Sally's hostility but maybe insufficiently aware of the anxiety that her hostility engendered in me. It is possible that my anxiety led me to curtail Sally's expression of anger prematurely or too abruptly. Given the knottiness of such interaction, I find it a daunting task to express in simple and vivid writing such an intersubjective commingling of our separate subjectivities.

Word usage and narrative tradition also make it difficult to describe clinical experience from a complexity sensibility. With respect to word usage, words function to define experience as specifically and concretely as possible. The concrete and specific nature of good words tends to establish

94   *Thinking and writing about complexity theory*

boundaries around them, boundaries that separate and distinguish one word from the other. Take the term "self," for example. Denotatively and connotatively this word describes a discreet and bounded entity. How, then, can we use this word "self" in clinical descriptions of diffuse relational states? How can we incorporate its current meaning with our understanding of the fluidity of self-experience, the porosity of boundaries, and the blending and continual reordering of self-experiences in intersubjective meetings?

Traditional psychoanalytic narratives, which tend to be conceptually and chronologically linear, create further problems in conveying a complexity sensibility, in expressing the non-linearity and unpredictability of the analytic process. Modern writers and poets experiment with literary strategies in the effort to depict simultaneity, recurrence, and the diffusion of identity in human experience. They use such devices as broken and ragged narrative frames, unmarked subjectivities, shifting points of view, unreliable narrators, and the rapid oscillation of both temporality and dimensions of psychic reality to convey psychological and relational fluidity. However, these strategies do not fit easily with the need for clarity and order in the presentation of clinical material.

Daniel Stern in *The Present Moment in Psychotherapy and Everyday Life* (2004) emphasizes the importance of attending to present moments in therapy work. Present moments are intense, heightened, truly-lived events, particularly when shared with another person. Although they are small—indeed, they constitute the smallest chunks of affective experience—and may last only a few seconds, these intersubjective present moments nevertheless capture the exquisite richness of "now" and provide opportunities for altering fixed relational positions. From a complexity sensibility, these are opportune moments for system perturbation and reorganization. If realized, these moments are at the center of change and development in life and in therapy. Therefore, Stern urges placing them at the center of analytic focus and concern. He challenges us to capture such telling moments in our writing about psychotherapeutic process, to render them in all their living complexity.

Stern's present moment is something like "a world in a grain of sand," a minute focus for viewing emergent patterns of organizing experience and interaction. A narrow focus concentrates the volume of contextual elements, which also helps in writing about analysis.

In my vignette, I broke up the chronology and linear narrative flow of the case in minor ways and sought to include non-verbal and sensory elements in order to convey feeling and mood. I also tried to focus on some present moments between Sally and me. Yet, my rhetorical repertoire is limited, insufficient to the large task of describing a case complexly and contextually. I am searching for more and better literary means. As we become more aware of the challenges of writing from a complex dynamic systems perspective, it will be fascinating to see what new and effective rhetorical strategies emerge.

Postscript

In response to Sally's voice message, I left her a message of my own. I told her that I regretted her decision to leave treatment and felt inclined to argue with her. However, I thought that we both could use some time to reflect on what had happened. Three weeks later I called her and was surprised by her warm and friendly greeting. Her voice sounded buoyant and animated as she told me how much she had appreciated my first call. She then said that she was interviewing some other therapists, but so far they were all jerks. She promised to keep me posted on her progress.

A few months after Sally's abrupt termination, I presented her case publicly. Frank Lachmann, a prominent New York analyst and infant researcher, responded to my vignette by suggesting that I call her up and yell at her. His idea seemed inspired to me, accurately mirroring how I had felt when I picked up Sally's message. In my imagination I rehearsed letting her have it. Did she know how much I hated playing out abandonment issues with her, and how much I particularly hated playing the role of abandonee? Yet, while I regretted not having made such a call at the time of Sally's leaving, I felt that too much time had elapsed since then. I was no longer directly in touch with my anger toward her and resigned myself to letting the relationship fade.

Imagine my surprise a few weeks ago when Sally left me another voice message: "I'd like to come back and work with you. Do you have time for me?" Perhaps, however, I should not have been so surprised; for by now I know, paradoxically, that surprise is an expected condition of complex systems. Systems change in jerky and unpredictable ways, after all, and emergent properties are non-linear and indeterminate. That Sally and I had maintained and worked on our complex relationship during our separation is evident from all the time I spent during the absence thinking and writing about us and from a similar process on her side, demonstrated by her call. Back working with Sally now, I still think about why she left the relationship in the first place, and why she decided to return. Maybe her hiatus from treatment allowed her room for self-regulation, and she is now ready for new interaction. In any case, I expect that she and I will create together some answers to these questions just as I am clear, with respect to these questions and to others that arise, that multiple forces are at work, some apparent and some invisible, and for even seemingly simple questions, the answers are complex, phenomenological, and emerge only in relationship.

References

Arnetoli, C. (2002) Empathic Networks: Symbolic and Subsymbolic Representations in the Intersubjective Field. *Psychoanal. Inq.*, 22 (5):740–765.

Aron, L. (1996) *A Meeting of Minds*. Hillsdale, NJ: Analytic Press.

Beebe, B. (2004) Faces in Relation: A Case Study. *Psychoanal. Dial.*, 14 (1):1–52.

Beebe, B. & Lachmann, F. M. (2003) *Infant Research and Adult Treatment: Co-Constructing Interactions*. Hillsdale, NJ: The Analytic Press.

Bucci, W. (2002) The Referential Process, Consciousness, and the Sense of Self. *Psychoanal. Inq.*, 22 (5):766–793.

Cilliers, P. (1998) *Complexity and Postmodernism*. London and New York: Routledge.

96 *Thinking and writing about complexity theory*

Carleton, L. & Shane, E. (2014) Gerald Edelmanas Project. *Psychoanal. Inq.*, 34 (8):847–863.

Coburn, W. J. (2002) The World of Systems: The Role of Systemic Patterns of Experience in the Therapeutic Process. *Psychoanal. Inq.*, 22 (5):655–677.

Damasio, A. (1999) *The Feeling of What Happens: Body and Emotion in the Making of Consciousness.* New York: Harcourt Brace & Co.

Edelman, G. (1987). *Neural Darwinism: The Theory of Neural Group Selection.* New York: Basic Books.

Edelman, G. & Tononi, G. (2000) *A Universe of Consciousness: How Matter Becomes Imagination.* New York: Basic Books.

Fonagy, P., Gergely, G., Jurist, E., & Target, M. (2002) *Affect Regulation, Mentalization and the Development of the Self.* New York: Other Press.

Gergely, G. & Watson, J. S. (1996) The Social Biofeedback Theory of Parental Affect-Mirroring: The Development of Emotional Self-Awareness and Self-Control In Infancy. *Int. J. Psychoanal.*, 77:1191–1212

Harrison, A. M. (2003) Psychiatric Theory and Practice: Using Sander's Theoretical Contributions to Assist Parents in Managing Aggression in Their Preschool Children. *Infant Mental Health J.*, 17:123–130.

Hebb, D. O. (1949) *The Organization of Behavior: A Neuropsychological Theory.* New York: Wiley.

Lyons-Ruth, K. (1999) Two Person Unconscious: Intersubjective Dialogue, Enactive Relational Representation and the Emergence of New Forms of Relational Organization. *Psychoanal. Inq.*, 19 (4):576–617.

Mitchell, S. (2000) *Relationality: From Attachment to Intersubjectivity*, Hillsdale, NJ: The Analytic Press.

Orange, D. M., Atwood, G. E., & Stolorow, R. D. (1997) *Working Intersubjectively.* Hillsdale, NJ: the Analytic Press.

Sander, L. (2002) Thinking Differently: Principles of Process in Living Systems and the Specificity of Being Known. *Psychoanl. Dial.*, 12 (1):11–42.

Shane, M., Shane, E., & Gales, M. (1997) *Intimate Attachments: Toward a New Self Psychology.* New York: The Guilford Press.

Siegel, D. (1999) *The Developing Mind: Toward a Neurobiology of Interpersonal Experience.* New York: Gilford Press.

Sroufe, L. A. (2000) Early Relationships and the Development of Children. *Infant Mental Health J.*, 2 (1–2):67–74.

Stern, D. (1985) *The Interpersonal World of the Child.* New York: Basic Books.

Stern, D. (2004) *The Present Moment in Psychotherapy and Everyday Life.* New York: W.W. Norton.

Weiss, J. & Sampson, H. (1998) Patients' Unconscious Plans for Solving Their Problems. *Psychoanal. Dial.*, 8 (3):411–453.

5   Waking sleeping beauty in the case of Emily

Mutual dissociation from a systems perspective

I'm going to present a dynamic systems or complexity approach to exploring my dissociation with a patient I'll call Emily. Complexity ideas are very useful clinically, providing a broad and flexible lens for viewing therapeutic material, and I will use Emily's case to illustrate a few of these ideas. Emily's case is deceptively simple—as though any serious encounter between two people could be simple—and the clinical incident that I'll describe is not particularly dramatic. Nevertheless, the incident, in retrospect, has transformed our work together. Not only did it emerge from all that had previously occurred between us, and not only did it illuminate the separate psychological organizations that each of us brought to our relationship, but it also revealed a mutual dissociative process. Each of us in our own way experienced a dissociation of feeling from thought. I believe that Emily and I jointly created the dissociation in our relationship. We shared its authorship. Before relating the vignette, though, I want to tell you something about Emily and our clinical work.

Emily is what old-time analysts meant by the term "an analyzable patient": she's smart, thoughtful, motivated, and able to contain her impulses, able to talk about them rather than acting them out. She is not a drinker, drug user, or overeater. In spite of a casual and low-key self-presentation—she dresses down and frequently sprawls comfortably on my couch—she is nevertheless disciplined both in her work and recreational life. Not only does Emily work out—her body is toned and muscularly defined—but she also finds time to read seriously, maintain friendships, and keep herself and home in meticulous order. She accomplishes all this as she juggles two kids, a husband, and a going, if somewhat lackluster, corporate career. While I often feel a bit disorganized and unkempt next to her, I admire her competence and equanimity enormously.

During our year and a half together, Emily has been respectful to me—especially appreciative of my emotional understanding—and quite responsible to our work. However, I do not feel that she is very attached to me—or, rather, I'd say she is avoidantly attached. Our encounters are short on affect and expressive energy. Instead there is some invisible barrier of politeness and reserve between us, a sort of pillowy barrier into which my efforts toward emotional contact sink lifelessly. At times, the relationship feels stifling like the atmosphere in an airless cave, and I feel baffled in both meanings of the word.

98 *Waking sleeping beauty in the case of Emily*

"Hang in here," I tell myself. "Stay present, attentive, curious, and trust the process. Trust that the process will help us out of the cave, help us discover new emotional vistas." I think of Emily as "Sleeping Beauty," and I want to help her awaken to life's color.

But participating in Emily's therapy is sometimes damned exhausting for me, and I wonder how I have helped to create such an oppressive, spiritless space with her? When in the grip of the cave fantasy, I feel tired of working so hard with little emotional reward—sort of like the scratched and bloodied fairy tale Prince, who, having struggled in the bramble forest for too long, despairs of ever reaching Beauty's Castle. I wonder if Emily senses my fatigue.

Emily has been in several previous therapies. She is psychologically sophisticated, knows some analytic ideas and language, brings in fascinating dreams, and says insightful and interesting things about herself. Yet, she has not spoken to me about her former therapeutic relationships, not once, not positively, not negatively. I worry that I may be a future addition to the unaddressed list, a dead letter, so to speak.

In spite of hard work and effort, Emily at 38 suffers from a chronic low-grade depression. She longs for deep connection and passion but, at the same time, feels that such experience eludes her. Her voice takes on a plaintive, whining quality when she speaks of the intensity that is missing from her life. It seems clear that our therapeutic relationship reflects this same dynamic of longing and frustration on both of our sides.

In college Emily had an intense relationship with a boy named Mike, a relationship which did spark heat and keen feeling. Yet, Mike, open, fun loving, and deliciously sexual, kept a long-time girlfriend back home. After graduation he left Emily for the other girl with hardly a backward glance. Although downhearted, she was not surprised. Mike's leaving confirmed for her what her mother had taught Emily during her growing up years: that she is second best and must adjust her life expectations accordingly. From her mother's perspective, other people—Emily's cousins, her girlfriends at school, the children of her mother's friends—are more gifted, talented, clever, imaginative, and special than Emily. Indeed, her whole first family, not just Emily, but father, siblings, and mother, too, are second best.

A corollary to being "second best" is that Emily must resign herself to failure, disappointment, and mediocrity. Although she hates the notion, Emily believes her mother. Ever since Mike abandoned her, Emily has endured with little fuss her share of heavy loss and disappointment, including the loss of an infant daughter. My sense is that Emily has not sufficiently mourned this lost child and that residual sadness over the dead little girl suffuses and colors her life.

Emily came to me for therapy after Mike, absent for fifteen years, contacted her. Separated from his wife, he initiated an erotic e-mail romance, full of cybersex and mutual personal disclosures. The hot correspondence reignited in Emily old longings and hopes, longings and hopes which Mike dashed when, after a few months of the correspondence, he reconciled with his wife.

Waking sleeping beauty in the case of Emily 99

"I felt alive with him," Emily says. And, indeed, during that period, Emily did look more sparkling and alive to me. Her everyday face has a dark, shadowed look—some mixture of grief, sadness, and worry—with heavy lidded eyes and the corners of her mouth down turned. Yet, while she was corresponding with Mike, there was a shine about her, a shine suggestive of excitement and openness. That shine disappeared into her customary gloom when he terminated e-mail contact, and I see it flash only occasionally in light or humorous moments between us.

Twelve years ago at 26 Emily married a go-getter, an energetic, ambitious, and controlling man. Her husband Dave sounds like a parody of the overbearing American business tycoon. While cunning, extroverted, and successful in the world, at home he is hyperactive, second-guessing, and critical. Often, he comes home from work and, without so much as changing his clothes, takes over Emily's meal preparation. Of course, he knows how to do everything better than Emily, including not only the cooking, but the domestic organization and child rearing as well. She and he agree that in most ways, she is second best to him—except interpersonally: in the family and with their friends Emily handles the affective relationships.

As one might expect, Dave is a better talker than listener, particularly when feelings enter a conversation. According to Emily, he becomes frightened and defensive and invariably preempts emotional encounters with advice giving, by walking away, or by instituting the "Mine is worse than yours" strategy. "So, you think you've had a bad day?" he might say, "Mine was much worse than yours."

After the death of their infant, Dave left Emily for several months, an abandonment that was never adequately explored but which has left a gaping breach in the marriage. Today Emily admires her husband's competence and his energy and devotion to getting things done. She also marvels—with some envy—at his self-confidence and entitlement. Yet, in our time together, she has come to recognize the absence of collaboration and emotional attunement in the marriage—on both sides. This absence troubles her to the core, but she does not believe it is possible to change things. More resignation.

With this background in mind, here is the vignette I'd like to address:

> Dave is up for a great job in a distant city. It is a prestigious job with a very large salary. Because Emily's company has a branch in that city, she may be able to arrange a job transfer—but maybe not. Emily claims to have no problems with or feelings about moving, even though her first family and best friend live in Los Angeles.

At our afternoon appointment I listen in a desultory way to droning details of the anticipated move. I hear no excitement or curiosity, no anger or resentment, in Emily's voice, only a dry and level narration of lists of things to do. I think to myself, "More loss and loneliness for Emily." I hate the details describing the dismantling of Emily's family, community, and professional life.

100 *Waking sleeping beauty in the case of Emily*

Although I feel angry for her, I am mainly aware of being lulled by her voice into drowsiness. I want to take a nap. To jolt myself awake, I ask Emily how she feels about leaving our therapy and me—we've met twice a week for a year and a half—and she answers with a warning edge, "It's premature to talk about it. The move is not a sure thing."

Outside it is raining, and perhaps it is the chilly grayness of the afternoon; more probably, it is Emily's own chilly grayness, her failure to respond to my question with even a whiff of feeling. It might also be the accretion in our work of many such emotional evasions, or the fact that I have my own attachment needs and abandonment anxieties and feel existentially threatened here. After all our work, my patient, who does not seem particularly engaged with me, may now leave me all together. At this moment, I do not expect even a backward glance from her as though I don't exist. All these factors in combination cause me to feel emotionally suffocated. Needing some air, I say, "Premature or not, I have feelings, lots of them, about your going." These words fall out of my mouth, and I gulp.

Emily is as surprised as I am. My statement has radically changed the emotional climate, has clearly perturbed our system. She answers tersely and defensively, "Well, unlike you, I try not to feel things if I don't have to." She falls into silence and averts her eyes. After a time, she giggles and looks back at me. I see a little gleam. Soon, she has regained her composure, "I guess that wasn't very gracious of me." She blushes, and then there is more nervous laughter. "Your words—they make me think of what my other therapists and even Janey (her best friend) have said about me—that I'm inaccessible, umh … hard to reach, closed. I think it's right. There's something wrong with me, defective. I'm not like other people. I don't have normal reactions. I suppose I'm flunking this therapy, too."

"Wow! Some energy, oxygen, an opening," I think. I guess out loud that she felt rebuked or shamed by my comment and so answered me angrily. "No, no" she says, denying hurt and anger. "Normal people would feel things clearly, would know their feelings. Why would I be mad at you for saying what you feel? You are certainly a part of my life here—part of the part I like, I mean. Of course, I'd miss you. But I don't, can't, let myself feel anything about it—since I can't do anything about it anyway."

I wait to see if she has anything more to say and then note that she has moved quickly to take total responsibility for the shift and resulting discomfort between us. I say with irony, "It seems that this rift is all your fault, Emily. Not only are you a lousy patient, you're also an odd-ball person. Since you're stuck being abnormal and can't change that or anything else for that matter, the least you can do is to shut up and shut down. Certainly, you mustn't have any feelings."

She laughs again, "I know better than that, but I do feel responsible." She seems very relieved that the hour is over and practically flees out of the office without saying goodbye.

Next session Emily picks up where we left off but in a very different mood. She speaks thoughtfully in almost a whisper as she watches the hardwood floor.

Waking sleeping beauty in the case of Emily 101

"I've puzzled about why I don't feel anything about moving away. You have feelings about my move, and I don't. It's weird. After all, this is not my choice. I like my life here, and my family is here and settled. And you're here too. But I do think Dave deserves to have his brilliant career. Really, he's been quite nice about the whole thing and says if it happens, if he gets the job offer, I can decide if we take it or not. Of course, he knows I would never say no. So why should I fret? It's a done deal one way or the other. Tuesday I felt you were expecting me to have strong feelings, and I just don't. Feelings like rage. I don't like those expectations from you, and I don't like feeling pushed."

"Rather than not having any feelings, Emily, maybe you simply can't think about feelings of loss here with me."

"I can *think* about loss, but I don't *feel* it. Maybe I choose not to. Oh, I don't know."

"Well if you have a choice and choose not to feel loss here, are there any ways that I contribute to or tip your choice?"

She thinks for a bit and searches me out visually. "Well, I'll be totally honest. I was thinking about whether to tell you this. Sometimes you look tired on Tuesday afternoons—like this week when I was talking about the move. When that happens, I think I'm boring you. You probably have many more interesting patients. I imagine they never bore you. I felt this same way with my old therapist, too. She often seemed tired or bored with me and so didn't push me enough. Hmm, I know you'll ask how that compares with you? You do probe and push, but I often don't like it. I don't want to feel bad feelings. That's why I snapped at you on Tuesday. I did feel bad; I left feeling terrible."

"You're right, Emily. I think I did push you Tuesday. In part, I pushed because I felt distant from you, distracted, and a bit sleepy. I wanted feelings from you. I wanted your feelings to wake both of us up. I wanted them even if they turned out to be angry ones. So, I am confirming your impression—although I hate when it happens, and I hate to admit it—that sometimes I dissociate when we are together."

Emily says, "This feels strange, talking to you about all of this so matter-of-factly. I want to know more, and I also want to leave."

"I want you to stay so we can work this out."

"You say you want to know me and to know my feelings. But it feels dangerous to me—especially if you're falling asleep."

"I sure understand that, and I acknowledge that you're very angry at me."

"Hmm."

"Emily, let's see if I have it right so far. It's bad enough feeling bad feelings by yourself; you don't want that, don't like that at all. If you can, you minimize or erase your bad feelings. And, then, if I am tired or bored, it's not likely that I'd care to attend to your bad feelings—that is, if you chose to have them and bring them here. If I were bored, not interested, or sleepy, then having bad feelings with me would be even worse than having bad feelings alone. Better keep mum about them.

102 *Waking sleeping beauty in the case of Emily*

What's new here is that you've confronted me about my behavior. I imagine the last thing you expected is to confront me and have me come alive and be interested, to have me listen to and respond to you. This comes as a surprise and is a bit dangerous. It seems that you are quite undecided about how or whether to continue this conversation."

"That's right," she says, and after a pause goes on, "To tell you the truth, nobody has ever been interested in my bad feelings. My mother was lost in her own bad feelings. I hated that and wasn't really interested in hearing her complain. So, I certainly understand why you wouldn't want to hear me complain. And, then, my mother had no patience with my feelings or me. Dave just gets defensive and angry. Sometimes he gets competitive with my feelings or just shuts down if I seem upset with him. So why in Hell would I think you'd really want to know?"

The above exchange, charged with old and present angers and new truths between us, made me very happy. It also woke me up. It felt to me like a whiff of fresh air, a small promise that together Emily and I might actually find an exit from our cave.

In the vignette a few central themes and questions emerge that organize Emily's relationships and our co-transference. For Emily these questions concern overarching themes of deep trust and commitment and her emotional strategies when trusts and commitments are violated. I imagine her asking me, "Do I have power and value in this relationship, or am I second best and powerless? Will you listen to and care about me, or will I just get dumped? Can I find and/or risk feeling and intensity here with you?"

As therapist, I, in turn, bring questions and goals from my worlds of experience that also organize the co-transference: "Can I function successfully to establish a trusting and feeling relationship with Emily? Can I tolerate what I anticipate: the emergence of deep grief and mourning as a result of Emily's history of abandonments and losses? Can I tolerate Emily's emotional denials, evasions, and deadness in order to create something new and alive between us? Or will I answer her emotional avoidance with my own?"

The two of us play out these questions in many variations. Each of us takes turns enacting the various and changing dramatic roles which these questions proffer. Particularly, the issues of trust and emotional vitality are central in the vignette. I suggest that in the joint project of waking up "Sleeping Beauty," paradoxically we have together created and experienced a claustrophobic life space, full of longing but until this point empty of deep feeling, passion, and meaning. This is the kind of life space that, until now, Emily has occupied alone.

Are there dynamic systems or complexity ideas which shed light on this discussion of Emily and me? I'll name a few. Complexity theory posits that two open complex systems—like Emily and me—are pre-wired for connection. Minds are inherently relational, interactive, and continually updated by experience. Each union of two minds is, then, a unique and cocreated dyadic system, all parts of which are mutually interdependent and mutually influential. The union is unique both because of the singular histories and experiences

Waking sleeping beauty in the case of Emily 103

of the partners and because of the particular context and ensuing process of their coming together.

All parts of complex systems are in a process of perpetual change, with each other and with other complex systems, a process of continual organization, deconstruction, and reorganization. In spite of this continual flux, dynamic systems tend toward ordered intricacy. In complexity parlance this process is termed the self-organization of complex systems. While movement and change are continuous and highly context-sensitive, complex systems nevertheless often find states of stability and equilibrium called "attractor states." "Attractor states" are preferred patterns of organization into which systems settle and which must be "perturbed" in order for new movement and organization to occur. In the case of Emily and me the creation of the claustrophobic cave, that space of emotional vacancy, is where our system had settled. Although I had consciously sought to influence her in the direction of vitality, the actual influence was toward a state of low energy for both of us. This was our attractor state.

How does complexity theory explain the perturbation and subsequent reorganization of our system after I confronted Emily's lack of feeling about our work, and Emily confronted my drowsiness? It pictures our system with an established history of intricate connections, connections in the nature of budding familiarity and trust. Although settled in an "attractor state" of mutual affective dissociation, the system also possessed the potential to confront the affective deadness and to change. Dynamic systems theory names this relatively open state, poised between order and chaos, the "tipping point." In keeping with the complexity notion of unpredictability, I would add here that both Emily and I were surprised by the long-term impact of our confrontation. At the time I certainly did not know that we were poised on any "tipping point" or that once the two of us had "tipped," the resulting effects would be large changes in the energy and tone of our relationship. According to systems theory, a small perturbation may create large effects.

By the time of the vignette, neither Emily nor I knew what sources in the system—Emily's history and experience or my own—accounted for our abilities both to dissociate from and to confront each other. Rather, by that time Emily and I were joint authors of the relationship, a circumstance that systems theory describes as the distribution of affect across the relational landscape. Emily and I were able to read and recognize each other and to know our relational dance in subtle, nonverbal ways. We had achieved with each other many "implicit relational knowings" about each other, or in Tronick's term, a "dyadic expansion of consciousness."

This astonishing observation that affects and "relational knowings" in dyads do not belong to just one party is an important contribution of systems thinking. What feels like *mine* is really *ours*! Dyadic affects and knowings become the property of both partners' history and experience. This conviction constitutes a denial of intrapsychic representation. As Coburn explains it,

104 *Waking sleeping beauty in the case of Emily*

> Instead of experiencing the "outside world" and then "internalizing" it, "representing" it, and arranging it in some manner for future adaptational use, sources of emotional experience are more usefully pictured as distributed throughout multiple relational systems. In that sense, in the explanatory sense, no one authors or owns their emotional experience."
>
> (Coburn, 2007)

And so, in our confrontation, our existing system was perturbed so that Emily and I paradoxically met each other with a directness and intensity that countered our dissociation and enlivened our interaction. Subsequent to this incident, our interactions have moved in the direction of more vitality, ease, and spontaneity.

What complexity thinking has added to my understanding of this relationship and to my therapeutic work generally is an enlarged sense of mystery and possibility. I no longer wonder whether change will occur in a given therapy, because changes are perpetual in a complexity sensibility. But I am less certain than I used to be that I can know the direction of that change. A complexity sensibility informs me that what I think I know and do is always less than or different from what is actually happening or what is possible. What I think will happen is always provisional and open to surprise. And what I think of as personal accomplishment always derives from larger relational systems.

Reference

Coburn, W. J. (2007) Contextualist Sensibilities in Psychoanalysis: A Discussion of Judy Pickles's Case Presentation. *Psychoanal. Inq.*, 27:139–144.

6 Stuck

Choice and agency in psychoanalysis

"You must believe in free will; there no choice."

Isaac Bashevis Singer

Introduction

This paper is about choice and free will in psychoanalysis. In it I want to illuminate a new kind of determinism: I'll call it contextual-complexity determinism. My argument is this: as postmodern theories increasingly embed the person in environmental and human contexts, the self or subject is under attack and is disappearing. As a result, the possibility of free will becomes problematic. Object relations, attachment theory, intersubjectivity, modern relational theory, dynamic systems—in all of these the self has been contextualized in biological, environmental, social, and relational systems; the self has been decentered, split, dissociated, and fragmented—"unreified" and even "fluidized"—reduced sometimes to shifting relational patterns and organizations, multiply divided, and otherwise deconstructed. Hence, the outlines of a bounded self and a cohesive agent have become more and more blurry. And, after all, what are agency and responsibility without a responsible self or agent? Don't we need an individual with a coherent self to exercise choice and responsibility? We have here a big problem! Currently, we find in the literature creative explorations of subjectivity, but subjectivity emanating from cubist, cracked, divided, and dissolving subjects.

Yet, to do our work we must believe that our patients and we possess enough autonomy and freedom—or, at least, degrees of freedom—to author our lives and initiate choice and change. As Isaac Bashevis Singer put it paradoxically, "You must believe in Free Will; there is no Choice." And so, we ask why one person can dream up, plan, and execute imaginative and complicated projects and activities, while another seems never to get off the dime. What does it mean to have agency and free choice? What does it mean to be stuck?

Let me begin with some clinical material:

1   Elaine's daughters, tired of their mother's "denial," insist that Elaine come to therapy. Elaine has not accepted her husband Edward's cancer death three and a half years ago. His clothes and possessions remain in the house just as he left them; the answering machine still responds with his voice: "We're not here …;" Elaine keeps Edward's unused car tuned and at the

106 *Stuck*

ready for him; and she is mired in "wrongful death" lawsuits. According to the children, their mother is out of touch with reality and exercising poor judgment. At our first session Elaine tells me, "I can't believe that Edward is gone, and I can't move on—whatever the girls mean by that 'moving on' crap. Nothing the girls say can change this." Elaine seems stuck.

2   Briana's life moves along on a staccato, discontinuous path. And there are a lot of potholes on the way. She has carried my number for several months before finally calling and urgently insisting on "the soonest appointment." She misses our first two scheduled appointments because, first, she forgets, and, then, she gets lost. On her third try, she rushes past me at the door into my office. Then, as I turn to join her in the office, she also turns and stops abruptly near the doorway so that I almost slam into her. In response to my gesture to be seated, she lurches for the couch, plops herself down throw pillow-like, almost falls sideways, rights herself, and then moans softly as though she has just finished an arduous race. Sitting down in my chair, I, too, am relieved that we have safely landed in our places. It turns out that Briana's life process is just as sticky-staccato—as unregulated and exhausting—as this entrance.

   Briana always means to begin, follow-through, or complete intended projects, but she is invariably late paying bills, and her house is "a mess." She is under-employed and lacks only three college classes to graduate. Yet, she cannot get it together to register for the classes or, once registered, to do the assignments. Thus, graduation is something vaguely out there, just beyond her reach. Her teenage son is out of control, sometimes violently so. Nevertheless, the efforts of therapists and psychiatrists to help with his development have failed because Briana is "too soft" on discipline, responds to the boy's temper tantrums with her own, and tolerates non-compliance of prescribed medication and behavioral agreements. She "wants it different," "knows what I should be doing," feels awful and blames herself mercilessly. But she is definitely stuck.

In their "stuckness" Elaine and Briana embody central questions with which psychoanalysis has grappled—or frequently sidestepped—since Freud. These questions relate to determinism and human freedom: to the possibility of self-agency, choice, and responsibility and to the necessary conditions for self-generated change. In grappling on a metaphysical level—what I will call "Big D" determinism—analytic theorists ask whether our behaviors and our lives are determined and, therefore, destined or fated. On a more local and certainly more comfortable level, analysts ask what therapeutic conditions foster or impede the *subjective experiences* of effectiveness and agency or helplessness and fatedness. I will call this second, experiential level "little d" determinism.

   The analytic sidestepping away from "Big D" makes perfect sense. What if our lives, our psyches, and our behaviors are determined? What if there is no such thing as an agentic self; no such thing as a choice? What if Elaine and

Briana have *no choice*? Imagine! If the constructs of self and choice and intentional action are illusory, our analytic efforts to help patients make and take responsibility for meaningful life decisions seem clearly absurd.

The questions of free will and choice are not abstractions for me; they are alive and charged with personal and relational meaning. Because my parents came down on opposite sides of these questions—my father negatively and mother affirmatively—I have struggled in confusion to define my own views. This paper is a continuation of that struggle. After all, without autobiographical resonance, why would anyone spend long hours researching and thinking about such illusive issues and then trying to torture words into some coherent meaning?

In the face of life challenges, changes—and sometimes catastrophes—my normally gloomy father would collapse into hopelessness and despair. At his most depressed, he would quote from *King Lear*, "As flies to wanton boys are we to the gods; they kill us for their sport." These were the days before rosy self-help books, days when serious literature often confirmed our deepest fears. My father's words, electric and implacable, generated in me currents of dread and anger. Mother, on the other hand, was a lemonade maker. No matter how sour a situation, she always eventually had a plan, a strategy, or a cheesecake in the oven. Before she died, my mother said, "My life has had many chapters. Some were hard, and some I created out of nothing. But all the chapters were sure interesting."

As children do, I believed both parents, simultaneously accepting my father's fatalism and my mother's trust in possibility and personal agency. Contradictory and perplexing, to say the least! Presently, I am a kind of nihilistic Pollyanna, hyper-alert to the dark, the distressing, and the difficult. On one hand, I hone in on system constraints: the complications and complexities and the *de facto* expectations, obligations, and restrictions, which inhabit living systems and inhibit choice. On the other hand, I also look for and expect to find chinks in those systems, spaces for individual agency. I remain ever hopeful of finding openings for new possibility, and, especially, for choice. The issues in this paper, then, are particularly meaningful to me, and I will explore here some metaphysical and psychological ideas about determinism, and, then, attempt to trace how they are dealt with or not in contemporary thinking.

Review of literature

From Freud to postmodern philosophy and contemporary dynamic systems, many theorists suggest that one or another form of "stuckness" is an objective, general feature of the human condition, the ultimate "deep attractor state."[1] Theorists describe "Big D" stuckness along a continuum with no choice or free will, at one end, to freedom with constraints, at the other. Freud, for example, believed in an objective determinism; he was a "Big D" guy, who held that

108   *Stuck*

> ... psycho-analysts are marked by a particularly strict belief in the determination of mental life. For them there is nothing trivial, nothing arbitrary or haphazard. They expect in every case to find sufficient motives where, as a rule, no such expectation is raised. (1910, p. 38)

Later he writes,

> [Are] there occurrences, however small, which drop out of the universal concatenation of events–occurrences which might just as well not happen as happen? If anyone makes a breach of this kind in the determinism of natural events at a single point, it means that he has thrown overboard the whole Weltanschauung of science. Even the Weltanschauung of religion ... behaves much more consistently, since it gives an explicit assurance that no sparrow falls from the roof without God's special will.
>
> (Freud, 1916, p. 28)

For Freud, then, "Big D" determinism—largely biological determinism—obtains, and he didn't concern himself much with questions of choice or will. For him, id energy—ruthless, rapacious, and raw—is the sole driving force, the motivation for all psychological life. For the mature Freud, mind, with its ego and superego structures, functions primarily to contain, modify, fulfill, and defend against the asocial and animalistic aims of the id drives. Choice for Freud comes at the tail end of the process of becoming conscious of one's conflicts, one's struggles with id drives. And it is meager choice indeed. Well-analyzed patients find strategies for containing their drives that are somehow better—more consistent with prevailing social expectations though not necessarily more satisfying or joyful—than former neurotic strategies. In analysis they learn to choose these better strategies.

Even with Freud, however, determinism is an ambiguous concept that may leave some possible space for choice. Freud argued that psychic events can be understood retrospectively: "So long as we trace the development from its final outcome backwards, the chain of events appears continuous, and we feel we have gained an insight which is completely satisfactory or even exhaustive." Yet, retrospective causality does not permit prospective prediction:

> ... if we start from the premises inferred from the analysis and try to follow these up to the final result, then we no longer get the impression of an inevitable sequence of events. We notice at once that there might have been another result, and that we might have been just as well able to understand and explain the latter ... in other words, from a knowledge of the premises we could not have foretold the nature of the result.
>
> (Freud, 1920, pp. 167–168)

Here, then, Freud leaves a small opening for the possibility of chance and choice to influence causal unfolding. Chance or "accidental" life encounters and the ego's responses to those encounters may alter a person's life direction and, thereby, change the causal matrix.

Like Freud, some current scientific investigators do not believe that free will exists. In framing mathematical models of complexity, for example, they propose that global causal or connective systems determine our lives and prevent the exercise of free choice (Grigsby and Osuch, 2007). These are "Big D" determinists, who depict matter, energy, nature, and human lives as embedded in binding matrixes that determine central aspects of physical, behavioral, and psychological unfolding. These matrixes may be linear, non-linear, relatively simple, or excruciatingly complex. While "Big D" determinism, however conceived, should be reckoned with both in conceptualizing issues of individual choice and freedom and in understanding human change process, it is mostly ignored in contemporary psychoanalysis.

Any discussion of "Big D" operates on what intersubjective system theorists call "the explanatory level of discourse": observed or theoretical descriptions of *states* or *conditions* (Coburn, 1999, p. 184). Such explanatory discussions are framed in "third person" objective terms. Free will and "Big D" determinism are theoretical constructs that exist on this explanatory level and are among those large existential questions about which there are plenty of beliefs but no certainty. My clinical tendency is to touch lightly on such questions or to skirt them all together, and this is precisely how my colleagues deal with the "Big D" question. Yet, one does not have to look far to see that there is a disconnection in our literature—and sometimes a downright contradiction—between theorizing about the self in relationship to global deterministic forces, on the one hand, and our treatment of people who feel stuck, on the other. This disconnection merits attention.

A more immediate and manageable way to think about "stuckness" is as a subjective, psychological *experience*, a "first person" knowing. According to Stolorow et al. (2001), this latter experiential or phenomenological level delimits the scope of psychoanalysis, eliminating the need to grapple with "Big D" questions in any way beyond the metaphorical. "Little d" is the personal experience of not having control, of being at the mercy of powerful forces, internal and/or external. "Little d" is a description of how some people organize and view—affectively and behaviorally—their life experience and expectations. For these people, much like Briana, making choices seems difficult and/or downright impossible. Consequently, while life may flow all about them, they live their lives passively or in a "one-step forward, one step backward" pattern. Like stones in a rushing stream, such people feel the current of life as something out there, eddying around or washing over them, rather than as a process in which they actively participate, a process which reflects creative choice, action, and responsibility.

I ask a question here that bears on the relationship between "Big D" and "little d" determinisms. In addressing "little d" questions, may we analysts simply ignore the "Big D" issue? Or rather, as John Searle (2008) insists, must a theory of subjectivity—a "first person ontology"—necessarily reflect and be

110   *Stuck*

somehow congruent with the explanatory level, with empirical/scientific description, with what Searle calls a "third person" ontology? I feel personal discomfort with clinical practices in which first and third person ontologies do not correspond, where what we do as clinicians may contradict what Ringstrom terms "the big altogether everything else" (2007).

In the rest of this paper I'm going to do two things. First, I'll present some contemporary thinking in search of the elusive subject and agent, in search of some version of a continuous self or a system of self-with-other. This search does not ignore the contextual nature of human development and experience—our foundational dependence on our human relationships and our historical, biological, social, and environmental contexts. Rather, it pictures the self, situated in particular physical and relational contexts, but still able to deliberate and choose life paths. Second, I will describe some of my clinical work with Elaine and Briana as that work pertains to questions of choice and agency.

Existentialists and mind/brain people

Against tendencies toward deconstructing the self, there are counter strains in contemporary philosophy, psychoanalytic theory, and infant research that emphasize alterity, difference, and the emergence of an agentic self. These counter strains are in the direction of constructing a post-Cartesian embodied subject, contextualized and embedded, to be sure, but also one with enough self-coherence to make choices and assume responsibility for them. I will explore some such efforts below.

In an excellent essay Frie (2002) discusses philosopher–psychologists of the existential-phenomenological tradition: Ludwig Binswanger, Medard Boss, Erich Fromm, Frieda Fromm-Reichmann, R.D. Laing, Eugene Gendlin, and others. As a group these thinkers concern themselves with the individual's relationship to the multiple contexts—particularly the relational contexts—of their lives. As Frie tells it, these clinicians

> … introduced the concept of a socially and historically constituted person; they emphasized the interpersonal and embodied basis of human experience; they questioned the myth of analytic neutrality and introduced the notion of a two-person psychology. At the same time, these clinicians sought to elaborate a concept of the *individual* self within a relational context and thus underline the importance and role of agency in therapeutic change. In essence, their aim was to reconcile such key modernist themes as agency, identity, and individuality with an emerging postmodern framework. (p. 636)

The existential-phenomenological tradition holds that while human beings are in the world and embodied, they can never entirely be reduced to any historical, cultural, linguistic, or social community. Human individuality and agency are indissoluble; and, Frie suggests:

Stuck 111

Even if we accept the notion of multiple constructed self-states, this self-system relies on an underlying continuity of selfhood that stands in the way of psychic disintegration and allows for self-perception and understanding over time. Thus, it would seem that there is need to temper the constructivist impulse … in order to leave a space for individual will and action which is related to our self-understanding. (p. 650)

The task of finding space for agency continues in philosophical and psychological literature that centers on defining the "underlying continuity" that Frie names. Theories suggesting that the human mind provides this "underlying continuity" appear in a number of philosophic explorations of free will. Cavell (2003), Hoffman (1998, 2000), and Searle (2008) all propose that it is a mental "space" or "gap" that allows for human reflection, deliberation, and free choice.

For example, Marcia Cavell (2003), an heir of the existentialists, argues that the exercise of freedom begins in the realm of "mind" and what she calls "reasons." Cavell uses the term "reasons" here in an idiosyncratic way. For her reasons emerge from minds that are embedded in larger human and social contexts; "mind" is not isolated from its physical and relational surrounds. Cavell says, "Reasons are a complex of mental states," constructed from wish, belief, desire, emotion, feeling, motive, and especially experience. Typically, reasons lead to intentional action performed in the external world. Further, Cavell argues, "In so far as our actions are caused by reasons, we are in the domain of choice and free choice; causality itself is no constraint" (2003, p. 516).

It seems that Cavell is both trying to flesh out the concept of reflective functioning and suggesting that choice derives from mental deliberation. I like her argument and would expand on it with this emphasis: depending on how mature and rich the subject's life experience, affectivity, relational matrixes, imagination, and conceptual repertoire, his/her reasons may reflect deep feelings and moral understanding. These reasons, once acted upon, become causes themselves, and subsequently they—and the actions that issue from them—become enmeshed in the workings of any given causal or connectionist system. They become part of the recursive feedback and associational nets that are integral to dynamic systems. As a result of our minds and our reasons, then, we are able to determine and affect our worlds just as our contextual worlds determine us.

Realized mental creations, reasons may initially enter the causal nexus, which includes both the physical world and other people, relatively unconstrained by external and internal forces. But agency and freedom are not absolutes; they may be compromised or constrained by many factors. "Agents are embedded in a causal nexus," Cavell says. Therefore, I add, they may be subjected to the pressures, power differentials, and competing needs of different parts of the complex causal system.

Irwin Hoffman similarly addresses the problem of choice and responsibility. In discussing his "dialectical constructivism," Hoffman sees both analyst and

112 *Stuck*

patient as responsible agents, people capable of moral self-reflection and of using their minds to make responsible choices. His ideas are similar to Cavell's although not as carefully explicated. Hoffman argues that "the individual's inevitable sociocultural embeddedness as well as the influence of unconscious dimensions of the transference and countertransference ... can be regarded as powerful influences without being wholly determining of the patient's experience and behavior (2000, p. 828)." He advances the idea of a "space for the individual will as a primary cause" of action, "a space between the source of influence and its impact, a gap in which I am present as an agent, as a choosing subject" (Hoffman, 2000, pp. 828–829). This space or gap clearly is a function of a deliberative mind and implies—although the implication is not explored—a degree of psychic separateness from one's contexts. Elsewhere Hoffman says that he is advocating an integration of modern and postmodern perspectives on human agency.

John Searle recognizes the absurdity of a human existence absent free will, and longs to find a naturalistic explanation for human choice. In Freedom and Neurobiology, Searle (2008) presents a hierarchy of human mental functions that issue from neurobiology and lead, again, to a theory about mind. According to Searle, mind—including intention, consciousness, reason, language, and probably free will—seems to be an emergent property of complex brain operations. The brain's operations are in continuous recursive interactions with one's internal and external environments, but ultimately mind "is essentially a problem about how the brain works" (2008, pp. 40–41).

Searle posits that free will may emerge in a neurological gap, one that functions as a space for deliberation between desire and action. Searle's "gap" echoes the ideas of Cavell and Hoffman about deliberative mental spaces and gaps. For all three thinkers, mental gaps provide space and time for reflective thought and initiated action.

On the explanatory level Searle also searches for room for indeterminacy within a "Big D" connectionist system, turning to modern physics in order to find such room. He speculates that free will may derive from the random indeterminacy existing at the level of micro brain processes. As he hopefully suggests, "The indeterminacy at the micro [neurobiological] level may explain the indeterminacy of the system, but the randomness at the micro level does not by itself imply randomness at the system level" of mind and will (2008, p. 76). Somehow, and Searle doesn't yet know how, hierarchical brain activity may transform micro randomness into organized choice at the macro level.

The tradition of recognition

Another tradition, that of "recognition"—from Hegel, Buber, and Levinas to Benjamin, Fonagy, and many infant researchers—not only bridges the fields of philosophy, psychology, and infant research, but also emphasizes the alterity of the other and the separate existence of self. It, therefore, establishes conditions necessary for initiative and choice. This phenomenological tradition—"little d"—advances the possibility of self as a responsible and/or constructive agent in human affairs.

It begins with Hegel for whom one's consciousness of self and other emerges through relational struggle. This is a dialectic of desire and striving for recognition, and it is through such recognition or mirroring that a consciousness of mind or self develops. In Hegel's vision, people wrestle recognition, one from the other, much as the Biblical Jacob wrestled the Angel for his blessing.

Martin Buber (1923) later transformed this process of mutual recognition into a philosophy of dialogue. Like Hegel, Buber believed that mind develops only in relationship, and we can only know another when we enter into relationship with him/her. For Buber, human subjectivity moves between two types of relationships: "I-It" and "I-Thou." "I-It" describes relationships in which people use each other instrumentally or as objects; in such relationships the other is largely psychologically unseen and unknown. The "I-Thou" stresses the mutual, holistic existence of two subjectivities meeting each other authentically in relationship. Buber's idea of mutuality and dialogue, of course, requires two separate participating selves.

Like Buber, Emmanuel Levinas (1969) also presents recognition of the Other as central to knowledge of self, the world, and transcendence. Rather than a relationship of mutuality and dialogue, however, Levinas envisions the encounter with the "irreducible Other" as creating an ethical relationship that demands respect and responsibility. Paradoxically, the encounter with the Other underlines not only our separateness, but also our absolute and essential human connectedness.

For Levinas the ethical dimension of relationship precedes all knowledge and derives from the experience of the face to face encounter. Meeting the other, encountering her face, reveals the awesome power of the Other's simultaneous nearness and separateness: "The Other precisely reveals himself in his alterity, not in a shock negating the I, but as the primordial phenomenon of gentleness" (1969, p. 150). For Levinas, failure to appreciate the alterity of the other is an act of violence. The epiphany of the face to face encounter is revelatory and binding, pure emotion and expression. The Other's face summons us, pulls us to it, and in its vulnerability demands protection from us. Our capacity to make ethical choice issues from this revelation and is intrinsic to Levinas' system.

In contemporary psychoanalytic literature, Jessica Benjamin, Peter Fonagy, and many of the infant researchers use and expand on the philosophical tradition of recognition. Within broadly contextual frames, all of these theorists leave room for separate selves who possess the senses of initiative, agency, and choice.

Jessica Benjamin (1988), drawing on ideas from Hegel, Levinas, and object relations theory, describes the development of relational recognition which she names intersubjectivity. It is a developmental achievement, resulting from a Hegelian struggle between two subjects. This conflict is between each subject's assertion of self and will, on the one hand, and the mutual recognition

114   *Stuck*

of the other's self and will, on the other. Resolution of the conflict allows the subjects to meet as "sovereign equals." In the process of struggle the partners create a third space that contains both an amalgam of and tension between both partners' viewpoints. In this Third there is room "for both subjects' separate but recognizable centers of initiative" (2005, p. 449).

During the developmental process both partners must relinquish internal or fantasy object relations and wrestle with wishes and efforts to negate the other. Through the struggle, they come finally to recognize the other's reality, the other's difference, and that the other is "an equivalent center of being." This last phrase echoes Levinas in its demand for respect and responsibility. Benjamin's concern for equivalence and respect is illustrated, for example, in her insistence that, like the baby, the mother is a subject, not an object. In relationships, Benjamin suggests, both partners come to view each other as assertive beings. Once achieved, recognition is still a condition of tension. As Benjamin states, "From the standpoint of intersubjectivity theory, the ideal 'resolution' of the paradox of recognition is that it continue as a constant tension between recognizing the other and asserting the self" (1996, p. 38).

Although Peter Fonagy draws from a different set of influences—attachment theory and object relations—he describes the development of recognition as a process quite similar to Benjamin's and names his process mentalization (Fonagy and Gergely, 2005). According to Fonagy, mentalization is a theory of mind, the ability to understand the mental state of oneself and others based on observed behavior. It is a form of mental activity that involves imagination and empathy and enables us to perceive and interpret human behavior in terms of intentional mental states. These states include needs, desires, feelings, beliefs, goals, purposes, and reasons. Mentalization begins with the baby's discovery that the mother is a separate subject with a separate mind, one that has its own intentions and aims but that can still comprehend the baby's. This discovery is also a developmental achievement, created optimally in the context of a secure attachment relationship with a parent who herself has the capacity to mentalize the child.

What is similar in Benjamin and Fonagy is an emphasis on difference in intersubjective relationships and the conviction that recognition and mentalization are functions of mind that enable its bearers both to understand the intentions of others, to understand their own internal and interpersonal environments, and to generate successful strategies for negotiating those environments. Such capacities are, of course, related to the senses of confidence, effectiveness, and agency that are the concern of this paper.

A complexity or systems sensibility: intersubjectivity and infant research

Because he directly addresses questions of the individual, freedom, and personal responsibility, I'll use William Coburn's thinking here as representative of intersubjectivity systems theory. His views are consistent with and reflective of the intersubjective field theory developed and elaborated in the voluminous works of Stolorow, Atwood, and Orange. Frie and Coburn (2010) approach the issue of choice and responsibility from a thoroughly contextualist perspective. His notion of the self is more radically systemic and contextual than any of the previous theorists. For Frie and Coburn, the self and individual emotional life is an emergent property of the "larger relational/socio-cultural surround" (2010, p. 7).

Coburn begins by acknowledging Heidegger's ideas that we are "thrown into life circumstances over which we have no control." Nevertheless, as one comes to understand and own the systemic contexts of his life, he/she may begin to imagine new life possibilities and choices.

Frie and Coburn argue that although we may experience our emotional worlds as bounded and our choices as generated from some private, internal source, individual choice, in fact, is "an emergent property of larger inter-penetrating relational systems, of which each of us is a constituent, and not as the product of one specific component or person" (2010, pp. 18–19). Paradoxically, as we increasingly come to own our "situatedness," the constituent physical and emotional circumstances over which we have no control, new life possibilities and choices may emerge. Frie and Coburn state:

> [I]n the absence of a situational awareness, included in which is a deepened understanding of the contextual forces (past, present, and imagined future) that conspire to situate us affectively in the very place we *find* ourselves, there cannot obtain an appreciation for the extent to which we can exercise what we think of as free will, autonomy, agency and individuality. (2010, p. 17)

Coburn has clearly identified the problem of contextual/complexity determinism; but, like all the other contemporary thinkers, he hasn't yet solved it, at least, to my satisfaction. While he contends with its slippery knot complexities, Coburn optimistically suggests that the therapeutic relationship works simultaneously to recognize the contexts of our separate-seeming but joined lives—to expand our situational awareness—and to foster an expansion of shared emotional tolerance. Perhaps an increased sense of agency follows.

Finally, self psychology, infant research, and attachment theory are areas of inquiry in contemporary psychoanalysis consistently more concerned with the construction than the deconstruction of self. In this last section of the literature review, I'll limit my focus to the infant research people whose work, like Coburn's, expresses a systems sensibility. Taken in sum, the important contributions of infant observers and attachment investigators over the past half century have created a fairly detailed architecture of the developing self, including the agentic self. Without directly addressing the issue of "Big D" determinism, the infant development and attachment people describe healthy developing selves as possessing the capacity for agency and choice both phenomenologically and in fact.

116   *Stuck*

The blueprints for a self are complex but comprehensible. The self develops from birth in continuous interaction with his/her primary caretakers. As Hastings puts it, "It takes [at least] two to make one" (Hastings, 2007, p. 369). The infant-caretaker system is multi-layered and recursive, taking into account the internal and external environments of both partners. Babies are active relational participants from the beginning. Initially, connections accrue and systemic self-organization develops through mutually regulated non-verbal exchanges. These include bidirectional rhythm matching of body and voice, modulation of vocal contour and pace, coordinated pauses, postural matching, gaze regulation, cross modal matching, and contingent responsiveness. Observations reveal that babies initiate more of these exchanges in the first year than their caretakers. Such observations indicate that agency is an inborn capacity that begins to develop from birth.

Besides "mutual recognition" and "mentalization," infant researchers use many terms to describe the relational processes—or aspects of the processes—that promote healthy self development. Here are a few: fittedness, secure attachment strategies, selfobject functions, affect attunement, affect resonance, mid-range responsiveness, self and interactive regulation, and mutual regulation. In contemporary usage, all of these terms assume bidirectional, contingent, and continuous interaction between baby and caretaker in which both similarities and differences between subjects are of central importance.

A sense of agency emerges, then, in repeated moments between mother and child when the mother recognizes and acknowledges the infant's somatic and affective states and intentional directions—or in Winnicott's term, the baby's "spontaneous gesture." For example, the baby cries from hunger, and the mother recognizes the baby's need and answers with nourishment and a "There, there." From such a responsive interaction, the baby feels not only physically satisfied, but his sense of efficacy has also been fed: "I made this happen; I made my mommy feed me!" Agency may be an inborn capacity; yet, for it to mature, it requires caretaker responses that recognize (Benjamin, 1988) and inform (Fonagy et al., 2002) the child about himself, physically and emotionally.

The lack of such responsiveness, "absence" in Hasting's term, constitutes "a danger signal which begins to deform both the child's self and the potential for [agentic] interaction. In its place grows a scar tissue of expectation: the expectation of neglect or abandonment or disintegration" (2007, p. 372). The child does not develop a sense of herself as a subject who can make a dent in the world. Poor self-esteem, low self-confidence, and impaired initiative may follow. Hence, one manifestation of caretaker "absence" is "stuckness."

Psychoanalyst/researchers like Stern, Beebe and Lachmann, Lyons-Ruth, and Judith Rustin infer links between these insights about the development of infant agency, on the one hand, and adult therapeutic action, on the other (Lyons-Ruth, 1999; Rustin, 1997). For example, analogous to effective mother-infant interaction, Rustin has ideas for the psychoanalytic relationship that may promote a sense of agency. She urges a bidirectional analytic stance that pays continuous and mutual attention to affect and state. She says,

> There is therapeutic action in a psychoanalytic stance that explicitly acknowledges the intersubjective matrix, emphasizes affect and state, and advocates systematic inquiry into the impact of the analytic activity on the patient. This stance and inquiry recognize and validate the patient's agency and empower him to shape the treatment in a way that fits, thus enhancing a subjective experience of agency in the patient. (1997, p. 59)

I agree with Rustin and will show how her ideas come alive in my work with Elaine and Briana.

Elaine

What happens when the experience of agency is foreclosed, when the environment is unbearably impinging, and when a sense of fatedness is overwhelming? Beyond hopelessness, helplessness, and depression—some obvious consequences of a sense of fatedness—Carlo Strenger (1998) presents an inventive psychological strategy that he calls "the ontological protest of subjectivity." In response to the oppressive sense of fatedness, Strenger says, the self has two possibilities. The first possibility is to renounce authorship of one's life and to settle for a life that is not personally directed, authentic, or meaningful. This is the psychological equivalent of renouncing one's dreams and entering, instead, the hated family business. This option echoes both Winnicott's (1956) notion of the false self and Brandschaft's (1994) idea of pathological accommodation. It also suggests a range of negative feelings and attitudes: fear, pessimism, lassitude, hopelessness, psychic deadness, and negation. My patient Briana tends in this direction.

The second possibility that Strenger presents is to engage in the "ontological protest of subjectivity." By this latter expression Strenger means not a passive retreat but an active rejection of reality. "Individuals who feel unbearably limited by fate … come to the conclusion that they can restore their sense of authorship only by recreating themselves" and/or aspects of their lives "from scratch" (Strenger, 1998, p. 628).

My patient Elaine has adopted the "ontological protest of subjectivity." Although to outward appearance, Elaine looked "stuck" when she first came to see me, she demonstrated an energy, defiance, and ironic stance behind her denial that belied the helpless/hopelessness of true "stuckness." And she seemed to invite me into the joke. As she put it, "Coming to terms, resolving my grief, who are they kidding? I'd rather be dead. I'll keep my relationship with my dead husband if I like, thank you very much."

Elaine describes her husband Edward in idealized terms and their marriage as rescuing her, fairy-tale like, from a Dickensian first family. She grew up a victim of her father's emotional brutality and sexual abuse and her mother's

118   *Stuck*

simultaneous, almost psychotic, witnessing and denial of his behavior. Although informed about the abuse, the mother was incapable of hearing, recognizing, or acknowledging Elaine's helpless distress. For example, here is a model scene: Elaine's father insisted that the girl bathe with him nightly until she finally refused at 15. As her father fondled her sexually, Elaine would space out and watch water beads melt and run in rivulets down the steamy lime green tile. In spite of Elaine's protests, the mother supported the baths, saying such things as, "It's the least you can do. Dad works so hard for us."

Then, in college, along came Edward, whom Elaine describes as decent and loving. Self-made and successful, he was also handsome, imaginative, generous, understanding, and protective. He exposed Elaine and their children to broad life horizons: a wonderful home, travel, art, music, political activity, and diverse social worlds. When he died of a sudden and deadly cancer in his early fifties, she was shocked and disbelieving.

Afraid of returning to the dark feelings of her early life—feelings of being trapped and "fated"—Elaine has chosen, as best she can, to deny Edward's death. She uses her mind, memory, and imagination as instruments of her "ontological protest," talking to Edward daily and enshrining his memory. Everywhere she goes, she finds him: e.g., in a rainbow after a storm or in a bird lighting at her window.

A part of our work has been to recognize the agency in her active denial of Edward's death—along with the dynamics of that denial—as well as the terrible grief and loss that propel it. My acceptance of—my participation in and even enjoyment of—Elaine's creative "spontaneous gesture" of denial has allowed her to choose an interesting compromise between denial and acceptance.

Together we have come to understand the dynamics of her denial as not only expressing Elaine's choice, but also as a benign echo of her own mother's destructive denial of reality. During the years that I have worked with Elaine, she has consciously chosen to maintain a strange living relationship with her dead husband while softening the ferocity of her denial. Outside of this primary relationship with Edward—which she refuses to relinquish—she has also developed her considerable artistic capacities as well as made some new friendships. Active in the world, she is nevertheless at home with Edward. Today, Elaine shrugs off her children's negative diagnoses and takes conscious responsibility for her choices. She does not feel stuck.

Briana

Like Elaine, Briana has revealed in our therapy conditions of serious absence in her first family. For Briana these conditions were active. She had a loving but absent father and an intrusive, unhappy mother, who felt inadequate and isolated from the world. As a consequence, the mother was critical and contemptuous of everything and everybody, including Briana. Briana does not remember maternal laughter, affection, or the encouragement of any spontaneous gesture. The mother's inability to see Briana as a separate subject as well as her blanket criticism of the child's every curiosity, smallest initiatives, and choice of friends paralyzed the girl. Briana grew up hyper-sensitive to criticism, emotionally disregulated, and oppressively self-doubtful. She did not conceive of herself as a separate mind or center of initiative. As one would expect, the mother herself was depressed and "stuck," also a legatee of cruel and critical parents. As the woman's sole companion and the inheritor of her caustic psychological world, Briana became a new link on a generational chain of misery.

Unhappily, the girl did not find people in her isolated social world to supply what was missing in her first family. Neither did she have the initiative to go out and actively seek people or compensatory experience in the larger environment. Withdrawal and passivity are frequently the consequences of growing up stuck.

This short background brings us to our therapy. From the outset, Briana asks me to make choices for her. What color eye shadow should she wear? What recipes should she prepare for her Christmas party? No matter that I don't wear eye makeup or, as a Jew, am ignorant about Christmas celebrations, Briana still assumes that I know what's good and can choose for her. Alone, self-doubts and lack of practice render even simple choices anxiety laden and daunting. Early in our work Briana also makes clear her dislike of thinking or talking about—or especially feeling—unpleasant emotions. Shame prevents her from either exploring such emotions or making sense or meaning out of difficult life experiences. Thus, she has no access to an affectivity that might provide life directions and opportunities to undo destructive patterns. This is especially clear in relation to her son Eric. "I want to tell you what happened this week," she frequently says to me, "but I don't want to talk about it."

Briana might then describe how Eric has confronted her emotional avoidance with goading insults in order to get a reaction, or else "acted out of control" with his own unruly feelings. Briana might confess finally, inevitably, to exploding at him. Shamefully, she'll tell me of Eric's temper tantrums and how, if she doesn't "hold herself tightly together" or leave the house promptly, she "has to" answer Eric with her own rage. The two might then engage in escalating emotional clashes, convulsive and crazy riffs that circle close to and just avert violence. In her disregulated emotional states, Briana feels helpless and ashamed but unable to choose any options other than flight or fight. Her family system is as stuck as she is personally. After such a description, Briana will abruptly change the subject. "Don't worry; I'm okay. I don't want to talk about it."

About six months into our therapy, during one of these mother-son brouhahas, the boy does become violent: he destroys his bedroom and the family room, bashing furniture and electronic equipment with a baseball bat. With the help of the school system, the family is able to send Eric to a therapeutic boarding school. While away, the boy responds well to the school's structure: its clear expectations and predictability. Sanctions and

120 *Stuck*

rewards at the school are consistent and reasonable responses to Eric's behavioral choices; and for the first time in his life, the boy begins to feel some control over and responsibility for himself. Briana is inconsolable. Remorseful and filled with guilt, she grieves the boy's absence. She feels none of her husband and daughter's relief and elation in the peace and quiet at home without Eric.

"He wants to come home," she tells me one day. "What should I do? I don't know what to do. If only I had known how to handle him, he would never be at that school."

"I thought he has an agreement to do the two-year program." I answer.

"Hmm, but I miss him."

The next thing I know, without our discussing the matter in any greater depth and against the advice of the headmaster of the school—against, indeed, Briana's own sense of what the boy needs—she impulsively arranges for Eric to return home after only ten months of his two year commitment. At our next appointment, Briana is apologetic and wary. She takes two throw pillows from the couch and hugs them to her middle as though expecting me to punch her in the gut.

With customary self-doubt, Briana tells me of her "decision" to bring Eric home. I try to listen and help her to sort out her feelings; but I am annoyed, and she knows it. To my mind this is not a "decision," as in a felt through and thoughtful process, but, rather, this is a repetitive impulsive discharge that has short-circuited Briana's reflective mind. I am annoyed at this failure of reflective functioning that together we have struggled to develop. I am annoyed at the power of bad old psychological and behavioral configurations. And I am annoyed that Briana did not think to consult with me. I say nothing to her about any of this; but in how many non-verbal ways, I wonder, do I express my annoyance? I have slipped professionally and feel my participation here today is an exercise in bad faith.

Next meeting, after placing the pillow barricade back in place, Briana tells me, "For the first time I didn't want to come here."

"I imagine you have feelings about our last session."

"I always feel that you're on my side—encouraging. Last time you were disapproving. I do that enough to myself and don't need you to do it. I don't want to come here anymore."

"You're right about last time, and I'm sorry."

"Really?"

"I was feeling bad for you and Eric and pissed that we didn't talk about the decision together."

Briana is surprised at my apology. She is silent for a moment but puts one of the two pillows back on the couch. "Wow. Thanks for saying 'I'm sorry.'"

"Hmn?"

"Nobody ever apologizes to me."

"If that's the case, it must have been hard to be angry at me and then a risk to let me know it."

"I didn't think about it that way." She pauses. "Yes, I don't like being mad." She pauses again. "But it also feels good to know how I feel and say it. I'm glad you get me."

A small disruption and a not very dramatic repair, this moment nevertheless marks the beginnings of self-reflection and self-assertion in our therapy. Here is Briana's early willingness both to share her mind and emotions with me and to take responsibility for them! In our subsequent therapy I have tried to maintain a two-fold focus: first, to attend to Briana's every assertion of agency in our relationship, to underline and emphasize deliberative decision making and choice whenever possible, whether hers or mine; and second, to work with her to widen our shared emotional territory, to expand the scope and depth of feelings open for exploration in our relationship. The early results feel promising. Briana has taken some small but important steps toward self-assertion. Passionate about food and cooking, she made the choice and has enrolled in cooking school to become a chef. "Imagine me! I've always wanted to do this, but I never dreamed I could."

Discussion and conclusion

I have asked in this paper how, at a time when the concept of self is vanishing from psychoanalysis, we as contemporary analysts might conceptualize an agentic self that has free will and choice. In something like the nightmare of the Solomonic baby, relational analysts currently depict the self as multiply divided. In addition, intersubjectivists and dynamic system thinkers often describe the boundaries of self as porous and/or melting into relational and environmental contexts. As a consequence, it seems that the self as baby is dissolving in its own bathwater. This is, indeed, a sorry situation for a profession that traditionally has sought to enliven its patients and help them to assume increased personal agency in and responsibility for their lives.

While sadly better at delineating the problem than solving it, I have tried to identify some strains and figures in contemporary philosophy and psychoanalysis that directly attend to issues of choice and agency: a line of existential-phenomenologists; some philosophers and psychoanalytic theorists—Cavell, Hoffman, Searle, Buber, Levinas, Benjamin and Fonagy; many infant researchers and attachment theorists; and Coburn, a thoughtful intersubjectivist. These thinkers provide different models of mind and relationship that bear on human agency and responsibility.

In my work with Elaine and Briana, I borrow from many of the theorists, using their ideas according to the specific needs of each relationship. For example, the space that Elaine and I created, where she could grieve her loss without totally banishing Edward from her daily life, took shape in the context of our growing emotional understanding. As a result of our increasingly rich and intense affective moments, Elaine and I came jointly to acknowledge and accept the finality of death—the ultimate fate of even the most vigorous person or vibrant marriage. This is a process that intersubjectivity theory

122   *Stuck*

describes very well. With both Briana and Elaine I attended to shifting affect states, tried to notice and encourage Briana's smallest spontaneous gestures, and recognized and honored Elaine's creative denial. These efforts with both patients echo intersubjective theory and the infant researchers, particularly Judith Rustin. Important moments in the work with Briana and Elaine, ones that bolstered each woman's sense of control and choice, derived from the convergence of memories, interpretation, collaborative analysis, relational ruptures and repairs, mutual understanding and appreciation, much laughter, and quiet reflection. The simultaneity of learning to be together in an easy, trusting, and relaxed rhythm; of retrieving history and memory and exploring the meaning of this past experience; and of enjoying together the power of mind and imagination to free one's spirit—all these factors advanced the development of reflective abilities. They also support self psychology's privileging of selfobject functions, infant research theories about self and interactive regulation, and "mind" theories about deliberative mental spaces and their role in the formulation and assertion of agency and will.

Although I have argued the need to think about the "Big D" question, I have not reached any conclusion about it in this paper. Neither do the thinkers that I have introduced here. While I long to believe in "Big D" free will, it remains a spectral presence in my life. I feel it but cannot prove its existence. In my clinical work I can only see the emergence of the "little d" experience of agency. And as thrilling as this emergence is to witness, it does not solve the existential anxiety of possibly living in a determined world without actual freedom and choice. In this essay I have also implied that I am not alone in my confusions and inconsistencies. Many colleagues also hold personal beliefs and engage in clinical practices that sometimes ignore or contradict their cherished theories. In spite of theoretical thorns, I have suggested that contemporary self psychologists, intersubjectivists and relational analysts, many of whom may not even think about "Big D" free will, nevertheless behave with their patients as though it exists. To paraphrase I.B Singer, we must; we have no choice.

Note

1 For example, in some mathematical complexity and evolutionary biology models free will does not exist. The generation of infinite or computationally complex behavior from the interaction of a finite set of rules and parameters creates the impression of free will. The unpredictability of the emerging behavior from deterministic processes leads to a perception of free will, even though free will as an ontological entity is probably an illusion. As an illustration, some strategy board games like Chess and Go have rigorous rules where no information is hidden from either player, and no random events occur. Nevertheless, these strategy games with their simple deterministic rules can have an extremely large number of unpredictable moves. By analogy, "emergentists" suggest that the experience of free will emerges from the interaction of finite rules and deterministic parameters that generate infinite and unpredictable behavior. Yet, if *all* these events were accounted for, and there was a known way to evaluate these events, the seemingly unpredictable behavior would become predictable. These theories view free will as a gift

of ignorance or a product of incomplete information, e.g., Epstein and Axtell (1996), Kenrick et al. (2003), and Wolfram (2002).

References

Beebe, B. & Lachmann, F. M. (2005) *Infant Research and Adult Treatment: Co-Constructing Interactions*. London: Routledge.

Benjamin, J. (1988) *The Bonds of Love: Psychoanalysis, Feminism, and the Problem of Domination*. London: Virago.

Benjamin, J. (1996) In Defense of Gender Ambiguity. *Gender Psychoanal.*, 1 (1):L27–43.

Benjamin, J. (2005) Creating an Intersubjective Reality: Commentary on Paper by Arnold Rothstein. *Psychoanal. Dial.*, 15:447–457.

Brandchaft, B. (1994) Structures of Pathological Accommodation and Change in Analysis. Paper presented at *the Association for Psychoanalytic Self Psychology*, New York City.

Buber, M. (1923) *I and Thou, trans. Walter Kaufmanm*. New York: Charles Scribner, 1970.

Cavell, M. (2003) Freedom and Forgiveness. *Int. J. Psych-Anal.*, 84: 515–531.

Coburn, W. J. (1999) Chapter 11: An Instrument of Possibilities. A Discussion of Dorothy M. Levinson and George E. Atwood's 'A Life of One's Own'. *Prog. Self Psychol.*, 15:183–190.

Epstein J. M. & Axtell R. (1996) *Growing Artificial Societies - Social Science from the Bottom*. Cambridge, MA: MIT Press.

Fonagy, P. & Gergely, G. (2005). *Affect Regulation, Mentalization, and the Development of Self*. London: Other Press.

Fonagy, P., Gergely, G., Jurist, E., & Target, M. (2002) *Affect Regulation, Mentalization and the Development of the Self*. New York: Other Press.

Freud, S. (1910) Five Lectures on Psycho-analysis. The Standard Edition of the Complete Psychological Works of Sigmund Freud, Volume XI (1910): Five Lectures on Psycho-Analysis, Leonardo da Vinci and Other Works, pp. 1–56.

Freud, S. (1916) Introductory Lectures on Psycho-Analysis. The Standard Edition of the Complete Psychological Works of Sigmund Freud, Volume XV (1915-1916): Introductory Lectures on Psycho-Analysis (Parts I and II), pp. 1–240.

Freud, S. (1919) The 'Uncanny'. The Standard Edition of the Complete Psychological Works of Sigmund Freud, Volume XVII (1917–1919): An Infantile Neurosis and Other Works, pp. 217–256.

Freud, S. (1920) Beyond the Pleasure Principle. The Standard Edition of the Complete Psychological Works of Sigmund Freud, Volume XVIII (1920–1922): Beyond the Pleasure Principle, Group Psychology and Other Works, pp. 1–64.

Frie, R. (2002) Modernism or Postmodernism?: Binswanger, Sullivan, and the Problem of Agency in Contemporary Psychoanalysis. *Contemp. Psychoanal.*, 38:635–673.

Frie, R. & Coburn, W. (2010) *Persons in Context*. London: Routledge.

Grigsby, J. and Osuch, E. (2007) Neurodynamics, State, Agency, and Psychological Functioning. In M. Piers (ed.) *Self-Organizing Complexity in Psychological Systems*. Brent, NY: Jason Aronson, pp. 37–82.

Hastings, R. (2007) The Development of the Person: The Minnesota Study of Risk and Adaptation from Birth to Adulthood: By L.A. Sroufe, et al.: A Review. *Int. J. Psychoanal. Self Psychol.*, 2 (3):367–379.

Hoffman, I. M. (1998) *Ritual and Spontaneity in the Psychoanalytic Process*. Hillsdale, NJ: Analytic Press.

124   *Stuck*

Hoffman, I. Z. (2000). At Death's Door: Therapists and Patients as Agents. *Psychoanal. Dial.*, 10:823–846.

Kenrick, D. T., Li, N. P., & Butner, J. (2003) Dynamical Evolutionary Psychology: Individual Decision Rules and Emergent Social Norms. *Psychol. Rev.*, 110(1):3–28.

Levinas, E. (1969) *Totality and Infinity: An Essay on Exteriority*, trans. A. Largis. Pittsburg, PA: Duquesnes University Press.

Levinson, D. M., & Atwood, G. E. (1999) Chapter 10 A Life of One's Own: A Case Study of the Loss and Restoration of the Sense of Personal Agency. *Prog. Self Psychol.*, 15:163–181.

Lyons-Ruth, K. (1999) The Two-Person Unconscious: Intersubjective Dialogue, Enactive Relational Representation, and the Emergence of New Forms of Relational Organization. *Psychoanal. Inq.*, 19:576–617.

Ringstrom, P. (2007) *Inductive Identification and Improvisation in Psychoanalytic Practice: Some Comments on Joye Weisel-Barth's Articale on Complexity Theory.* Accepted for Publication.

Rustin, J. (1997) Infancy, Agency, and Intersubjectivity: A View of Therapeutic Action. *Psychoanal. Dial.*, 7:43–62.

Searle, J. (2008) *Freedom and Neurobiology: Reflections on Free Will, Language, and Political Power.* New York: Columbia University Press.

Stern, D. (2004) *The Present Moment in Psychotherapy and Everyday Life.* New York: W.W. Norton.

Stern, D. B. (1996) The Social Construction of Therapeutic Action. *Psychoanal. Inq.*, 16:265–293.

Stolorow, R. & Atwood, G. (2014) *Contexts of Being: The Intersubjective Foundations of Psychological Life.* London: Routledge.

Stolorow, R. D., Orange, D. M., & Atwood, G. E. (2001). Psychoanalysis—A Contextual Psych… Gill. *Psychoanal. Rev.*, 88:15–27.

Strenger, C. (1998). The Desire for Self-Creation. *Psychoanal. Dial.*, 8:625–655.

Winnicott, D. W. (1956). On Transference. *Int. J. Psycho-Anal.*, 37:386–388.

Wolfram, S. (2002) *A New Kind of Science.* Wolfram Media, Inc.

7 Malignant loneliness and its clinical implications

There is a pain—so utter—
It swallows substance up—
Then covers the Abyss with Trance—
So Memory can step
Around—across—upon it—
As one within a Swoon—
Goes safely—where an open eye—
Would drop Him—Bone by Bone.
Emily Dickinson #599

Sometimes I feel like a motherless child
Sometimes I feel like a motherless child
Sometimes I feel like a motherless child
A long way from home, a long way from home
Sometimes I feel like I'm almost done
Sometimes I feel like I'm almost done
Sometimes I feel like I'm almost done
And a long, long way from home, a long way from home.
Harry Burleigh

Desolate and alone
All night long on the lake
Where fog trails and mist creeps,
The whistle of a boat
Calls and cries unendingly,
Like some lost child
In tears and trouble
Hunting the harbor's breast
And the harbor's eyes.
Carl Sandburg, Lost

Sometimes a pressed flower looks colorful and alive when, in fact, its center is desiccated and lifeless. Although she appeared alive and resilient, Susan was such a flower. She had fashioned a rickety but workable life structure in spite

126 *Malignant loneliness and clinical implications*

of a history of severe loss, criticism, neglect, and rejection in her first family. Notwithstanding such bad early treatment and her persistent underlying sadness, Susan was curious about life and responsive to her relational experiences. However, when she found herself totally alone, it turned out the scaffold was not strong enough to support her. I was young, inexperienced, and hopeful and didn't realize that her loneliness was life threatening.

I should have known better because early in our relationship Susan opened her purse to show me the gun she always carried. "It's in case of danger," she told me, and I believed her. When she lost her important connection to life and a reason to live—her cat died—she shot herself. The danger, it turned out, was her subjective experience of unremitting loneliness. Although Susan killed herself sometime after our termination, I still feel her loss not only with sorrow, but also with responsibility and deep regret. This paper on severe malignant loneliness is dedicated to her.

I have felt for some time that loneliness is a more human and experience near way to think about certain extremely painful psychic states, states that we name more generally and abstractly with terms like "trauma" and "annihilation anxiety." Here I'll echo and expand on Frieda Fromm-Reichmann's 1959 description of "the deep threat of the uncommunicable, private emotional experience of severe loneliness" (Fromm-Reichman, 1990), She argues that clinicians often overlook or confuse malignant loneliness with other less life-threatening conditions. This happened for me with Susan. Thus, how an analyst reads and responds to unspeakable and life-threatening malignant loneliness is a serious clinical issue and the point of this paper.

First, I want to differentiate the life-threatening pain of severe, malignant loneliness from other forms of aloneness: solitude, solitary contemplation, creative engagement, and social alienation. These kinds of subjective aloneness are bearable states, sometimes painful, sometimes pleasurable and fairly common to human experience. Unlike malignant loneliness, these bearable states are open to reflection and verbal expression. Bearable aloneness especially touches introverted natures, artistic and creative people, spiritual seekers, and minority and marginal social group members. The state seems to derive from some combination of a person's temperament and/or family, social, political, and cultural experience.

Malignant loneliness, on the other hand, is unutterable, muffled by its intense personal pain and shame; frequently hushed by dissociation and/or substance abuse; and ultimately silenced by suicidal action. As Fromm-Reichmann says, "… loneliness seems to be such a painful, frightening experience that people will do practically everything to avoid it" (p. 306). Moreover, she adds:

> People who are in the grip of severe degrees of loneliness cannot talk about it; and people who have at some time in the past had such an experience can seldom do so either, for it is so frightening and uncanny in character that they try to dissociate the memory of what it was like, and even the fear of it. (p. 313)

Malignant loneliness and clinical implications　127

Finally, she tells us:

> Anyone who has encountered persons who were under the influence of real loneliness understands why people are more frightened of being lonely than of being hungry, or being deprived of sleep, or of having their sexual needs unfulfilled. (p. 315)

This silence must be why one turns literature, to poems like the ones here by Emily Dickinson, Harry Burleigh, and Carl Sandburg, and to the work of other artists to give voice to aspects of the extremely lonely state. Dickinson's poem captures the dangerous, annihilating pain and necessary dissociation that occurs in malignant loneliness. The Burleigh and Sandburg poems advance metaphors that attempt to express its excruciating anguish: homelessness, darkness, fog, plaintive whistles, and the lost, motherless child.

Other aesthetic modes like the film "Lars and the Real Girl" also seek to grasp the intensity of this state. In that film Lars embodies malignant loneliness and his lifesaving, but socially isolating, dissociation from its torment. Frigid cold is the ruling metaphor for his situation. He dwells away from the warmth of the family home in a cold garage in a cold Northern clime, an environment that mirrors his emotionally and psychically frozen state. He moves stiffly in his body, cannot look directly at people, and is almost inarticulate. At work, a direct greeting strikes him dumb, and at home he sits staring into darkness for hours, alone and rigid, frozen in body, frozen in spirit. Abandoned at birth by his mother's death and neglected by a grieving father, who "didn't want anyone around," Lars at 27 cannot avail himself of any kindness or affection and is caught in a literally painful dilemma. On one hand, he longs for human connection; but, on the other hand, he recoils in pain from overtures for personal, and especially sexual, contact. He says that being touched feels like frostbite: "Like a burn. Like you go outside and your feet freeze. And you come back in, and it burns." Because nobody sees or understands or feels into the extremity of Lars' situation, he is psychically alone.

Now, after a brief survey of what psychoanalysis has said about malignant loneliness, I'll return to my patient Susan. Finally, and most importantly, I'll argue that malignant loneliness poses unique clinical challenges and requires careful recognition and therapeutic response during treatment as well as continuous connection after treatment is complete. Continuous connection is a radical challenge to traditional ideas of analytic termination.

A literature review reveals that loneliness has received little attention in mainstream psychoanalysis. Because of the field's emphasis on intrapsychic drives, loneliness has been largely ignored in traditional psychoanalytic thought. This is also the case with other socially created emotions like jealousy, love, hate, and loss and with socially created vitality states such as passion and joy. Isn't it ironic that while the great emotional states of love and loss, longing and loneliness, have been the major subjects of poetry, fiction, movies, and popular music, psychoanalysis has narrowly focused on self-referenced internal drives?

128 *Malignant loneliness and clinical implications*

In my writings I've tried to remedy this situation, recasting important human emotions in relational contexts. In fact, I turn to the concerns of country songs as good indicators of what psychoanalysis has overlooked. Take for example Hank Williams' "I'm so Lonesome I Could Cry," a song in which Williams provides a tumble of metaphors to capture his own malignant loneliness: a bird whose sad song renders him "too blue to fly"; a weeping moon, hiding in shame behind a cloud, and a weeping robin whose sorrows bestow, respectively, shame and the loss of a will to live; an endless night in which time crawls slowly and is punctuated by mournful train whistles and plaintive bird song. Such metaphors in accretion come as close as possible to rendering the unutterable in words.

It fell to interpersonal analysts—a group outside mainstream psychoanalysis, who predicated psychological development and disturbance on real relational experience—to address loneliness as a relationally-derived emotion. In addition to Fromm-Reichmann, Sullivan posits that loneliness is "profound deprivation" that threatens security. He suggests that failure of parental attention—Sullivan terms it "audience"—as well as the experiences of being bullied and socially ostracized in mid-childhood may result in lifelong profound loneliness. For Sullivan extreme loneliness is more painful and psychologically dangerous than anxiety (Sullivan, 1970).

Attachment theory and infant research theorists address issues of abuse, neglect, and the absences of mentalizing experience and emotional resonance in infancy and early childhood. They suggest that suffering from these faulty interactions may result in intense loneliness in adulthood. Terry Drake (2015) turns to these thinkers to argue that childhood neglect often creates the "naked terror" of acute adult loneliness. To buttress her argument, she provides a comprehensive literature review that includes the ideas of Winnicott, Bowlby, Spitz, Erickson, Harlow, Main, Kohut, Brandchaft, Howe, Daniel Stern, and Stolorow. I recommend it.

Let me return now to Susan, who first struck me as a sad and prim little gothic waif. Petite and sweet faced, her eyes ringed with black kohl, Susan dressed in the goth garb of the early 1980s. However, unlike most counter-culture costumes of the day, her black clothes were always scrupulously and strangely cleaned and ironed. She proudly kept her old black clothing pristine by adding a special vinegar to the wash water, vials of which she routinely brought me in order to keep my own black pants from fading. Susan was an inveterate caretaker and worked diligently to save, preserve, and maintain whatever was in her care. In a short time, I fell into her domain.

"It was so hard for me to stay clean living in the car," she explained. When Susan was 17, her mother, a pious Catholic and busy socialite, and her father, a wealthy, conservative businessman, violently disapproved of the girl's left-leaning politics and hippie lifestyle experiments. Although she had always felt alienated from her first family, her turbulent adolescence witnessed Susan struggling to assert some kind of authentic identity.

Malignant loneliness and clinical implications   129

However, in response to Susan's insistence on choosing her own path, the parents threw her out of the house. Susan lived for several months in an abandoned junk yard car, during which time she befriended a derelict man, who raped and then cast her off like all the other junk in the yard. Alone, filled with shame and suicidal, Susan did not turn to her parents or any of her teachers at school for help. "It was terribly lonely," she tells me.

This frightening and dangerous time shattered whatever trust, security, and confidence Susan had developed to that point in her life. And over the years, this literal experience of homelessness had transformed into the psychological conviction of being alone and without a home. By the time she came to therapy she lived in a fixed state of existential anxiety and doubt. With respect to her family, ten years after her banishment, Susan had never reentered the family house, and the parents would only deign to meet Susan on holidays at the parents' country club. She would approach these occasional meetings with apprehension, hope for repair, and anxiety hives.

While her vulnerability was palpable—a constant dark and frightening rumble beneath the rest of her life, a disturbance that I noted but didn't understand then—Susan was also amazingly resourceful. And she struggled to, and mostly succeeded in wearing a happy face. She finished high school while living in the car; and by the time she came to therapy, she had almost completed college part time and on her own dime. Susan worked as assistant to a successful punk musician, who was also a writer and entrepreneur. She adored him and did everything for him from cleaning his toilet to organizing his schedule to paying his bills to illustrating his book. She was proud of her importance to her boss and her contributions to his success and was always careful with him to appear cheerful and upbeat. Ironically, in his ambition, self-centeredness, and exploitation of her, this young man was much like Susan's parents. He did, however, pay her very well, and Susan had pride in her growing bank account.

When the musician decided abruptly to move to New York and leave Susan behind—unfeeling and without a backward glance—she was desolate and suffered a complete emotional collapse. The desertion occurred about a year and a half into our therapy; and at this repetition of past betrayals and abandonments, Susan was left with nobody in her life except for her cat and me. Although I realize now that I intuitively grasped Susan's fragility and tenuous hold on life, at the time I was puzzled by and didn't understand the intensity of my own worried and distressed feelings for her. In dreams and between appointments Susan would often occupy my mind. I'm reminded of a fascinating research study that Beebe and Lachmann describe. The study used a psychiatrist to evaluate strategies for predicting future suicide attempts in subjects who had committed previous suicidal acts. While the psychiatrist failed to predict future attempters using conscious, rational measures, he unconsciously but accurately anticipated future suicides through non-verbal physical displays: i.e., muscular activations, negative facial expressions, and

130 *Malignant loneliness and clinical implications*

rapid, pressured vocal rhythms. With Susan I think I was engaged in a similar intersubjective process in which I registered non-verbally the emotional danger to Susan's life, danger that was not consciously apparent to me.

Six months after her boss's desertion, Susan was still in the throes of deep grief: she hardly ate or slept, was almost mute, and had little interest outside of getting through each day. Yet, her mathematics and accounting abilities and practiced extroverted skills had earned her a banking job. About the job she said, "You know it's important for me to support myself, but I feel like a mutant sport at work. It's all so alien to who I am, and I hate going there. I'm looking for something else, but my mother is glad I'm working at a bank." Again, I think of the vibrant dried flower: the outside may look fine, but on the inside it's dying.

A few months later Susan tells me, "I'm worried about finances, and until I get health insurance, I'd like to take a break from therapy. I'll be back when there's some money in the bank." If only I had said "NO! You're important, not the money. You can't go." Instead I encourage her to do what she thinks best. She doesn't return and, then, about a year after our termination, Susan calls me on a Friday at 1 p.m., the regular time of our former visits. She says, "This is when we used to meet, and I want to say goodbye and thank you. My cat died last week." When I pick up the message about an hour later and call back in panic, a detective answers, "It's too late."

A heartbreaking lesson but one necessary to share! Susan's kind of isolation, joined with a history of trauma and a sensitive and sad nature, preclude traditional termination. To underline the point, traditional termination for such people may be terminal! The decision to oppose termination begins with the therapist's sense, which I described earlier, of a dark, destructive rumble beneath the person's life, a rumble like the vibrating sound before an earthquake—which also echoes in the therapist's gut. With such patients whatever one does to maintain human connection is indicated. Continued regular treatment; predictable, if spaced, sessions; check-in conversations—any of these is desirable and may avert a tragedy like Susan's death. Of course, such a commitment is at odds with—what seems to me—an outdated traditional view of termination as fixed and final and desirable. This view contradicts everything we know about the continuing value of relational connection in a person's life, whether that connection is regular, sporadic, or simply lives in one's imaginative sense of self.

Educational objectives: At the conclusion of the presentations, listeners will

1 Be able to describe different forms of loneliness and differentiate them from the malignant, life-threatening kind.
2 Be able to use an understanding of malignant loneliness in diagnosing and treating patients.
3 Be able to assess the continuing clinical needs of the malignantly lonely person over long periods of time.

References

Beebe, B. and Lachmann, F. M. (2005) *Infant Research and Adult Treatment*. New York: Other Press.

Dickinson, E. (1970) ed., Johnson, T. H., *The Complete Poems of Emily Dickinson*. Cambridge: Harvard University Press.

Drake, T. (2015) *Naked Terror: The Role of Childhood Neglect in Adult Loneliness*. Unpublished Dissertation, Los Angeles: Institute of Contemporary Psychoanalysis.

Fromm-Reichman, F. (1990) Loneliness. *Contemp. Psychoanal.*, 26:305–329.

Sandburg, C. (1970) *The Complete Poems of Carl Sandberg*. New York: Harcourt Brace, Co.

Sullivan, H. S. (1970) *The Psychiatric Interview*. New York: W.W. Norton.

Williams, H. (1993) I'm so lonesome I could cry. In Cusic, D. (ed.) *The Complete Lyrics of Hank Williams*. New York: St Martins Press.

8 Bad faith and analytic failure

I'm told that we learn more from mistakes than from successes. I'm not so sure about learning from them, but I'm certain my mistakes remain in memory with more clarity and brilliance than my successes. Having practiced dynamic therapy for over forty years and taken on writing a book about my work, I find myself reviewing my professional life with lots of feeling and a fair share of chagrin. My chagrin has motivated me to think about personal analytic failures, and suffice it to say, I remember lots of mistakes and cases that either never found traction or went awry.

Remembering my therapeutic missteps, however, does not make me feel especially incompetent. I don't generally engage in self-accusation or self-punishment, and this presentation isn't a masochistic exercise. Rather, I think, as flawed creatures we all make mistakes and sometimes suffer expected analytic disruptions, and I'm not an exception. However, this memory paper is focused on a particularly serious breach over which I carry guilty and shameful feelings.

Here's how I will proceed: keeping in mind that not all mistakes constitute failure, I have divided the less serious therapeutic mistakes and ruptures into groups that constitute venial therapeutic sins. Afterward, I'll address the serious breaches that represent for me the mortal sins of analytic practice.

So, here are the venial sins. The first group consists of poor match-ups: temperamental or co-transferential mismatches that hinder the consolidation of a therapeutic alliance. The second group is composed of therapists whose unanalyzed personal issues result in analytic snares such as shared evasions and collusions with the patient. For example, how many therapists withhold important observations from their patients out of personal fear, shame, or anger and then explain their dissembling as an effort to spare the patient's feelings? Such behavior keeps the therapeutic work less than optimal.

Then, there are the small, undermining disruptions—mostly therapist errors—that are eventually available to conscious scrutiny. These include clumsy and premature responses; misunderstandings and faulty interpretations—I made more of these in the old days when I tried to too hard to be smart and knowing; and some insensitive or ill-timed jokes before I learned that—at least for me—easy humor between therapist and patient first requires establishing

Bad faith and analytic failure   133

therapeutic trust, mutual good faith, and confidence in the other's good intentions. Over time I have mostly learned to recognize these sorts of disruptions, to acknowledge them, and hopefully to repair them with patients.

Also, there are enactments—these may not be sins at all, venial or otherwise. They are intense interactive situations where some disowned or dissociated aspect of patient or analyst or both creates intense emotional disequilibrium. Dialogue is disrupted and confusion reigns until a member of the dyad can begin to identify and explore with the partner the meanings of the enactment. Done successfully, the resolution of enactments may advance the therapy. Ignored or handled clumsily, enactments can abort treatments.

Finally, there are also unforeseen outside conflicts and life events that may disrupt treatment. Such outside intrusions are usually nobody's fault. Yet, while they are beyond the control of either partner, they are particularly vulnerable to therapist mismanagement. I think here about situations such as sudden illness or family interference or economic calamity or geographical dislocation. My case today is an example of a disrupting outside event that I managed badly.

With respect to poor match-ups, patients mostly vote with their feet and leave early. With respect to the therapist's personal blindness and lack of development—which are, by definition, out of awareness—these can make treatment impossible. Mostly, though, they simply limit the scope of a treatment, limit where the therapeutic couple can go. Therapeutic partners often express genuine satisfaction for treatments that have been enormously helpful to the patient, but which have also skirted some uncomfortable and unexplored therapist issues.

As for the other kinds of mistakes, they now seem like expected events or venial sins, situations to heal and learn from rather than death blows to therapy. I return to Kohut's idea of rupture and repair as vehicles for growth and development, both in the therapeutic relationship and in the analyst's professional and self-development. And because, as I said earlier, we are all imperfect creatures, hopefully striving for enlightenment, I also believe our mistakes are intrinsic to learning and expanded understanding. After all, the Phoenix must burn before it can emerge from its own ashes.

But then there are real Analytic Failures, our professional mortal sins. To my mind these are all similar in that they represent Bad Faith. Bad Faith is a legalistic term that also has currency in Existential philosophy, particularly the writings of John Paul Sartre. In the legal realm bad faith is an intentional dishonest act that violates contractual obligations. It consists in consciously misleading someone to enter into an agreement without the intention or means to fulfill it. For example, Trump's promise to restore good jobs to out of work coal miners and steel workers—when their industries are either dying or automated—is an act of bad faith.

In philosophy bad faith is used somewhat differently: it represents an individual's betrayal of one's genuine self through fraudulent choices and actions. Bad faith situations occur when people, under pressure from social and

134 *Bad faith and analytic failure*

cultural forces, adopt false values and disown their innate freedom. Subsequent bad faith thoughts and actions are termed "inauthentic" and are closely related to such ideas as self-deception and pathological accommodation. That is, Sartre believed that acts of bad faith represent a disavowal of the essential freedom and choice that all humans possess; they mark a refusal to be an agentic subject in one's life and, instead, represent an act of submission to be an object or thing. Returning to our national political nightmare, we are currently witnessing bad faith in our House of Representatives and Senate on a daily basis.

In the therapeutic relationship my idea of bad faith borrows from both traditions. Analytic bad faith occurs when the analyst's self-interest or self-protection trumps the patient's needs and interests. This violates the foundational agreement of therapy and usually involves some combination of failed empathy, compassion, authenticity, and therapeutic will. Borrowing from the Existential definition, bad faith also occurs when the analyst falls back on stereotyped analytic responses that mask the therapist's true thoughts and feelings.

Bad faith failures generally begin out of our awareness—as all enactments do—but they also may be consciously chosen acts of cowardice. In addition, they also may be sins of omission. By this I mean the analyst's failure to engage the patient with whatever affective material is immediately present—failure, for example, to engage with co-transference or enactment situations—confirms an act of bad faith. Fear of the patient's or one's own rage is a common example of such an evasion. Bad faith analytic failures not only challenge our moral and ethical core, but our conception of the therapeutic contract and pursuit as well.

I hope my acts of bad faith—personally and professionally—are few, but I do remember one major therapeutic failure whose shadow haunts me across thirty-some years. In telling this story I admit to feeling personally and professionally vulnerable and wanting to justify myself by claiming youth and inexperience. However, the case seems a good illustration of the bad faith that we—even those of us who are old and experienced—are prey to.

This is the story of Mark and me. I'm pretty sure his name was Mark. I had to rummage in my memory to find his first name and still can't locate his last. Such is the power of disavowal and intentional, if unconscious, forgetting. Nevertheless, I can't forget his story and our relationship. Mark was an average 17-year-old boy of average intelligence, average good looks, and average aspirations: he wanted a girlfriend, a car, and lots of dope. A cute, regular-featured beanpole with sandy hair and freckles, he was pleasantly non-descript in his faded jeans and tee shirt presentation. But he was born into the wrong family.

My shameful forgetting of Mark's name echoes Mark's mother's view of the boy. To her he was a dimly remembered afterthought. Mark's mom was a professor of philosophy, a heady woman of superior intellect who had little time and attention for or curiosity about her decidedly average, almost 18-year-old son. Mark was the accidental issue of one of those "zipless fuck" couplings, fairly common in California commune culture of the 1960s. The mom had only a vague, a "maybe it could be," idea of who Mark's father was.

Bad faith and analytic failure   135

Mark's older, brilliant sister and the mother's current boyfriend were both interested in Mark but mostly lost to him because of their own demanding lives. No wonder, then, that Mark felt like a neglected child, without either symbolic access to his feelings or a clear sense of identity or worth. Mark and I had met for about six months before he murdered his mother and sister on Christmas day in the late 1970s.

The mother's boyfriend brought him to therapy after noting a familiar depressive teen-age boy syndrome: social isolation and withdrawal, lack of motivation for activities or sports, slipping grades at the end of eleventh grade, the absence of a future vision, flat affect, and poor communication skills. Mark spent lots of time in his room smoking dope.

After checking me out for a short time, Mark really got into our therapy. He liked coming and talking and being heard, and he never missed a session. As a thirsty flower after rain, Mark bloomed. This metaphor is apt because Mark loved botany and growing things—particularly marijuana. He spent time in the library—this was before the internet—researching indoor and outdoor growing methods and planning his marijuana farm. In response to my attentive listening, he soon became very talkative, taking an enthusiastic teacher-like stance with me, educating me about the wonders of weed and its cultivation. His animated teaching was probably reflective of his professorial mother at her best.

Because he needed money for growing indoor equipment, Mark soon found a job in the gardening department at Target—or maybe it was K Mart then—and made friends with a few work mates. He also tentatively began to think out loud about the problems in his family relationships and his longing for a father. Things were looking up for Mark, and I felt good about the mirroring self-object and mentalizing functions I seemed to be furnishing him.

At our last appointment two days before Christmas, Mark seemed uncharacteristically happy. He told me he was going to his grandmother's for Christmas dinner and then gave me two gifts. In addition to a small box of See's Candy—his favorite—he also brought a small marijuana plant for me. He had planted it in a red pot covered with little hearts. Truly, I was surprised that he had fussed. I thanked him for both presents and for his thoughtfulness but said that I couldn't accept the marijuana. I understood that he loved dope and wanted to share it with me, but I felt differently about drugs. I wouldn't have them in my home because I didn't want my young children exposed to them. Mark seemed disappointed, and I apologized. Later in the day, my own son, about 9 at the time, found the little pot of pot at the front door. To my surprise he knew what it was. "Someone really likes you," he said. I understood that Mark had left the plant in spite of my refusal, and that he and I were in an enactment over the gift and its meanings. But we were just at the beginning of our relationship, and I assumed there would be plenty of time to work things out.

The mother's boyfriend contacted me the day after the murders and gave me a short description of the event. I was so shocked and sickened that, at first,

136 *Bad faith and analytic failure*

I couldn't register the information. I had to call him back a few hours later—after I had stopped shaking—to hear the news again and to find out how to find Mark. When I visited the boy in jail, he was pale and also shell-shocked.

Here is the story Mark told. After an awful argument early on Christmas morning, the mother and sister left for the grandmother's holiday party, leaving Mark home alone. The boy wasn't able to articulate the deep rejection, loneliness, and rage that I imagine he felt on their leaving; in fact, he spoke as in a trance, with dead eyes and a cold and stony tone. During his mother and sister's absence, the boy tinkered with the mother's Christmas gift to him: a rifle and ammunition. I remember thinking, "What kind of crazy Christmas present is that for an unseasoned adolescent?" Mark shot his mother with the loaded rifle immediately on her return. He described her on the floor, her body twitching for a time before she died.

Although Mark remembered feeling left out after his mother drove off that morning, he didn't remember—nor did he have in the telling—any feelings about the murder. His sister, home from college for the holidays, then gave the boy her car keys and some money and urged him to drive to Mexico; yet, after driving a few blocks, Mark realized that his sister had witnessed the mother's murder. He returned home and killed her. KILLED HIS SISTER! This part took my breath away; it was impossibly horrible. I felt so sad for the sister—deeply identified with her—and, therefore, was disturbed and enraged for me and filled with shame for Mark. I knew that Mark—in whatever his dissociated state—would have killed me with ease had I been in the sister's place. While I had compassion for his plight, the killing of his sister disrupted my ability to empathize with him. I was overwhelmed emotionally, and my state prevented me from considering Mark's needs or the needs of our therapy. In that moment the minimal conditions for a therapeutic relationship were gone.

I remember feeling icy and shivering as I passed through security at the county jail, and I also remember how institutionally dingy and ugly the surroundings were. The vomit green wall color was a punishing welcome to a nightmare environment. Mark looked particularly young and scared, and for that I felt compassion. I also felt frightened for him, for his vulnerability in the prison culture that would likely be his next home. Yet, his emotionally barren and self-justifying account of the murders that followed turned my stomach and made him repellent to me. The matter-of-factness with which he explained his decision to kill his sister—"She might tell," he said—chilled my heart. Mark expressed no guilt or regret; and I was too aghast to consider the pain/shame driven defensiveness or shock that might account for his dispassion and dissociation. Truly my heart went dead to him. While I wanted to do my duty—whatever that might be—mostly I wanted to get away and never see Mark again. This was, of course, a violation of my therapeutic agreement with him, to deal honestly with the affective therapeutic issues: Bad Faith!

Oh, I stayed and listened to Mark for a reasonable amount of time. But it was dead listening. He told me that his lawyer had recommended a guilty plea.

Bad faith and analytic failure   137

Mark's age would mitigate his sentence: he could expect to spend twenty-five years in prison, and then get parole in his forties. Afterward, he would have years of freedom. I remember thinking that this was all self-deception: Mark's life was over. I felt a heaviness and sadness about my conviction. For the rest of the time I spent with him that day, I engaged in various forms of in-authenticity. Without conviction, I reassured Mark that he could make a life for himself in prison and urged him to read and study and find interest and work there.

In retrospect, I feel especially ashamed of this teachy-preachy advice which, however constructive, masked my horror and functioned to protect me from what the boy had done. It also protected me from exploring with him any affective dimensions of his act and its aftermath. I had abandoned our therapy. Even at the time I felt fraudulent and defensive as I delivered my unsolicited advice—a phony, wise-old-woman pose masking fear and terror and disgust. I also felt guilty telling Mark that I would write to him but could not visit him in prison. What I meant to say was, "I am so horrified by your act that I want to obliterate all memory and thought of you." This, of course, is exactly what Mark had heard all his life from his mother's actions, from her coldness and contempt and rejecting behavior. I repeated his trauma! After a few letters from Mark and a few desultory responses from me, the correspondence ended, and I do not know what happened to the boy. Sometimes I imagine running into him on the street and not recognizing him, a brutalized and hardened middle-aged man.

While writing about and reliving this sad chapter in my professional life, I have tried on innumerable different, more truthful and therapeutic scenarios. Here is one sample:

> Mark, I see you growing into manhood, but I also know you as a younger boy. This is the boy I see right now, and I'm talking to him. You look scared, and I imagine you hate what you did and hate yourself. I also hate what you did, but I don't hate you. Right now I just feel so sorry for you and for your family. I know you will pay in your life for what happened on Christmas, and I hope in time you will be able to do penance and find some peace. In our work I wish we could have talked more about anger; I think we were beginning to do this and regret that we didn't have enough time together. I apologize.

Conclusion

It wasn't Mark's murderous act that defines this therapeutic failure but rather my bad faith. Of course, I had reasons to lose my professional self over the murders. I was a relatively young therapist at the time and the mother of a young and growing family. Mark's murderous act terrified me and threatened two pillars of my personal life as well as my respect for human life. But these are explanations not excuses. By acting inauthentically from my emotional distress and disgust, I violated the foundational therapeutic agreement: to privilege the patient's emotional life, to deal with present emotional issues, and to protect the treatment. And so, remembering this experience has pushed me to rethink and reaffirm my obligations and responsibilities as an analyst.

Because I believe that analytic partners co-create a special, perhaps sacred, space that is separate from each partner's life outside the space; and because I view this space as one of openness, spontaneity, and intimacy—conditions that makes psychological growth and development possible—I think the analyst's primary task is to guard this space, to keep it safe from empathic failure and dishonesty. Whatever the analyst does that restricts or prevents him/her from fulfilling this protective function represents bad faith. And when the function fails, damage to the therapy is devastating. Once injured feelings quiet and space emerges for reflection and dialogue, therapists and patients may sometimes repair enacted instances of bad faith. But when repair does not occur, analytic failure is inevitable. Such was the case with Mark and me.

9 Temporal disturbance in the case of Maya
Musical dissonance, and the failure of future vision

Time is troubled for my patient Maya and for me with her. In this paper I will describe the nature of the temporal disturbance as well as the process by which I have come to understand it. My understanding began with unquiet bodily stirrings in encounters with Maya. These led to associations and images, which, in turn, created some new ideas for me about time. Underpinning my thinking is a complexity model of change that borrows modernist ideas about empathy and affect attunement from contemporary relational self psychology and intersubjective systems theory; about implicit process and relational knowing from infant research and attachment theory; about self-other de-differentiation in the co-created analytic third from relational theory; and, particularly, about a model of mind or self that is by nature relationally entrained and entangled from cognitive and neuro-science.

Using these ideas, I'll try to show how, within an established therapeutic space, I register crucial information about the other in my body as well as in my mind. For example, in the effort to understand my complex and worri-some patient, I access and filter interactional cues—along with accompanying internal quivers and quakes—through my imagination and associational fancy, a process that sometimes prompts the emergence of images and metaphors that capture important aspects of my patient Maya and our analytic relationship. My sense of disturbed time with Maya is an instance of this process and of how new understanding may result from imaginative interplay.

Maya's cutting has stopped; her active suicidal gestures have ceased; and her several "accidents" are hopefully behind us. What's more, after two hospita-lizations and more than a year and a half of therapy, she has completed—with trepidation—a semester of college part time, has begun the school year with a full load, and has cautiously entered new social situations. Finally, recently Maya claimed to feel "much better," more in control of her relentless anxiety and destructive impulses.

Yet the memory of several suicidal episodes; the continuing jumpy, dis-junctive nature of Maya's states and mood shifts; the sometimes dramatic discrepancy between her life experiences, on one side, and her emotional responses and physical reactions, on the other; and her unpredictable, changeable, and impulsive behaviors with me and in the world—all these

140 *Temporal disturbance in the case of Maya*

shake me viscerally and leave me profoundly off-kilter, puzzled, and afraid. I fear that the frightening events in Maya's history are not mere memories, but rather are living potential events in the present. And I'm sure that my fear infects the ambiance of our meetings. All this makes for a very unfortunate feedback loop!

Because our attachment is unsettled and our rhythms only sporadically in synch, it often feels that we are navigating a tottering boat with a sputtering engine and faulty rudder. Any unexpected breeze may drive the boat off course or aground. Maya is very hard for me to reach in a consistently empathic way; and, in fact, for me it seems as though we have been marking time—have been in a temporal holding pattern—until we can find a meaningful way to connect and genuinely begin our work. In the context of her suicidal thoughts, my sense of time suspended explains some of the peril and personal unease, urgency, and insecurity I feel. I want to seal our connection so that we can move ahead together. For Maya, well..I'm not quite sure how Maya feels about our work. What I do know is that she moves in and out of our intersubjective connection—our analytic space—unpredictably but with regularity.

Nineteen years old, beautiful and bright, Maya entered treatment with suicidal wishes and the habit of cutting herself. An avid participant in websites devoted to cutting techniques, Maya's behaviors had escalated to deep cutting that threatened her arteries. Two years ago, after she approached her roommates dripping in blood, her university furloughed her. I met her during the black depression that ensued.

Maya is the only child of hard-working, intellectually accomplished, and religiously devout immigrant parents. Both parents are intensely engaged with work, religion, and their transplanted ethnic community. Born in California, Maya struggles with conflicting identifications that are common to second-generation immigrants—chiefly, the conflict between being a traditional daughter and an American teenager. For example, she consciously repudiates her religion and many received behavioral stipulations from her tradition; but in doing so, she describes herself as feeling anxious and guilty toward her parents as well as socially "neither fish nor fowl." She declares that she belongs nowhere. Her ambivalent cultural identifications are one source of her pervasive loneliness.

Maya also suffers from neglect and abandonment issues. Both of her parents are driven professionals whose life passions are focused on work. For them parenting was secondary to their work lives, and unintentionally they neglected Maya throughout her childhood. Maya remembers as a little girl staying at day care until nine or ten at night and all the waiting, all the endless waiting for her parents: waiting to be picked up from day care, from school, from lessons, and more waiting, to no avail, for them to attend her events. Maya recalls playing Benjamina Bunny in a first grade production; when her parents didn't come, she pretended that her friend Tara's parents were her own. In early adolescence she was a latchkey kid, watching T.V., playing

Temporal disturbance in the case of Maya 141

video games, and waiting still for her parents. These stories of stress trauma—an accretion of quotidian abandonments—are exquisitely painful for me to hear. They suggest that family neglect has left Maya without a coherent sense of self or worth, has left her doubtful, highly anxious, unable to regulate or comfort herself in the face of small and large life trials, and profoundly lonely.

In our work so far, Maya alternates between being a good, compliant patient, genuinely responding to my empathic inquiries but then "forgetting" appointments and abruptly withdrawing from emotional contact with me. I suspect that she is enacting with me her ambivalence about human relationships: conflicts between her need and longing for understanding, recognition, and intimacy, on one side, and her expectations and fear of abandonment, on the other.

Maya's frequent withdrawals leave me feeling dropped, confused, worried, and angry. My stomach lurches and gyrates with her rapid mood shifts. In the context of her looming threat of suicide, two metaphors—each of which has a temporal dimension—help me as I puzzle over our lack of secure connection. The first metaphor is of music. There are rhythmic and harmonic disturbances in our meetings, particularly absences of sustained melody, tonal dialogue, and "pattern closure" between Maya and me. Our therapeutic music often has the quality of movie music in some disaster films: the kind that accompanies the hero in a peaceful major key just before the villain pounces, the alien attacks, or catastrophe befalls in a percussive explosion of dissonance.

The second metaphor concerns disruptions in narrative continuity between us, and what I'll call the collapse of "future vision." Future vision, the imaginative projection of oneself into the future, is a term I'll talk more about below. In my imagination the collapse of future vision expresses itself in blurry or wavy images of Maya, forms emblematic of instability and uncertainty. Together the problems in sustained musical and narrative unfolding represent disturbances in time. They are expressed outside the therapy by Maya's inability to follow through on tasks and her repeated impulsive behaviors and inside the therapy by the sudden severing of emotional congruence between us. The disturbances radically disrupt Maya's—and my own—senses of possibility and hope.

Disruptions in my sense of time—in our music and narrative process—upset me and cause me to doubt myself as analyst and helping person. And because a sense of time is foundational to planning and executing life plans, I also worry about its absence in Maya's functioning. Worry about Maya lodges in my body and emotions more than in my brain; after all, she is demonstrably "much better." But there are just too many times when she and I seem to be in harmony, on the same wavelength—and I feel hopeful about Maya's moving into a positive future—and suddenly her music shifts and her rhythms veer off from mine. She may become very high and fast or low and deadened, and I am disconcerted and dumfounded by her abrupt emotional disconnection from me. Not only do I have to recalibrate my nervous system and my expectations

142   *Temporal disturbance in the case of Maya*

at such moments—that's real and bad enough—but I also have to adjust my long-term inner vision, my "future vision" of her and of our relationship. These dramatic shifts fall shadow-like; they are personally disturbing and also, perhaps, expressive of Maya's deepest doubts and fears.

Disturbance in the musical unfolding

I live in Los Angeles and love the conductor of our orchestra, Gustavo Dudamel. Dudamel frequently plays the music of Danish modernist composer Louis Andriessen. Several years back, my regular concert-going companions cancelled out, and I attended a performance of Andriessen's work alone. I'm recalling this performance because the feelings of distress and dis-ease, which it elicited in me, are similar to feelings I experience with Maya. As I sit with Maya in certain of her states, I think of Andriessen.

The piece that has stayed with me—because it both disquieted and fascinated me at the same time—was full of dissonant themes and a strange lack of emotional closure. It started with a rising theme, a simple phrase that presented itself without any answering musical phrase. Then it repeated itself and built on its repetitions with changes in volume and intensity—again without any musical dialogue—until I could barely stand the growing tensions in the music and in me. Then, instead of breaking the tension at some point with some musical resolution, the composer moved jaggedly to a new theme, which quickly began its own repetitive pattern. I could not sense any links between the first and second themes. Many such jagged shifts and new themes followed. Although each new theme was musically arousing and unique, often harmonically beautiful and challenging with unexpected instruments and complicated rhythms, each one built to an emotional pitch with no satisfying resolution. Like a staircase that ascends to nowhere, there was no landing place, only a potential sheer drop. With my companions' empty seats around me, I felt increasingly unsettled, more and more alone and anxious. And then the piece came to an abrupt end.

Andriessen, like many modern composers, was playing with my expectations of what should happen within musical space and, thereby, foiling my temporal sensibility. Of course, all interesting music plays with expectations to some extent, altering rhythms, themes, pitches, and tones for emotional effect, but generally it resolves the resulting tensions as it moves along or, at least, by the end. Andriessen's piece challenged my established ideas of how a musical phrase operates. That is, I expect internal dialogue between the elements of a musical piece and also between a musical piece and its audience. For example, according to my sensibility, a musical phrase, however complicated or re-petitive, will eventually invite a complementary musical response—in other words, as with gravity, when a musical phrase or theme rises, an answering phrase or theme will eventually descend. And to my ear, however complicated a composition may be—rhythmically, harmonically, thematically, and/or emotionally—at the end its parts should somehow cohere. In other words, in their unfolding the musical elements create an arc in time, "pattern recognition and closure," a temporal process satisfying to one's ears and mind and heart. The Andriessen ended without internal dialogue or any final resolution with its listeners.

As with music, therapy also sets up expectations of responsiveness and relationship and temporal expansion. In doing so, it also creates a *process in time*. As in the unfolding of a musical piece, so in an analytic relationship we develop expectations for the rhythms—the gives and takes—and the arc of therapeutic unfolding. With experience we attain tolerance for all kinds of differences, deviations, and quirky riffs; nevertheless, we hold some general notion about the rhythm and trajectory of an established therapy. Over time we expect some predictability. Over time through dialogic expansion, we expect development and change.

Failures in rhythm and timing can be painful and even traumatic as in cases of dysregulation and non-responsiveness. What's more, without dialogue and thematic linkages, therapy goes nowhere but merely exists in an existential eternal present. This is the point I've been leading to: time disappears.

The story Andriessen told was of creative struggle in the context of existential alienation and disconnection, and this, too, is my story with Maya. It tells of neglect and psychic disconnection and how it is enacted between us. This is why my emotional response to the therapy with her is so similar to my feelings about the disturbing music. In our therapeutic work I try to hold time for the both of us. While Maya often flails in a timeless present, I sift through memories from her life and attempt to make some narrative sense of them. When I express unease about this disjunction, Maya does not yet respond. Sometimes she seems to be listening, but usually she changes the subject.

Here now are some ways in which Maya is my Louis Andriessen. Rarely leaving room for my verbal responses, Maya uses our sessions more for monologue than dialogue and prefers me to leave her themes unanswered. When I make an inquiry or comment, she will frequently ignore me or change the subject. Thus far the only predictable rhythm we have established is the certainty that what we build in one moment will collapse in another.

I never know which of Maya's many contradictory moods will dominate a session, moods that jump from excited curiosity and discovery to blank and desolate emptiness to jittery angst. Sometimes she lounges on the couch in a comfortable curl while at other times she sits on its edge, shaking her leg and tapping her foot nervously on the floor. From week to week she careens between celebrating brilliant achievement—conquering a challenging philosophical text, for example—and experiencing bleak failure—feeling so distracted and disregulated that she can't get through a simple school assignment. Her language echoes her discontinuous states. In positive states her logic and syntax are coherent, but in distressed and/or excited states her narrative jumps from one disconnected subject to another with fragmented sentences and tangential associations.

144 *Temporal disturbance in the case of Maya*

Also, from week to week I never know what friends Maya has taken up or discarded from a continuously revolving circle of people—or why. At times she delights in hanging out with friends; at other times she claims to loath the company of the human cretins in her world and matter-of-factly describes snubbing or dropping her acquaintances; and at still other times she laments her loneliness and the fact that nobody cares about her.

I often experience Maya's relational shifts personally. Between sessions and sometimes even within sessions, Maya can move abruptly from what feels like a collaborative, resonant connection to a sense that we are strangers who hardly know each other. It's as though all memory of good interaction disappears; we have no memorial linkages to tether our disruptions. So, when the connection breaks, our music comes to an abrupt end. Gaze, rhythm, vocal tone, vitality affects, etc.—our many modes of meeting—lose synchrony. Then, it's as if Maya and I are playing out the "Groundhog Day" scenario, beginning our relationship over and over again from square one. *As in an Andriessen composition time disappears.* I sink psychologically, and my fantasies and hopes about our relationship evaporate like so many floating soap bubbles. My own senses of doubt, distrust, and doom cast emotional shadows on the relationship. While I imagine that these feelings mirror Maya's own senses of doubt, distrust, and doom, they are now front and center in our created therapeutic dyad. I fear that one day I will be a casualty of her patterned relational roulette.

Worst of all, I never know what dangerous adventure she will recall for me. Several months ago, before she even sat down for our session, she handed me her iphone on which a video was poised to play. The video showed a large wave washing Maya off a rocky perch at the ocean and her falling into the turbulent surf below. Miraculously Maya survived the pull of undertow and battering of waves, survived with a badly bruised body but no head injuries. The video of the incident—which a friend had shot on Maya's iphone—enhanced the terror of the story. I suddenly became sweaty. Yet, Maya's verbal description had the quality of an interested but cool and detached storyteller: "What I noticed is that each time a wave threw me towards the rocks, I fought … realized I didn't want to die. I was surprised." Then she added, "I won't ever go to the ocean again."

My body reaction to her narrative was adrenaline anguish, a hot and clammy flush, as if I were furnishing missing emotional music to Maya's spare lyrics. So often, as in this instance, we act in emotional counterpoint to each other rather than in harmony. When Maya fell into the sea, she and I came at the scary scene from different perspectives and with different psychological strategies and organizations. My visceral fear reaction came in a flash and preceded my ability to think about Maya's fall by several beats. I was only aware of the hot flush, tingling in my neck, the chill coursing down my back, and the dreadful sense that this "accident" was intentional. In contrast, Maya's thinking apparatus seemed fine, but her fear responses were absent, presumably dissociated. Only later, when I could finally think and begin to deconstruct the incident, did I wonder how and why Maya's friend came to film the incident.

One result of our "out-of-tuneness"—all of our frequent emotional and psychic mismatches, all of my "not knowings" and all of her "not feelings"—is the prevailing sense of peril with Maya, and I approach her with more wariness than I would like. I notice attending more to Maya's trailing edge material for clues to explain the peril. I want to make a song with her that has an expanded temporal dimension; but even when I note forward edge growth, I hold my breath and feel skeptical about its taking firm root. Not only are Maya's fantasies of the future largely grandiose and perfectionistic, leaving me at some level doubtful of their success; but I am also afraid that she will interrupt time by killing herself. Yet, I know that, in spite of my doubts and fears, for the success of our enterprise I must maintain a hopeful, developed vision of Maya in time.

Here is a sample of interaction with Maya that, I think, catches our "out—of-tuneness":

Vignette: After forgetting our previous session because of excitement and preoccupation with the first week of school, Maya breezes into my office. "I'm sooo sorry about last week, and I have so much to tell you." She shines with happiness and vitality. Before I can ask about the missed appointment and before she is even seated, she snaps opens her new Mac Air computer. The "wallpaper" on the presentation page is an enlarged photo of a young woman. Maya has photo-shopped the image of the woman's upper body and head, morphing it into a large and craggy rock formation. She has created a rock woman. Huge waves and foamy spumes of sea water crash against the body and spray the rock woman's face. My first association to the photo is, of course, "the accident" at Malibu. As I begin to comment on the screen saver, Maya abruptly slams the computer closed and launches into an animated, disjointed recitation of her life happenings. The rock woman and I are disappeared.

Her new classes and how she already knows and could teach the content of the chemistry and biology courses; a poem she has just posted on Tumblr; her idea for a new blog that should attract thousands of hits; how awake and alert she feels now that she is using a stimulant drug along with some Klonopin for emotional balance; her ability to study for hours without distraction or sleepiness; the gorgeous boy, whom she glimpsed at her local Starbucks, a vision of perfection who somehow, she knows, is destined to be her boyfriend—all this information tumbles out in a rush.

I feel knocked back and almost buried under the press and volume of her disjointed excitement. At once, I register Maya's elation and optimism—it's contagious. She wants me to recognize how well she is performing and how hopeful she feels. But I also feel her manic and grandiose state with foreboding. I especially feel frightened and confused about the tranquilizer she mentions. Only a month earlier Maya tried to asphyxiate herself under the influence of Klonopin. We agreed then that she would never take the drug again. But here it is! What dosage? Where did she get the prescription? I feel my stomach sink, my chest heave, and anxiety rise.

146 *Temporal disturbance in the case of Maya*

Taking a deep breath, I say to Maya that she seems happier, more energetic, and more positive than at any time since we began working together. "But what about the Klonopin? Where did it come from?" I ask. She tramples my question, asserting that it feels so good to have school, some place to go and some things to do every day. During the past two years of recovery, she has been lonely and bored and "floating on time," as in her latchkey years. "I had these same great feelings when I went off to college two years ago. It was the last time I felt happy, normal."

As I listen to Maya, my sympathetic nervous system is aroused: flushed cheeks, beating heart, light-headedness. I recall to myself that two years ago, right after arriving at college, Maya began the dangerous cutting that earned her suspension from university and landed her in the hospital. I want to grab her, hold her, calm her down. This is not Winnicott's symbolic holding that I desire. I am worried that our relationship isn't strong enough to withstand the onslaught of her disregulated moods; hence, I want to hold Maya literally and physically. I want to protect her fragility from the destructive crash that I fear may follow all this frothy excitement. Two days later I am very upset but not surprised when Maya's mother calls to tell me that Maya has cut herself after many months of abstinence.

Narrative upset—more disturbance in time

Besides music, I have been thinking and reading about other temporal dimensions in therapeutic work (e.g., Gentile, 2006; Knoblauch, 2011; Leowald, 1960). Goldin, for example, speaks of the breakdown of narrative flow and the narrowing of "temporal bandwidth"—a constriction in the sense of time—in addictive patients. I think there are similar problems with time in many other kinds of distressed patients and in our treatment of them as well: for example, future time shrinks or disappears for the grief laden and depressed as well as for those with problems maintaining focus or attention.

Maya, who is not an addict but who does seems to have problems in sustained attention, evinces an unsettled, accordion-like sense of time. For her time widens and narrows and assumes the colorations and volumes of her shifting mood states. Sometimes the future is brilliant and full of promise; at other times it is dark and desolate or even non-existent. My own sense of time is quite vulnerable to Maya's changes, a reflection of the implicit dimension of our relationship and a condition that poses a challenge in our co-transference. In a vivid dream, which caught this enactive dynamic, I was trapped inside a bellows that continually expanded and contracted beyond my control. When the bellows contracted and squeezed me, I could not catch a breath or glimpse any light or color. I felt stuck, mortally endangered—no way out. The dream captures Maya, me, and us; and it also raises the particular problem of future vision—for Maya, for me with her, and for our therapeutic relationship.

For both patient and therapist the construction of a "future vision"—the projection of a person into an imagined future—is a complex relational and developmental process. Once established, however, fantasies of desire, promise, and hope inform a person's motivations, choices, and actions. Future vision begins as "a gleam" in the parent's/therapist's eye and moves into fantasies that place the person, more developed and realized, in some future context. Then, over time the gleam is communicated mostly in non-verbal but sometimes in explicit ways.

While some theorists caution therapists against having life goals for their patients (e.g., Bion, 1967), I believe that holding in mind long-term possibilities for the other is an aspect of a mirroring selfobject transference or of genuine relational knowing or, indeed, of any loving, intimate relationship. Over time the therapist's future vision, if consonant with the patient's real capacities, will inform the patient's senses of possibility and self and help her to construct her own future vision. In time a conjoint future vision becomes an often unspoken part of the intersubjective therapeutic mix. If or when future vision fails in any part of the dyad, the therapy is in trouble.

The parental relationship provides a model of future vision. I think of the predictive power that a parent's dreams and aspirations have for a child, how a mother and/or father's stable, positive expectations and fantasies for the future may organize a child's self-concept, channel her motivations into constructive action, and then help direct her behaviors and achievements into an expanded future. How layered and complex the parents' future vision for the child; how consonant with the child's capacities; and how and with what attitudes the vision is channeled into a developmental program—these dimensions help shape a person's growth and development and senses of safety and self. In my Jewish tradition, a prayer of future vision is said at the naming of a new baby: "Just as this child has entered into God's Covenant, so may he/she enter into Torah, a good marriage, and a life of good deeds." Not only does this prayer reflect the values of the culture, it also implies traditional educational and religious programs and practices that lead to the expressed wishes and expectations.

I speculate that Maya's unstable sense of time was organized and continues to be supported in her family. The thickness and complexity of one's future vision—and therefore its stability—frequently vary with the parents' expectations for and imaginings of the child's future. They vary, too, with what is included and what is excluded in those imaginings and how values and behaviors that promote a particular future vision are modeled, encouraged, and reinforced.

In Maya's transplanted immigrant family her parents limited their future vision of her primarily to academic achievement and "making it" in America. They emphasized Maya's scientific and mathematical abilities and her obedient and polite manners while dismissing her considerable literary and artistic gifts as well as the importance of her social-emotional world—all the influences and pressures on her of American adolescent culture and social practices. The skimpiness of their view of her has left the girl psychically and emotionally lopsided, off-balance. Then, as a result of their absences, the parents provided Maya with little scaffolding, concrete instruction, or practice in helping her to realize their vision. Additionally, discussions about their future vision have

148 *Temporal disturbance in the case of Maya*

always been deathly serious, framed in dire warnings about the consequences of failure, and certainly lacking in enthusiasm and joy. As a result, Maya is clear about what they want, very vague about how to get there, and radically ambivalent about the whole thing.

Because she was a gifted child, Maya easily met her parents' expectations until puberty. She was the golden child in their immigrant community where she received the blessings, predictions, and burdens of making a brilliant future. But with absent parents, who did not adequately channel her development, a broader access to American culture at her public high school, and too much floating time, Maya lost her life path and did not develop habits of discipline. Her grades fell short of dazzling excellence, and she was filled with shame for dashing her parents' expectations as well as those of her immigrant community and her own.

From detailed inquiry Maya and I have begun to construct a new future vision, one fashioned from our joint imaginings. It pictures an active woman riding her bike to work: possibly a medical center where she is doing research or practicing as a physician. She has a partner at home with whom she shares her intellectual curiosities, her love of art and music, and lots of sex. Their home has overflowing bookshelves, an easel at a window, lots of electronic toys, and maybe a child. The woman feels centered in her life and has access to a broad array of emotions. This vision is cobbled from Maya's expressed wishes, my values, and also my sense of Maya's capacities. On her best days Maya imagines this scenario; however, she currently stumbles at each step toward realizing it.

Adjusting or abandoning or losing fantasies of the future—one's "future vision"—is painful and often more difficult than negotiating the real present. Because persistent psychic fantasies often form early in life and reflect unquestioned familial or cultural assumptions, they are often hardier and longer-lived than one's current psychic or external realities. For many in divorce, for example, it is easier to be done with a difficult and disappointing spouse than to relinquish the fantasy of a forever marriage and home. Maya is continually losing, regaining, and losing again her future vision, a dynamic that, in my view, materially contributes to her recurring despair, suicidal thoughts, and self-destructive behavior.

Maya is like other people who grow up in families without a stable future vision or in an environment where some established future vision has failed. These are people who develop without a sense that their parents see or project them into the future with a realistic sense, who grow up with either no, limited, or unrealistic parental expectations or expectations that are incompatible with a child's nature or personal resources or life environment. Such people are, at once, forced to navigate their lives alone while frequently feeling themselves to be "up a creek without a paddle."

Thus, children from families with faulty future visions or—as in Maya's case—a limited one that was not structured or nurtured, are generally diminished in some way or another. For some, their temporal horizon is very

Temporal disturbance in the case of Maya 149

limited. Such people may be oriented to the past, a realm of regrets, of "shoulda, coulda, wouldas"; they may have no or truncated or impoverished future fantasies; or they may simply live day to day in a kind of empty present. For others, their self-created future visions may be either so unstable as to fail frequently or so expansive as to be grandiose. Maya falls into this latter category. For Maya, who holds tenaciously to an idealized future vision, her golden, perfectionistic, often inflated fantasies of achievement and recognition come in and out of focus and sometimes totally collapse.

In my own growing up, my parents' life troubles frequently distracted them and interrupted their respective future visions of me. As a result, I looked to teachers and my friends' parents for mirroring direction; and it was wonderful in my twenties to find a therapist who could hold me in the present and also project me positively into the future. Through that relationship particularly I was able to mobilize my resources and chart my life. I have hoped to provide a similar positive future vision for Maya, but she makes it damned hard and frustrating.

For parents who dream their child into a positive future, watching the gradual unfolding of their expectations is satisfying and reassuring. What happens, however, to the child and/or to the parents if those fantasies are continually interrupted or radically changed? Isn't the loss of our stable future vision often the source of confused identity and profound grief? Stolorow writes about the trauma, apprehension of "finitude," and diminution of the future that results from the upending of "absolutisms of daily life" (Stolorow, 2007). His idea of trauma parallels this notion of a failed future vision, and his discussion of "finitude" and death, while mostly about acceptance, sometimes has a depressed even suicidal vibration.

Certainly, at those moments when my positive future vision of Maya collapses, I feel bereft. Then I remember and am flooded by her past destructive episodes, and fear and gloom shrouds our relationship like fog. Because with Maya I have repeated experiences of shattered future vision, I naturally surmise that I am picking up Maya's fear, her own lack of stability and safety, her own recurring loss of self and future vision. Here is an example of how her sometimes grandiose or perfectionistic construction of a "future vision" is vulnerable to frequent breakdown and destruction, both for her personally and for the two of us in our therapeutic work.

After the previous session in which she seemed buoyant and positive about school prospects and her boyfriend, Maya is in the dumps. She arrives twelve minutes late for our meeting. "Can't study for the exam tomorrow." Maya shakes her head and then sits in immobile silence. She has a stricken look on her downturned face. "Paralyzed." More silence. "Staring. Can't stand anybody. Everybody's ugly. Me too. Can feel folds of my belly fat." She pinches the skin on her tummy, which is hard and flat. "Rob (the boyfriend)—liked him last week; hate him the most." Long silence. "Got a 97 on the calculus test. Somebody got a 103 with extra credit. Should get a perfect score in that class—but can't study. Can't sleep either. Oh, who cares? The existentialists are right: nothing matters."

150   *Temporal disturbance in the case of Maya*

This is an example of narrative and temporal collapse; a wall of inert negativity blocks all sense of possibility and agency. Maya's language loses syntax and her first-person pronouns, her "I," largely drops away. In her communication to me she also loses affective words, substituting for them concrete body sensations, perceptions, and states. It's no wonder that she is inclined to use a concrete razor blade to deal with these bodily feelings rather than to treat them psychologically.

Theoretical underpinnings

I draw from many overlapping theoretical sources in my work with Maya, beginning with Heinz Kohut (1984). In emphasizing the analyst's importance in fulfilling the patient's selfobject transference needs, Kohut stressed the centrality of relationship in the consolidation of self-experience. This emphasis underlines the importance both of the analyst's presence and of affect in analytic work and human development. And Kohut's idea that the analyst's use of the empathic tool—the imaginative capacity to experience the world from another person's perspective—can help to change the emotional organization of another person's mind has had far reaching implications for psychoanalysis.

Broadening Kohut's one person model, I borrow from Fosshage's expanded notion of empathy as he stresses the importance of implicit modes of understanding and adds two new listening perspectives (1997, 2007); and I also draw from Intersubjective Theory's ideas about emotional attunement (e.g., Orange, 1995; Stolorow, 2011). While for Kohut empathy or vicarious introspection was the analyst's capacity to decenter—to step into the other's shoes, so to speak—in order to experience the world approximately from that person's perspective, for me, empathy also takes into account my own empathic introspective processes. That is, beyond empathy for the other is attention to my own subjectivity. To do good work, I must attend to my own mind and body in all their complexity, in their array of emotions and many states of being. It is then that I feel free to use my own ideas, feelings, and imaginative associations—all the intuitional flutters and flickers and the resulting mental allusions and images—to access, experience, and share the subjectivity of the other. It is also then that I can register the patient's active efforts to be understood, efforts that are often communicated nonverbally. In short, for me, true vicarious introspection includes at least three dimensions: beyond Kohut's decentered vicarious empathy, it includes the analyst's use of her own subjectivity—her uniqueness, her difference, her imagination—as an aid to imagine the other empathically and also to receive the other's non-verbal communications. It follows, of course, that the dyadic partner engages in a reciprocal process: as Aron puts it, "a meeting of minds (1996)."

The complexity model of mind that I currently imagine—fluid, interactive, and intersubjective—is different from Kohut's notion of one separate mind

Temporal disturbance in the case of Maya   151

entering another's perspective while still remaining intact and unchanged. In moving beyond Kohut to understand the workings of relational understanding—which he encouraged his followers to do—I have recruited relevant ideas from allied fields as have many other relational thinkers. Although beyond the scope of this paper to elaborate, these fields include (1) philosophical and sociological ideas about field theory and evolution (e.g., Orange, 1995, 2003; Stolorow, 2002, 2007), (2) scientific notions about context and interactive connectionist networks such as dynamic systems or complexity theory (e.g., Coburn, 2014; Damasio, 1999; Edelman and Tononi, 1999; Weisel-Barth, 2006), (3) findings from infant research and attachment theory about mutual regulatory and contingency systems in the development of mind and relational expectations (e.g., Beebe and Lachman, 2002; Beebe et al., 2005; Boston Change Process Study Group, 2010, 2013; Fonagy et al., 2001; Lyons-Ruth, 1999; Main, 2000; Sander, 1995), (4) relational ideas about two person psychology (e.g., Benjamin, 2004; Mitchell, 1997; Renn, 2012), and, especially, (5) discoveries in cognitive and brain science that highlight the importance of implicit communication systems, mirror neurons, and shared circuitry in human empathy and understanding (e.g., Cacioppo, 2004; Decety and Lamm, 2006; Gallese, 2003; Iacoboni, 2008; Marks-Tarlow, 2012; Pally, 2010; Ramachandran, 2011; Schore, 2003a, 2003b).

For reasons of space I'll limit the present discussion about implicit relational knowing to some stunning ideas from neuroscience, ideas which have bearing on my work with Maya. Specifically, recent explorations of mirror neurons and shared circuitry suggest that the capacity for empathy and social "mind reading' is a basic human capacity. Mirror neurons, first discovered in 1996, are specialized sense and motor neurons in the brain that are linked to registering subjectively the actions and intentions of another person. It turns out that the Mirror Neuron System is only a subsystem of the larger neuronal system of Shared Circuitry. Shared circuitry occurs in brain areas that regulate touch, pain, emotion, behavior, and even those that integrate the senses of self and mind (Pally, 2010).

Briefly, the term "Shared Circuitry" refers to all the neuronal systems in the brain that subjectively register and resonate with action and affect in others and seem to play a part in self-other understanding. Significantly, these circuits operate in the same brain regions used for self-experience (Pally, 2010). The insula and cingulate cortex, for example, are upper brain regions that contain the specialized neurons. These regions regulate sensory and motor data, affective information from the limbic system, and physiological feedback systems; they serve to integrate self-other affective information. The insula and cingulate cortex direct this information to behavioral planning systems in the frontal cortex and, in sum, seem play a central role in the creation both of emotional consciousness and resulting behavioral responses.

Significantly, at the same time that we can tap into the other's experiences through shared circuitry, we can also differentiate ourselves from the other. Shared circuits and mirror neurons exist "as a subset of the total neural circuitry that belongs only to the self" (Rustin, p.155). We are, thus, always

152 *Temporal disturbance in the case of Maya*

negotiating self-other information as we move through life. Pally (2010) concludes that together mirror neurons and shared circuitry support "... the intersubjective nature of relationships, the centrality of empathy, and the use of the self in understanding others as well as the role of the body in mental life" (p. 382).

From the many research and theoretical ideas I have named—particularly the notion of Shared Circuitry—here is an outline of some contemporary relational ideas that help me make some sense both of how I know what I know about Maya and where my metaphors and associations about time come from: (1) We have nonverbal as well as verbal capacities for "mind reading," for knowing other minds; (2) We are capable of empathically accessing another person's perspective and can feel the pain and joy of others, sometimes immediately and intensely; (3) We can subjectively anticipate the behavior and intentions of others; (4) Minds speak to each other nonverbally and out of conscious awareness, and their communications often occur in images and metaphors. They tell each other or create together intimate stories about themselves. These processes work reciprocally and simultaneously and help to explain how our patients come to know us; (5) Bodies do the same: as Freud put it, "He that has eyes to see and ears to hear may convince himself that no mortal can keep a secret. If his lips are silent, he chatters with his fingertips; betrayal oozes out of him at every pore" (Freud, 1905); (6) At the same time that we can tap into the other's experiences through shared circuitry, we can also differentiate ourselves from the other. Hence, even in an intersubjective world we still retain the experience of privacy and separateness.

Conclusion

In describing the case of Maya, I have tried to illustrate a modernist model of empathy and attunement, one that includes the analyst's empathic attunement to her own subjectivity and her receptivity to the patient's non-verbal communications. In using my capacities to attune both to Maya and to my own subjectivity, I became aware of and attended to temporal disruptions between Maya and me. In the process two metaphors emerged: music and "future vision." While these metaphors arose from my own imagination, I also think of them as emerging from my interaction with Maya and, therefore, as our joint creations. Subsequently, the metaphors have been very helpful to me in understanding Maya's mind.

I have tried to show how the disruptions in my music with Maya—disruptions in themes, rhythms, tone, dialogue, and pattern closure—both help me understand Maya's inner process and affect our interactions. I have also tried to illustrate some distortions and disruptions in Maya's sense of temporal narrative flow: how her sometimes grandiose or perfectionistic construction of a "future vision" is vulnerable to frequent breakdown and destruction, both for her personally and for the two of us in our therapeutic work. I know that whatever my fear at such moments of breakdown, I must struggle with my own negativity in order to maintain a positive vision of Maya's future possibilities and hold onto her forward edge leanings.

References

Aron, L. (1996) *A Meeting of Minds*. Hillsdale, NJ: Analytic Press.

Beebe, B., Knoblauch, S., Rustin, J., & Sorter, D. (2005) *Forms of Intersubjectivity in Infant Research and Adult Treatment*. New York: Other Press.

Beebe B., Lachman, F. (2002) *Infant Research and Adult Treatment: Co-constructing Interactions*. Hillsdale, NJ: Analytic Press.

Benjamin, J. (2004) Beyond Doer and Done to: An Intersubjective View of Thirdness. *Psychoanal Q.*, 763:5–46.

Bion, W. (1967) Notes on Memory and Desire. *Psychoanal. Forum* 2(3): 272–273, 279–280.

Boston Change Process Study Group (2010) *Change in Psychotherapy: A Unifying Paradigm*. New York: W.W. Norton.

Boston Change Process Study Group (2013) *Enactment and the Emergence of New Relational Organization. J. Am. Psychoanal. Assoc. N.Y.*, 61(4): 727–749.

Cacioppo, J. (2004) *Social Neuroscience: Key Readings in Social Psychology*. New York: Psychology Press.

Coburn, W. (2014) *Psychoanalytic Complexity*. New York: Routledge.

Damasio, A. (1999) *The Feeling of What Happens: Body and Emotion in the Making of Consciousness*. New York: Harcourt Brace.

Decety, J. and Lamm, C. (2006) Human Empathy Through the Lens of Social Neuroscience. *Sci. World J.*, 6:1146–1163.

Edelman, G., Tononi, G. (1999) *A Universe of Consciousness: How Matter Becomes Imagination*. New York: Basic Books.

Fonagy, P., Gergely, G., Elliot, J., & Target, M. (2001) *Affect Regulation, Mentalization, and the Development of the Person*. New York: Basic Books.

Fosshage, J. L. (1997) Chapter 4 Listening/Experiencing Perspectives and the Quest for a Facilitating Responsiveness. *Progr. Self Psychol.*, 13:33–55.

Fosshage, J. L. (2007) The Analyst's Participation in Cocreating the Analytic Relationship. *Int. J. Psychoanal. Self Psychol.*, 2:147–162.

Freud, S. (1905) *Fragment of an Analysis of a Case of Hysteria (1905 [1901]). The Standard Edition of the Complete Psychological Works of Sigmund Freud, Volume VII (1901–1905): A Case of Hysteria, Three Essays on Sexuality and Other Works*, pp. 1–122.

Gallese, V. (2003) The Roots of Empathy: The Shared Manifold Hypothesis and the Neural Basis of Intersubjectivity. *Psychopathology*, 36:171–180.

Gentile, K. (2006) Timing Development from Cleavage to Differentiation. *Contemp. Psychoanal.*, 42:297–325.

Iacoboni, M. (2008) Chapter 1. "Monkey See, Monkey Do." Chapter 6. "Broken Mirrors." In *Mirroring People: The New Science of How We Connect with Others*. New York: Farrar Straus Giroux.

Knoblauch, S. (2011) Contextualizing Attunement Within the Polyrhytmic Weave: The Psychoanalytic Samba, *Psychoanal. Dial.*, 21, 4:414–427.

Kohut, H. (1984) *How Does Analysis Cure?*, eds. A. Goldberg & P. Stepansky. Chicago: University of Chicago Press.

Leowald, H. (1960) On the Therapeutic Action of Psychoanalysis. In *Papers on Psychoanalysis*. Hew Haven, CT: Yale University Press, 1980, pp. 221–256.

Lyons-Ruth, K. (1999) The Two-Person Unconscious. Intersubjective Dialogue, Enactive Relational Representation, and the Emergence of New Forms of Relational Organization, *Psychoanal. Inq.*, 19, (4):576–617.

Main, M. (2000) The Organized Categories of Infant, Child, and Adult Attachment. *J. Amer. Psychoanal. Assn.*, 48:1055–1095.

Marks-Tarlow, T. (2012) *Clinical Intuition in Psychotherapy: The Neurobiology of Embodied Response*. New York: Norton.

Mitchell, S. (1997) Chapter 2 The Therapeutic Action and Chapter 5 Varieties of Interaction. In *Influence and Autonomy in Psychoanalysis*. Mahwah, NJ: Analytic Press.

Orange, D. (1995) *Emotional Understanding*. New York: Guilford Press.

Orange, D. (2003) Antidotes and Alternatives: Perspectival Realism and the New reductionisms. *Psychoanal. Psychol.*, 20:472–486.

Pally R. (2010) The Brains Shared Circuits of Interpersonal Understanding: Implications for Psychoanalysis and Psychodynamic Psychotherapy. *J. Am. Acad. Psychoanal. Dynam. Psych.*

Ramachandran, V. S. (2011) *The Tell-Tale Brain: A Neuroscientist's Quest for What Makes Us Human*. New York: Norton.

Renn, P. (2012) *The Silent Past and Invisible Present: Memory, Trauma and Representation in Psychotherapy*. New York: Routledge.

Rustin, J. (2013) *Infant Research & Neuroscience at Work in Psychotherapy: Expanding the Clinical Repertoire*. New York: Norton.

Sander, L. (1995) Identity and the Experience of Specificity in a Process of Recognition, *Psychoanal. Dial.*, 5:579–593.

Schore, A. N. (2003a) *Affect Dysregulation and Disorders of the Self*. New York: Norton.

Schore, A. N. (2003b) *Affect Regulation and the Repair of the Self*. New York: Norton.

Stolorow, R. D. (2007) *Trauma and Human Existence*. New York: Analytic Press.

Stolorow, R. D. (2011) *World, Affectivity, Trauma*. New York: Routledge.

Stolorow, R. D., Atwood, G. E., & Orange, D. (2002) *Worlds of Experience: Interweaving Philosophical and Clinical Dimensions in Psychoanalysis*. New York: Basic books.

Travarthen, C. (1993) The Self Born in Intersubjectivity: An Infant Communicating. In U. Neisser (ed.) *The Perceived Self* (pp. 121–173). New York: Cambridge University Press.

Weisel-Barth, J. (2006) Thinking and Writing about Complexity Theory in the Clinical Setting. *Int. J. Psychoanal. Self Psychol.*, 1:365–388.

10 Courting the "real" and stumbling in "reality"

Confusions and hazards of relational practice

To be in an analytic relationship is to be in an affective hothouse, the atmosphere heavy and humid, the temperature intense. The resulting emotional vulnerability to which relational partners are prey can make psychoanalysis a confusing and dangerous game. From the analyst's perspective I think about danger first in relation to aggressive and angry feelings that emerge between analytic partners. Unless they are skillfully negotiated, such feelings—the stock and trade of traditional psychoanalysis—can derail relationships. I also think about knotty and vulnerable emotions like analytic tenderness and love, feeling states that grow between analytic partners and that relational psychoanalysts increasingly address (e.g., Aron, 2005; Davies, 2009; Grand, 2009; Mitchell, 2000; Stern, 2011). Such tender feelings can also derail relationships.

Passionate and intimate emotions between analytic partners may conflict not only with traditional analytic theory and professional expectations, but also with other contexts in the analyst and patient's respective lives. Nevertheless, I can't think of a long-term patient for whom I haven't felt some love and/or tenderness and/or passion. Mirror neurons, emotional contagion, intersubjective mind-sharing—however one thinks about them, tender feelings seem to be natural byproducts of two people intentionally opening themselves to each other and receiving back willing response.

The intense feelings as well as shared emotional states, which emerge in the crucible of relational analytic space, change patterns of relational expectations and open partners to positive representations of the therapeutic dyad. The structure, contents, and dynamics of these new relational representations, in turn, open new behavioral possibilities; they expand repertoires of interaction and connection inside and outside of the therapy. Many and diverse theorists speak of positive expansive psychological changes that issue from "new" relational experience (e.g., Alexander, 1950; Lyons-Ruth, 1999; Shane & Gales, 1997; Stern, 1994, 2002; Summers, 2001, 2012; Tronick et al., 1998).

Yet, when emotional collisions occur, the intense relational feelings also expose the analytic partners to disappointment, disillusionment, rage, and an array of other dark feelings. That in which we invest deep feeling and project healing powers can, in its failures, hurt and break our hearts. I will try to illustrate here one particular source of analytic hurt that arises from the clash of

156 *Courting the "real" and stumbling in "reality"*

separate realities, that arises from discrepancies between what goes on inside the private, co-created analytic space, on one side, and the patient's and analyst's respective external contexts, on the other. Such clashes of realities, which occur when external contexts intrude on private analytic space, account for some of the particular vulnerabilities in the analytic pursuit and are the subject of this paper. At least, this approach helps me in unraveling some of my own tangled feelings and ideas about the pleasure, healing, but also threatened danger and pain from the passionate feelings that bloom in long therapies.

Thinking of vulnerability and love and the collision of competing realities reminds me of the disastrous end to an important therapy relationship, one that I mourn even now. My twelve-year relationship with Lara, including her serving as my first control case (See Chapter 1) was deep and loving and heart shattering in its end. Here is a brief taste of the beginning of that end. I received a phone call:

> "I know what you did," she says, "How could you?" Lara hurls her accusation through the phone line. It knocks me off center. Although I don't know what she's talking about, I'm suddenly flushed with confusion and anxiety, my everyday shell of coolness and coherence cracked by the force of her charge. If Lara is accusing me, I must be guilty of something.
>
> Lara continues, "I saw Dr. Kim today, and she told me about Duke—that you killed him. How could you? And you lied to me. How could you do that? And you didn't ask me to help."
>
> Now I know what she's talking about, and I am speechless. To use a neuroscience metaphor—and maybe a reality—connections to my Broca brain region are suddenly severed; I can barely think, and words fail me. Finally, I manage a sallow, "The dog. We need to talk about Duke."
>
> Lara agrees, saying, "When I can look at you again, we'll talk about how you're not as good as you think you are." Lara and I never do have the face-to-face talk.

The abrupt loss of Lara has left me, years later, still devastated, ashamed, and unresolved. Because of guilt and shame, I haven't discussed the loss with colleagues except as a "stranger than fiction" anecdote; but in a conversation about the vulnerabilities of relational analysts, this lost loving relationship pops up and demands attention. Telling about its messy and painful ending will be my clinical example and the focus of this paper.

The telling also provides me an occasion to focus on the strangeness and power of the space we relational analysts create with our patients and how the creation of that space contributes to psychic change. The therapeutic space, the arena of change, is strange because while it may feel exquisitely sensitive and "real"—full of passion and tender feeling—it may also be shockingly separate from what I'll call the "reality of other life contexts." As analysts we stand astride and often shift between at least two separate realities: analytic reality and the reality of life outside the office. And so, in this paper I want to think out loud about how confusing it sometimes can be to be a relational analyst.

The first thing that occurs to me is that the illusory, provisional, and exploratory nature of analytic space invites my patients and me to become increasingly open and human together. Patients come to treatment with well-established, unconscious patterns of expectations about relationships, varying degrees of dissociation, differing capacities for mentalization or inter-subjectivity, unique emotional regulatory systems, and singular histories of behavioral responses to human interaction. Sometimes these patterns seem fixed and unmovable.

Nevertheless, minds open and dynamic changes do occur in analytic space. There partners deconstruct emotional and cognitive patterns of relational expectations and responses that formed in important early attachment re-lationships. Play is a hallmark feature of the space: two partners playing at or experimenting with being emotionally present, attuned, honest, and direct, playing at softening and refashioning formerly fixed assumptions. There is a kind of illusory or "as if" quality to this private space—safe and "not-quite-real"—where partners are free to name affects, recover and integrate dis-sociated experience, and risk and practice new kinds of emotional interaction. All this occurs through back and forth, recursive interaction that stimulates associations, shifting self-states, and enactments. Over time strategies that work relationally become part of new interactive patterns, and old, maladaptive strategies slowly lose their power and standing. The process is humanly lib-erating.

Because analytic partners attend to, register, and share subtle and shifting feeling states and perceptions—and their origins and derivatives—all the stuff of intimacy develops in analytic unfolding: private language and jokes, joint dramas, images, and stories. With intimacy, emergent feelings between the analytic partners deepen, thicken, and intensify, and these feelings bind the partners emotionally. Often the experience of this kind of intimacy is ex-quisitely pleasurable for both partners, frequently more pleasurable than many more superficial relationships in "real life."

At its most simple, this is my story of therapeutic change; and when analysis succeeds, it is deeply satisfying for analysts as well as patients. But the work is hard. In the analytic play-space there is so much for the analyst to do, requiring her to shift continuously and almost simultaneously between different states of being. A fully active and emotionally involved participant in the therapeutic interaction, the analyst must also be a continually vigilant observer, searching out co-created unconscious material and finding words to talk about it. At the same time that she is empathically exploring the patient's experience, the analyst must also negotiate the murky, quasi-conscious pull of her own feelings. Catching the unconscious in action—her own, the patient's, the dyad's—is a bit like chasing phantoms. It's also like going to a party where one simulta-neously dances and watches the dancing, or has an animated conversation with someone while, at the same time, observing one's own face. It's impossible: a

158 *Courting the "real" and stumbling in "reality"*

multi-layered task requiring multiple simultaneous perspectives. But impossible or not, this task is at the heart of the relational analytic endeavor.

There are many theoretical terms to describe aspects of the mutative process that occurs in analytic space such as selfobject transference (Kohut, 1978), emotional understanding (Orange, 1995), "moments of meeting" (Stern et al., 1998), dyadic expansion of consciousness (Tronick et al., 1998), recognition (Benjamin, 2000), and mentalization (Fonagy, 1998). And whatever metaphors we use for the experience of analytic play—riffing, cooking, dancing, making music, improvising, being emotionally attuned or intersubjectively linked, etc.—what we feel is heightened creativity. And nothing feels better or more humanly "real" than to be in the midst of one's own creative flow. Such shared experience naturally generates fantasies about the relationship in both patient and analyst. The term "illusion" is used to capture the unique fantasies generated in the analytic play space.

The practice required for change and, then, the actual relational changes that do occur between patient and analyst in the analytic play space usually precede changes in the patient's "real world." One source of analyst vulnerability and frustration is our tendency to forget how glacial and fragile and uncertain is the movement from emotional and interactional change in the analytic space to psychological and behavioral change in the patient's life. In some cases, changes in the patient's external world may be ultimately impossible.

So, to review: positive shifts that develop in the analytic relationship do not immediately or necessarily translate to changes in the patient's "reality life contexts." Long after defenses relax and new rhythms, collaborative emotional regulation, and dynamic understandings establish themselves in the analytic dyad, the patient may still be reactive to old relational cues and configurations in the world of "reality." And old relational behavioral patterns may persist. This is especially true of trauma survivors.

We analysts certainly know shocking moments in long established analyses when, as a result of some dyadic exchange, a patient's archaic modes of relating in the "reality outside of the analytic context" suddenly flood the analytic space. These archaic modes may compete with, contradict, and/or drown out newly organized relational practices. Such moments are often destabilizing and distressing for the analyst as well as the patient. Beyond expectable vicissitudes in analytic interaction between recognition and non-recognition—which are an uncomfortable part of all dyadic process—these destabilizing moments can feel surprising and acutely painful. They often contain the material of dramatic enactments.

Immersion in the illusionary space may also distract the analyst from his own life contexts. That is, the magnetic draft of the play space may draw the analyst away from her everyday life, pulling her toward intense relational feeling, unconscious enactments, complex understandings, and fantasies about the analytic partner. Over time analysts may naturally succumb to the lures and provocations, and, of prime importance here, the provisional, "as if," illusory

Courting the "real" and stumbling in "reality" 159

nature of the play space. Passionate feelings accompany authentic analytic encounters and mutual recognition there; the feelings seem absolutely "real" and solid. But these feelings are specific to the analytic space, and our experience of emotional "realness" in the analytic relationship may be very different from how we—and how our patients—function in the "real" world outside the analysis. The contrast or clash of "realities" is often a source of confusion and conflict for both dyadic partners. The analyst is as likely as the patient to be the agent and/or the victim of just such a clash.

As is by now clear, I have been playing with multiple meanings of the pesky word "real." To refer to the subjective sense of presence with and recognition of the other, to "moments of meeting" or to the meeting of minds in the analytic space, I am using the phrase "experience of the real." (See also Coburn, 2001). Of course, even within the analytic space, partners move in and out of "the experience of the real" or, as Jessica Benjamin puts it, they move between "recognition" and "destruction" (Benjamin, 2000). I also use the term "reality" to refer to the contexts of the lives of patients and analysts outside the therapeutic space. This linguistic confusion parallels and embodies the confusion that I have felt as analyst between the "experience of the real" in the analytic play space and "reality" in the rest of my life and the lives of my patients.

Here's a short and funny example that issued from just this confusion. A colleague and I attended the wedding of a young man and woman who were our respective patients. My relationship with the bride was long-standing and very dear because she and I had struggled together with her history of sexual abuse, abandonment, and intractable, life-threatening bulimia, an illness that had finally remitted. Because we had worked through her father's death and her mother's drug addiction and depressions, I rejoiced that she seemed to have found a loving partner.

I did think long and hard about attending the wedding, discussing it both with my patient and my colleague. However, because the analytic relationship felt so "real" and dear, so solid and tight and surrogate mother-like, I decided to go. For his own reasons so did my colleague. Imagine how hurt and deflated—and, in a short time, amused—we both felt to be seated with my patient's hairdresser and manicurist, her partner's trainer, and the couple's housekeeper. Hired help all of us!

Although I know that I hadn't imagined the intimacy with this young woman in the created therapeutic space, I was very wrong about what reciprocity existed in the "reality" world outside the therapeutic space. Had I worked in a traditional psychoanalytic mode, I would never have been at the wedding in the first place. Because of the emphasis on rational understanding, interpretation, and fixed ground rules in traditional practice, boundaries tend to be clear, and mixing socially is out-of-bounds. Thus, as a traditional analyst, I would not have had to confront discrepancies between my expectations and feelings developed in the therapeutic space and what actually occurred in the patient's "reality context" outside the analysis. In short, boundaries in

160 *Courting the "real" and stumbling in "reality"*

relational analysis can be cloudy and damnably confusing, and feelings—mine, for example—easily hurt.

Let me turn now to the therapeutic loss of Lara with which I began this talk. I have previously written about Lara (See Chapter 1), an exciting, enticing, difficult woman whom I had seen as a control case and in analytic therapy for many years. Impulsive and emotionally explosive, the child of a schizophrenic mother and a cruel, powerful, alcoholic father, Lara came to our therapy with a history of wild and violent friendship, sexual, and love relationships. She fueled her chaotic life—and episodes of high drama—with drugs and alcohol.

During our long and volatile relationship, we not only dealt with Lara's history of explosive and splintered relationships and her fascination with danger and violence, we also grieved the suicide of her younger brother, whose death she blamed on her father's brutality. A carpet-bombing of criticism and challenges and continual therapeutic disruptions marked the early years of our work. Through the difficult first few years I tried to function as a mirroring and idealized selfobject, emotionally empathic and curious about her mental states. Over time, though, we began to negotiate differences in our respective perceptions and perspectives, and through this differentiating work Lara developed new reflective skills—what she termed "self talk." These skills derived from the accretion of mentalizing experiences in our relationship. Learning reflective skills enabled Lara to make better choices in her life. At the time of our rupture, her impulsive and self-destructive explosions had quieted both in and outside our analytic space. Lara had come to idealize our relationship and to think of me as her dearest person. And as midwife to her perilous and torturous psychological birth, I felt intensely connected with and loving toward her.

Then came the Dog Nightmare.

One of the stabilizing factors in Lara's life and our therapy was her love of dogs. For the first several years of our work she brought her large, lumbering and very sweet Yellow Lab to our sessions. Charley's presence helped to calm and regulate Lara's hyper-aroused emotional states. Lara and I both appreciated his loving nature; and when Charley died of old age, we mourned his passing together.

Lara and I also shared puppy brothers. One day she arrived for a session—red-faced and in an agitated state. She held two 5-week-old puppies in the palms of her hands. She had found them wandering in a parking lot near my office—"Some murderous bastard deserted them!" she fumed. Scooping them up, she brought them to therapy, and I—enchanted and under the spell of the adorable, helpless pups—agreed to find a home for one of the dogs. Which I did: the puppy, Otis Redding Barth, is presently my family's 14-year-old beloved Shepherd. Lara kept the other pup, and our sharing these dogs deepened our emotional bonds. My impulsive decision to keep the puppy, which confused the boundaries between analytic space and our respective "real" worlds, also began an enactment that ended in a therapeutic disaster.

Courting the "real" and stumbling in "reality" 161

When Otis was about 3, he entered into a domination struggle with my older male dog, Duke Ellington. Duke, a lovely, submissive guy, had a trace of coyote in him; and in the face of Otis' challenge, he became aggressive and violent. He attacked me twice at feeding time, the second time biting me seriously. After the second attack, I took him for medical tests, all of which were negative. Given the ferocity of the second attack, my vet suggested that I put Duke down. "The taste of blood is a death sentence for a family dog," she said.

The vet's suggestion was unthinkable. I promptly found Duke a new home, one with a single master and no other dogs. Once I placed him, my heart finally stopped pounding. Several months later, however, Duke threatened the new master, who called me in a panic and demanded that I remove the dog. Then I did the unthinkable: I picked up the dog, registered his joy at our reunion, took him for a walk, and bought him a Big Mac. After that I sat with Duke as he was euthanized. Helplessness, grief, and the sad conviction that "my best" here was shamefully inadequate—these are my lingering feelings and thoughts about this horrible episode.

So with all our intimacy and dog connections, why did I not know that Lara and I shared the same vet? And what are the odds that my vet would tell Lara about Duke's death?

Duke was gone about a year when Lara calls me in great distress. "I know what you did," she says. She tells me that I have been dishonest in not telling her that I had put the dog down; tells me that I owed her the right to rescue the dog and save his life; and tells me that I am not the "perfect" person that I think I am. She is angry and inconsolable, does not want to talk to me, and says that she needs a break from therapy until she absorbs this shock. I feel sick, helpless, and miserably responsible. I feel responsible both for the ridiculous, unforeseen, and accidental circumstances in the veterinarian part of this story and, of course, for my impulsive violation of analytic boundaries in adopting the puppy.

Things go from bad to worse in our subsequent exchange of emails. Lara is crushed by her disappointment and disillusionment with me. She wants to talk, knows that she should talk about what has happened, but just can't. Her great complaint is that I didn't turn to her for help, and she defines my not talking to her about Duke as "dishonest." My efforts to acknowledge her perspective, to delineate the boundaries between my outside life and our therapy, and to comfort Lara fail. Shattered idealization creates inner turmoil for her and turns to hate and contempt toward me. She wants to withdraw. Repetition and retraumatization and old behavioral responses returned! I feel the dreadful rumble of our relationship imploding.

Over a few weeks the emails continue, are repetitious, and Lara remains unable to see or talk to me in person. Finally—in less fluent and coherent language than this—I am able to say the following: "O.K., I get it, Lara. You feel that I am a murderer; that I killed Duke. I imagine it feels a lot like your father in relation to your brother. You also imagine that you could have fixed

162   *Courting the "real" and stumbling in "reality"*

things for Duke just as you still imagine you could have saved your brother. I also want to fix this mess between us, wish I could fix it, but I don't think I can. If it's possible to heal, we can only do it together. I want to try. Maybe you need more time to think about this." Then I add, "But if you have to, you are free to go." Lara thanks me and says, "I feel relieved." I have never seen her again. A few years later, perplexed by a life dilemma, she emails me for help. We have a good exchange, and Lara writes, "I remember why you have been so important to me." This is our last interaction. Ach!

Discussion

Is there a more glaring example of external contexts intruding and fracturing the illusions and constructions in the analytic play space? And is there a more chilling cautionary tale about the pitfalls of relational spontaneity and about the vulnerability of the relational analyst to illusion? When the "reality" world outside the therapy intruded and she learned that I had put my old dog down, Lara was retraumatized and suffered intense pain. She retreated to early, dysregulated ways of managing violent behavior, and we were not able to repair our awful breach. The ragged sundering of our relationship became another iteration in her long history of ragged endings. And for years I have felt some combination of disappointment, sadness, guilt, and deep regret.

I have tried to process the episode from several different perspectives. From the perspective of Duke's master, I feel regretful and guilty and sad because I was the agent of killing a living creature. But also, from that perspective I am convinced that in the interests of my family, other animals, the safety of others, and my own security, I did a responsible, hard thing. From the perspective of observer of the passing scene, I shake my head at the improbable absurdity of my vet's telling Lara about Duke's death. I will never know how the conversation came about or what was said because rules of confidentiality prevent me from confronting the vet. Needless to say, my dogs now have a different doctor.

From the perspective of analyst, when I adopted the puppy, I overstepped a boundary between play space and the "reality world outside the analysis" and entered into an enactment with Lara around parenting and caretaking and mutual responsibility. She and I created a "play" family with "real" animals. For several years I was able to keep the two realms relatively separate although I never felt comfortable with my impulsivity.

In retrospect, the factor that influenced my decision to keep the puppy rather than to adopt him out is, paradoxically, the very same one that contributed to my initial connection with Lara. I am an animal lover, and so is she. In fact, I am the kind of animal lover, who threatens to become a crazy old dog lady. A dog's innocent, affectionate, and forgiving nature; a dog's pleasure in sufficiency; and a dog's capacity for developed empathy—these qualities embody values that I deeply respect, strive for, and too often fall short of. And I love participating in the simultaneous unfolding of a puppy's development and my own deeply connected relationship with the animal. My nuclear family, extended family, and many of my friends treasure our dogs. A lot of my social life—hikes, picnics, and just hanging out—includes my dog families. The first night that the puppy Otis shared the bed with my husband and me—and didn't pee—I fell in love with him.

For Lara's part, her first and only experience of mutual love happened with animals. Until our therapy, Lara simply hated and distrusted other people, especially the ones she loved and needed. Our mutual love for dogs provided both an essential link in our therapeutic relationship and an opening for Lara to consider new possibilities with other humans. Indeed, my feelings for her dog Charley provided emotional adhesive in our early therapy. And so besides simply falling in love with Otis, I imagined that a puppy raising collaboration with Lara would advance our connection. It might not only create a new focus for examining issues of trust, empathy, caretaking, and balance in relationships, but also furnish an enduring bond between us when Lara finally left our therapy. It might also serve as an inoculation against anticipated loss.

Of course, at the time I took the puppy I was unaware of many of the factors informing my choice. Yet, even then I had a sense of doing something subversive by adopting the dog. In retrospect, I overestimated the stability of emotional change that had occurred for Lara in our play space and also magnified the rosy romance of our relationship, the strength of our analytic love. Thus, in spite of my best intentions, I upset the delicate balance between maintaining professional clarity and responsibility for the analysis, preserving my privacy outside the analysis, and participating authentically and spontaneously and lovingly in the dyad.

Because of the fractured analysis and terrible repetitive pain that has ensued for Lara, I am deeply sorry. For my loss I am still heartbroken. This awful incident has reminded me of both the perishable nature of the relational analytic pursuit and all its contextual contingencies. While some of these contingencies we can manage or negotiate, over others we have little or no control. I hope this lost relationship hasn't made me gun shy to risk honest presence in my work, but certainly it has made me wary of spontaneous choices and actions that may confuse analytic play space with competing reality contexts outside the analysis. As in the case of Lara such confusion may interfere with my ability to protect the analysis for my patient.

References

Alexander, F. (1950) Analysis of the Therapeutic Factors in Psychoanalytic Treatment. *Psychoanal. Q.*, 19:482–500.

Aron, L. (2005) On the Unique Contribution of the Interpersonal Approach to Interaction. *Contemp. Psychoanal.*, 41:21–34.

Benjamin, J. (2000) Intersubjective Distinctions: Subjects and Persons, Recognitions and Breakdowns. *Psychoanal. Dial.* 10 (1):43–55.

Coburn, W. (2001) Subjectivity, Emotional Resonance, and the Sense of the Real, *Psychoanal. Psychol.*, 18:303–319.

164 *Courting the "real" and stumbling in "reality"*

Davies, L. M. (2009) Love Never Ends Well: Termination as the Fate of an Illusion: Commentary on Papers by Jill Salberg and Sue Grand. *Psychoanal. Dial.*, 19:734–743.

Fonagy, P. and Target, M. (1998) Mentalization and the Changing Aims of Child Psychoanalysis. *Psychoanal. Dial.*, 8:87–114.

Grand, S. (2009) Termination as Necessary Madness. *Psychoanal. Dial.*, 19:723–733.

Kohut, H. and Wolf, E. S. (1978) The Disorders of the Self and their Treatment: An Outline. *Int. Lara. Psycho-Anal.*, 59:413–425.

Mitchell, S. (2000) *Relationality: From Attachment to Intersubjectivity*. Hillsdale: Analytic Press.

Orange, D. (1995) *Emotional Understanding: Studies in Psychoanalytic Epistemology*. New York: Guilford Press.

Shane, M. and Gales, M. (1997) *Intimate Attachments*. New York: The Guilford Press.

Stern, S. (1994) Needed Relationships and Repeated Relationships: An Integrated Relational Perspective. *Psychoanal. Dial.*, 4:317–346.

Stern, S. (2002) The Self as a Relational Structure. *Psychoanal. Dial.*, 12:693–714.

Stern, S. (2011) The Therapeutic Action of Analytic Love: Commentary on Joye… *Int. Psychoanal. Self Psychol.*, 6:489–504.

Stern, D. N., Sander, L. W., Nahum, J. P., Harrison, A. M., Lyons-Ruth, K., Morgan, A. C., Bruschweiler-Stern, N., & Tronick, E. Z. (1998) *Int. J. Psychoanal.*, 79 (Pt5):903–921.

Summers, F. (2001) What I Do With What You Give Me. *Psychoanal. Psychol.*, 18:635–655.

Summers, F. (2012) Creating New Ways of Being and Relating. *Psychoanal. Dial.*, 22:143–161.

Tronick, E., Brushweller-Stern, N., Harrison, A. M., Lyons-Ruth, K., Morgan, A. C., Nahum, L. P., Sander, L., & Stern, D. N. (1998), Dyadically Expanded States of Consciousness and the Process of Therapeutic Change. *Infant Ment. Health Lara.*, 19:290–299.

11 Katherine

A long, hard case

Introduction

Each of us probably has one worst/hardest case, a patient whom, "had we only known," we never would have taken on. Mine is Katherine, the subject of this paper. My complex relationship with her—we've seen each other serially for over thirty years—has been "through thick and thin." Notwithstanding some lovely "thick," we have survived a preponderance of "thin." Our relationship has endured in different iterations and with varying frequency of meetings and changing therapeutic aims. It has forced me to examine and reexamine the complex connections between life contexts, theories, and clinical choices, forced me to ask exactly what Katherine and I are doing/are creating together. I have had to define for myself what constitutes a contemporary psychoanalysis

Katherine is a person to whom I am deeply attached, whom I love, and whom I also have hated intensely. Yet, in trying to tell our story, I find myself writing several disjunctive stories within stories. This is because our long relationship actually comprises several disparate relationships—complete with changing characters and contexts and evolving emotional needs—and like so much of life, it emerges as an endlessly changing patchwork rather than as a smoothly flowing tale. In fact, it seems to me that Katherine and I have been in multiple therapies together. This patchwork quality—the shifts and changes and multiplicity—of some long-term therapeutic relationships is a major interest of this paper.

However I think about Katherine and me, as a single story or as multiple chapters, I have surrendered to an intersubjective intimacy with her that, while precious to me, sometimes also feels professionally suspect. At least, I worry about that. As a result, our work together has challenged, stretched, and sometimes shredded my basic identity as psychologist and analyst, pushing me continuously to revise my foundational analytic assumptions and beliefs. I will present here some of my resulting thoughts about the experience of profound intersubjective connection and the psychoanalytic pursuit.

Let me begin with a dialogue and a narrative that occurred during Katherine's last suicidal depression about five years ago. This was the worst of many depressions that Katherine suffered and that I witnessed, and the dialogue is a good example of a "thin" moment in our relationship.

166 *Katherine*

Notes from June 2005

Early this morning I pick up Katherine's middle-of-the night suicide call, and then I battle an aggressive busy signal until afternoon, vainly trying to reach her. The operator says her phone is off its hook.

"Thank you so much for not calling me back. I so appreciate your caring. Click." This is the blunt and sarcastic message that Katherine has just left for me. I immediately call her back, and this time the phone rings into voicemail. Foiled again! I leave my own edgy message, "For God's sake, Katherine, I've called and called, and all I got was a busy signal. I'm worried about you."

I am upset by the frequency of Katherine's angry messages. My head feels hot inside and full to bursting. For protection, I make jokes to myself. I call Katherine's daily voicemail barrage her "love songs," music in a minor key, played on a cracked and broken instrument. "Dr. Joye, what kind of doctor are you? Why can't you help me? Click." "Just tell me one thing I have to live for. And don't say Eliza. She'd do just fine with her father; she doesn't need me one bit. Click." "I don't want to be here. Click." "Just give me one good reason to endure this. Click." "I suppose you're off having a fine day. I think I should go to the hospital, but you're not there to tell me how to do it." Click, click, click.

When I finally reach her, I find a different Katherine, contrite and vulnerable. Her softened tone sounds entirely different from the sharp, angry, challenging voicemails.

"Dr. Joye, thanks so much for your message. I'm having trouble with the phone company—the unpaid bill—and they shut off my calls and voicemail. I got mad and threw the phone. I had to fight with some desk jockey until I got my service back. And then I felt so paralyzed, I couldn't pick up your calls."

"Bad day."

"Duh! I can't find a reason to be here. I have fifty dollars in the bank, and it's the first of the month bills. My head is godawful, the buzzing. Eliza would be better off without me."

And then she tells me what she did last night for her daughter Eliza. The girl belongs to a bicycle club that had scheduled a midnight ride through the city. Not feeling comfortable with the 13-year-old going alone, and not wanting to disappoint her, Katherine had borrowed a bike and followed the group for twenty-five miles in the dark. She, Katherine, who in her depressed state can barely get off the couch, has done this! After a moment of silence, Katherine says, "I appreciate your call. Thanks so much. I'll see you on Monday."

I feel tears pulse in my throat as I hang up, and then I notice the time. It is after 6 p.m., and Saturday, my day off, is shot.

Her ragged state shifts, anger, self-loathing, senses of betrayal and abandonment, exquisite psychic pain, suicidal longings, deep attachment capacities, and ambivalent attitudes toward agency and responsibility; my impatience, annoyance, resentment, and concern for her—all are present in this enactment. When I presented this dialogue at a professional conference, some colleagues commended me for hanging in with Katherine, for pursuing her through the dark tunnel of her depression in order to reach her and check on her safety. But others challenged me. What do I think I'm doing here? This is not psychoanalysis! What's with my scolding tone in the message I left? Why would I take so much responsibility for reaching her, for chasing her until I'm out of patience? What about her responsibility? Why don't I confront her angry tone and aggressive behavior? And the unkindest question of all: how does such a long treatment result in such emotional shambles?

Some history

Rescuing Katherine from suicide long ago has left me tethered to her. Having saved her life once, I feel unaccountably, unwillingly, but undeniably responsible for it. And I expect that I already felt that way even before the suicide attempt. I guess this is a problematic condition for a psychoanalyst. Or is it?

Katherine's certainly has not been an appealing life or one to which I like being bound. It began in poverty and squalor, neglect, and sexual exploitation. As a child Katherine was taught neither how the world works nor moral and ethical choices and values. In her home there was no inspiration, curiosity, or hope. The music and poetry of life drowned there in censure, sarcasm, and curses. Katherine grew up in spiritual poverty, a lost child in a large family where the boys left home early; where the girls had babies in their teens; and where one sister drowned because the baby's father, Katherine's stepfather, left the 3-year-old to bathe alone while he ran out to buy some needed smokes.

Katherine fled to the United States, made it through college, and has struggled to work productively. However, in addition to terrible luck, she suffers from chronic depression, periodically broken by acute black periods and a patterned history of lousy choices. Her life exemplifies the predictive strength of negative identifications and expectations. Here is an example: a friend's older brother raped Katherine when she was 14. Since that night she calls herself "a f—k in the dark," a sickening metaphor that captures feelings of self-loathing and worthlessness, the sense of being exploitable, alone, and nothing. Katherine has consistently chosen men who treat her that way. For thirty years she has withdrawn from or behaved coldly toward most people, hoarding her deepest affections and then squandering them on a man we call "Him."

"Him," the object of Katherine's desire, is a gifted, sexy, and charismatic musician who steals her money, sees other women, and marries some of them serially. Periodically, he deserts Katherine as he did during the Christmas preceding the depression recorded above. That Christmas without Him—without his call, gift, or fleeting thought—began Katherine's emotional slide. I have loathed the torch Katherine has carried for Him and its sickening song: "Oh, my man I love him so-o-o!"

Thirty-two years ago when she first came to see me, lithe and lovely and new to L.A., I had heart and hope for Katherine. This was early in her pursuit

168 *Katherine*

of Him but not too soon to read the writing on the wall. She entered therapy in despair and rage over his first desertion. She had the opaque, "I-dare-you" eyes of the seriously depressed.

To me she brought her pain and depression, and on me she displaced her rage. For the first seven months of our relationship our meetings took a predictable shape: after a few brief niceties and the imparting of some scanty information, Katherine would settle into a cold and rocky—and sometimes sad—silence. Although she was either unable or unwilling to respond to my many inquiries, she would stare and/or glare unhappily at me. In each session as consuming silence swallowed up all inquiry, Katherine would become increasingly anxious and frustrated. Then, the minutes would tick by glacially; and shortly before the session's end, with a troubled scowl on her face, she would storm out abruptly, leaving me with reverberations from my slammed office gate. Invariably Katherine would call me later to apologize, tearful and remorseful, enacting, I came to understand later, the dynamic arc of an abusive, frustrated, emotionally arid, and claustrophobic relationship. A psychological Apache dance with me as one of the Apaches!

At the time I was fairly new to the therapy game, just beginning a private practice with the excited curiosity and sense of new discovery in every encounter. Probably, my excitement and curiosity made it possible for me to tolerate—barely—what seemed like a vast desert of silence. Although jangling, Katherine's noisy leave takings were relieving punctuations for me to these painful silent expanses. Yet, even at this early stage in my clinical development, a part of me was interested in observing and understanding the meaning of the sudden shifts in Katherine's moods and behaviors. I could not yet conceptualize and name the legacy of trauma: dissociation and disregulation of affects, psychic states, and behaviors.

In reaction to my training at an orthodox psychoanalytic facility—where the therapeutic ideal was a bad version of intellectualized ego psychology—I had taken enthusiastically to Bowlby's new notions about universal attachment needs and to Kohut's ideas about the centrality of affect and selfobject experience both in development and therapy. With Katherine, Kohut was especially helpful; his ideas lent me some structural support. In working with her I tried to be—and mainly was—interested, empathic, and inquiring. I also was frequently confused and discouraged by my patient's lack of progress and about my role in ameliorating her distress.

In hindsight, Kohut's idea of empathy as the ruling therapeutic tool—and the shape it provided to my thinking and clinical behavior—helped me to stay present with Katherine through a slew of doubts about our progress, the process, and my therapeutic competence. The steadying power of theory! That empathy, this basic and necessary therapeutic tool, may operate differently for every dyad and may underlie many forms of therapeutic action was not yet clear to me. Nevertheless, although I now have many additional ways to conceptualize my relationship with Katherine, self psychology provided me

Katherine 169

a scaffold for my early work with her and cemented my appreciation for the utility of theory when one feels mired in relational quicksand.

After many months, Katherine suddenly asked me, "How can you stand this?" This was her first relational gesture toward me, my first inkling that I might exist as a separate person for her. I told her that the silence and angry exits were hard for me, but that I wanted to know her. I added that she often seemed lost and alone, hidden, and I trusted that some part of her wanted me to find her.

Slowly, Katherine responded to my interest and attention. Having somebody intent on knowing her came to matter so much to Katherine that if she didn't have carfare—in the days before she owned a car—she would walk the eight miles from Laurel Canyon to my Encino office. Her responsibility for getting to our twice-weekly sessions assuaged my doubts about the value of what we were doing. I told myself, "Something about this must matter if she knocks herself out to get here." It seemed that whatever nurturing I was offering, Katherine was thirsty for it.

The central issue that sealed our relationship concerned Katherine's multivalent feelings about her mother, and my recognition and acceptance of those feelings. The mother, who suffered two bad marriages and delivered seven children, was a caretaking slave. Katherine remembers her never-ending labor: sewing clothes, preparing meals, and washing and hanging out to dry the large family's mountain of laundry. In addition, the mother occasionally held outside menial jobs to make ends meet. All of this left her pretty much physically exhausted and emotionally empty when it came to Katherine and the other children. She was undemonstrative, emotionally vacant, and, worst of all, passive and silent in the face of her second husband's cruelty toward Katherine. For example, while Katherine was at school, the rage filled stepfather shot the girl's beloved dog. The mother feigned ignorance about the killing and never talked to Katherine about the killing or attempted to comfort her.

The mother seems also to have been intellectually dry and incapable of imagining Katherine's curious mind let alone nourishing it. As though she had run out of fuel for living, she was similarly passive and stalled in the rest of her life. Katherine doesn't remember her mother reading anything or listening to music or ever dressing up, save for one evening out with the stepfather when Katherine was 4 years old. The barrenness of the mother's mind deprived Katherine of vital mirroring experiences, leaving her psychically desolate and emotionally and behaviorally disorganized—in short, hopelessly confused about the meanings of her life experience.

On the good side, the mother was kind, never critical or blaming, and she appreciated Katherine's needed domestic help. "You're a good helper," was the only compliment that Katherine remembers from her mother. As the second oldest and most responsible child, Katherine assisted the mother with the housework and the little children; she wanted to support her mother emotionally.

170   *Katherine*

And so, in the transference when Katherine enacted with me the wild oscillations in feelings toward and responses to her mother: affection and responsibility, longing, pity and contempt, withdrawal and silence, and outright hatred and rage, she registered that I not only understood the swings, but also could emotionally tolerate these gyrations in feeling, mood, and behavior. I imagine that my tolerance was expressed mostly non-verbally in my facial expressions, vocal rhythms and tone, and the myriad cross-modal matchings and recognition tokens and gestures described by infant researchers. Certainly, back in the 1980s I didn't have the language that I have now to describe recognition/mentalizing processes.[1]

Although this paper is primarily a description of Katherine's and my relationship, I will insert here a word about therapeutic action. Whatever its origins, my capacity to recognize and accept the full sweep and depth and thickness of Katherine's emotions; my capacity to understand and articulate her intentions and motives; and my willingness to participate in enactments with her until their meanings emerged—all of this profoundly affected her, providing a balm for her lifelong loneliness and emotional suffering. The impact of careful listening and emotional joining and understanding amazed me at the time; in fact, it still does.

As our relationship deepened over time, Katherine simultaneously began to acknowledge the pain of her first family and seemed better able to reorganize her feeling states and to regulate her ragged mood and behavioral shifts. And I think my recognition—expressed in myriad implicit ways as well as articulated explicitly—also confirmed intuitions and truths that she already knew in a shadowed way. Our illuminating them intersubjectively enabled her to own them consciously and, thereby, to feel more real and able to manage her adult life. This is the healing process that Winnicott, Benjamin, Fonagy, Hastings and many others write about. Katherine and I lived it together; and in doing so, she began to call me her "American mother."

For my part, I had my own mother issues. Although vastly paler than Katherine's, mine had some similar themes. My mother was a busy and vibrant woman who had scant emotional interest in her bookish little girl. Like Katherine, I became the good and helpful child in the hope of earning her attention and love. Until her death, I stayed close to home and to my mother, mostly in a caretaker's role, always trying to improve the quality of our attachment, to negotiate some degree of intimacy and recognition with/from her, and to avail myself of the vitality that she lavished on others. This strategy worked: as our roles shifted over the years, I did receive more affection and love—and even glimmers of recognition—from my mother.

Comparing my experience and accommodating coping responses with Katherine's, and noting her will to life and health and new experience—a will that drove her at a young age far away from her impoverished family and culture in spite of strong counter forces—I was left feeling admiration and awe for her fierce pursuit of a better life and for her courage. Yet, I also realized that, however imperfect and strained, I did have a psychic home with my mother while she had none with hers. Therefore, the fact that she and I came to create a sense of home together seems to be the miracle of our long relationship.

With the lilting language that is her Irish inheritance, Katherine began to keep a journal in our first year together. It was lively and original, thoughtful and humorous. This journal contrasted dramatically with the long, sullen silences that began our relationship, and the muttered anger and slamming of my gate that accompanied her early leave-takings. Over the years she has entrusted me with twenty-three volumes of this journal for safekeeping. I came to feel that this was another way that I helped to hold her relational life; for a while I became a guardian and champion of her memories.

Early on, Katherine lapped up new experience—books, music, theater—as a desert nomad drinks at an oasis. I picture her glowing face that first year as she described an Ella Fitzgerald concert. However, her vivid journal and joy in aesthetic experience stand in stark contrast to the general way she conducted her life. When she began therapy, she did not get along with people, socially or in any of her short-lived jobs. In her sessions she told me repetitive stories of hurtful and enraging interactions with people: stupid people, mean people, people who either didn't understand or respect her or who behaved in snobby and superior ways. She shifted between shyness, bleak feelings of self-doubt, moments of grandiosity, and times of awful contempt for others. In response to perceived bad treatment, Katherine would sometimes explode. Her raging outbursts would regularly blast through the depression that dammed her life, a depression of despairing moods like viscous, muddy logjams clogging her natural flow.

During her on-again-off-again relationship with "Him," there have been other men like him. Men, who have attracted Katherine, have invariably been handsome, cool and smooth, at first, and then, later, cruel and dismissive. Once she read me a love letter from a different sort of man, an obviously smitten romantic. The letter was light and funny, complimentary and engaging, filled with smart and apt images and illusions. I imagined its author to be one potentially great guy. Katherine was scornful and disgusted that a perfect stranger could "wear his presumptuous heart on his sleeve." She, of course, spurned him with the same cruelty and disregard that she herself suffered at the hands of her slick boyfriends.

I was initially attracted to Katherine mostly because she was different from me in compelling ways. Her heart was more bruised than mine, and both her gumption and attachment needs greater. And, of course, there were many other subtle but magnetic qualities—complementary to mine—that attracted my subjectivity but elude concrete description. These qualities reside in the realm of the implicit.

Here are some concrete differences. Of a different national and cultural background from me, she was far from home and often homesick. I, of course, was rooted in and engaged with my native culture. Over the years Katherine has learned and taught me a great deal about her cultural history, traditions,

172　*Katherine*

and art. Katherine was also as different from me physically as one could imagine. While I am short-statured and have average good looks, she is unusually beautiful: very tall with long graceful feet and hands that made me think of dance and music. In her early twenties Katherine's slender body and young girl's perfect rosy and innocent face had attracted modeling offers in Dublin, London, and New York. Her haughty refusals, we came to see, reflected her self-doubt rather than any lack of desire. Her beauty intrigued me; powerful beauty arouses my envy and curiosity.

Katherine also thought, behaved, and even smelled differently from me. Her scent was foreign, complex and musky, and at its center a reminder of exotic plants and damp earth. At its edges, there was a faint sweetness that lingered in my office for hours after a session. Katherine shared this scent with two important people in my life, and I am sure that is one reason I felt drawn to her. What we had in common was love of language, doubt-ridden longings for self-improvement, aesthetic passions, intense desire for new experience, and pleasure in shared personal moments.

I hated Katherine's cruelty; yet, this cruelty also aroused and drew my curiosity and somehow tightened the bonds between us. I am a fairly mild and mostly kind person. Whether because of compassion for its childhood sources or unexplored and disowned aspects of myself or both or some other reasons, I found Katherine's cruelty shocking and magnetizing of my attention. And while I knew that it derived from—in fact, imitated and illuminated—her life of bad treatment, I still hated and was fascinated by it. She seemed to take pleasure in hurting others, particularly the inflated Los Angeles types that one finds in the entertainment industry. While relating to me some cutting personal put down she had made to this man or that, she would come alive, the vitality sudden and surprising and filled with color. She only expressed shame or guilt when she had injured an innocent creature. In the grip of what she used to call her "slash and burn" mode, Katherine has abused stray cats in her care. Once in grief—I feel sick remembering—she confessed to throwing some newborn kittens against the wall, and, then, horrified, picking up the dead, twisted creatures in the hopeless wish to revive them. Such impulsivity and rage, reactive to her sense of impotence and resonant of the hated stepfather, testify to Katherine's inheritance of trauma and violence. At times I have been the focus of Katherine's cruelty and always, later, of her remorse and penitence.

Suicide

Our big rupture occurred twenty-two years ago during Katherine's first profound depression, an episode cued, of course, by a disappointment with "Him." By this time, over six years into our work, Katherine was functioning better in her work and personal life, some of the sharp, unregulated edges of her feelings and behavior having softened a bit. She could also name and understand the underlying reasons and meanings of her depression. Yet, although she had come to trust my constancy and concern, our relationship did not provide enough ballast to keep Katherine from sinking into a deep depression with an attendant loss of agency. Katherine felt herself to be drowning and powerless to save herself. I felt worried and a rumbling foreboding.

At this point I suggested that she try a new kind of antidepressant receiving widespread public attention, and Katherine agreed to take Prozac. Although I had only read a little about SSRI medicines, my worry for Katherine and my interest in scientific brain exploration prompted this recommendation. Nevertheless, this simple suggestion caused me conflict because recommending an antidepressant in 1987 defied prevailing psychoanalytic practice. I suppose I was looking over my shoulder for the analytic truant officer, who would punish my truancy from some psychoanalytic ideal. While intellectually distrustful of doctrinal purity for its own sake and the ways in which orthodoxy of all kinds constrains possibilities, back then I was emotionally a worried psychoanalytic child wanting to please my analytic elders.

At first the Prozac seemed to work miraculously. Katherine said, as lifetime depressives new to the medicine often do, "This must be how normal people feel." Then, just as suddenly as it worked, its potency failed, and Katherine was deeply depressed again. I learned later that all along she had been drinking a lot of alcohol, been taking the medicine in a haphazard, spotty way, and then had simply discontinued its use. Nevertheless, her dramatic first response to the drug strongly confirmed that at least part of what Katherine and I were dealing with was her brain chemistry.

On New Years Eve 1988, I picked up a message from her, "I've taken the bottle of Prozac, another bottle of Seconal, and I'm sipping champagne. This isn't a bad way to die. Happy New Year." When I called her back, my heart in a knot, nobody answered. Without thinking, I automatically called 911 and reported her suicide.

Katherine could not forgive me for meddling. Two days after the suicide attempt, finding herself surprisingly alive and impossibly debt-ridden—what with all the new medical bills—she screamed at me by phone for ruining her life. "Drop dead," she cursed. When she left the hospital, she refused to see me; and for about five years I lost touch with her. With my physical ties to Katherine cut, I felt both relieved and quietly worried about her during that time.

My intervention on Katherine's suicide attempt somehow has joined me irrevocably to her. The decision to call the police, although mandated legally for psychologists, nevertheless felt to me like a final commitment of responsibility to our relationship. It turned out to have a similar meaning for Katherine. And so, while I didn't see Katherine for many years after the intervention, I kept her in my mind and heart. Many years later, after she was a parent, Katherine admitted that beyond her anger about my calling the police, she knew my action was an ultimately loving and responsible one.

174 *Katherine*

New contexts, new treatment strategies

Finding herself pregnant, Katherine called me again eighteen years ago. During the conversation she told me that she was doing well professionally; and, given that the birth father was a jerk, she had decided to have and raise the child as a single parent. She said, "I'm going to need mothering help, and you're it." I heard many things in this direct and presumptive demand: her clear need, her old distrust of the world, her self-doubts and fears along with a wish to be a good mother, her assuming of adult responsibility, and her respect for my nurturing capacity.

Over the succeeding years, I did consult with her regularly, sometimes in my office and sometimes by phone, and mainly kept her parenting as our therapeutic focus. My memory of the dead kittens furnished all the motivation I needed to help her in mothering her little girl. I hoped that together we could break the generational chain of mutilated babies in her family. At the same time, I trusted that Katherine's native resources and our relationship—the real working space that we had created together, which Katherine had begun to call her "American home"—would carry us through her daughter Eliza's childhood.

In the course of the parenting work, we did reconstructive personal exploration and first family exhumation. Yet, looking back, I see that during this period, we mostly dealt with the practical exigencies of Katherine's life. I felt conflict over this choice because of my competing professional identities. I wanted, at once, to be a good therapist to Katherine and also to meet some imagined psychoanalytic ideal. While I intuitively understood that contexts matter and should organize one's therapeutic strategies; and while the contexts at this time required practical focus, I still felt torn and guilty. Over time I have reconciled the conflict, coming to believe that my choice to focus on Katherine's mothering was consistent with maintaining a genuine empathic bridge with her; it reflected what I imagined Katherine wanted and needed from me.

Eighteen years ago Katherine needed lots of practical help. Her baby was born with a serious birth anomaly—since resolved—that required the attention of medical specialists; and, of course, Katherine experienced all the attendant worry and stress that such conditions confer on parents. I helped her to negotiate the knots of the medical world and to develop interpersonal skills that advanced good relationships with helping people, relationships that, in turn, advanced Baby Eliza's interests. My help included advice giving and role-playing, neither of which is analytic in any traditional sense. But for a lonely, frightened soul in alien territory with a daunting task to accomplish, I believe that my practical help was the "affectively needed" response. To go a step further, I also believe that withholding my practical know-how would have been morally wrong.

Perhaps I was afraid of another suicide episode, or maybe, remembering my own first years as a floundering mother, I determined that Katherine mainly needed practical life consultation and child-rearing support. My sense jibed with the focus of inquiry that Katherine set in our sessions: usually she would begin with some immediate, concrete question or challenge, and we would problem-solve. The process included Katherine's memories and associations but in the context of the immediate practical concern. In any case, I do not remember this period as one of formal intense therapy with Katherine, and I joke that my role with her became some combination of quasi grandmother, quasi life coach, quasi charm school instructor. So, what was I to her? As she puts it, I became her "peep" (as in people). In retrospect, this period—in which my connection to and concern about her and her child grew—enlarged the expanse and depth of our intersubjective relationship. As Katherine came to imagine her child's mind, it seems she also began to imagine mine.

The theoretical and clinical flexibility that I adopted with Katherine—our tailoring our therapy to the needs and contexts of her life—often felt to me like a sinful betrayal of some imagined psychoanalytic father. In my imagination, this father was like some massive Old Testament prophet, who punished disobedience with potent weapons of guilt and shame. I subsequently learned that disobedient analysts have surreptitiously made adaptations to analytic ground rules since the birth of the field.

Notwithstanding the changes in frame, I believe that overall I maintained a consistent analytic sensibility with Katherine: trying to keep our relationship openly curious about the meanings of her life experience and attentive to the vicissitudes in our relationship, the strains and nicks and variations in the thickness and flexibility of the connection. In fact, my long relationship with Katherine supports my conviction, as Howard Bacal has so eloquently urged, that every analysis is unique and requires procedures specific to the needs and contexts of the dyad (2003); and, as Donna Orange has suggested, we must hold our theories lightly. I would add that sometimes we have to juggle multiple theories for the benefit of our work.

S—t happens

Things might have continued in this way indefinitely had an uninsured drunk driver not critically injured Katherine a decade ago. At that time, with some lapses, Katherine was living more successfully than at any previous period in her life. Although still collecting grievances, she was managing a professional life, had some friends and community connections, and was taking good care of her daughter Eliza, an easy, sunny, and gratifying 9-year-old. Indeed, she had developed into an interested and engaged mother. For me, Katherine's development seemed to validate the usefulness of our strange, long-term therapeutic relationship.

At first, the accident arrested her life; and, then, in a short time, it hurled Katherine into a maelstrom of physical and economic trials. The initial physical toll was dreadful: a broken hip, shattered arm, and fractured skull, all of which healed quickly. The long-term effects seemed devastating. The accident had left

176 *Katherine*

Katherine with extensive and elusive brain injuries. Initially, she lost double digits of I.Q points along with the ability to remember, plan, and sequence tasks very well. Her vision and hearing were impaired and her gait wobbly. She was expressively aphasic; and a strange static in her brain, noisy and relentless, caused her to feel disoriented in public and irritable in private. Because she could not concentrate for long on any task, just planning her daughter's day tapped all her resources. Saddest of all for me, Katherine had lost her great writing gift. Miraculously, though, the substance of Katherine—the whatness, the whereness, and the humanity—seemed still intact. I attribute this to the integrity of her emotional brain, those structures deep inside the brain somehow spared in the neurological wreckage of the accident.

The accident and its avalanche of consequences confirmed for Katherine every negative expectation that she had collected and harbored over a lifetime. In spite of her dark vision, at first she mobilized healthy resources to recover physically in order to care for her child. Unable to work, she received a pittance of money from Workman's Compensation, an insufficient amount to provide economically for herself or her intellectually and musically gifted teenager. The resulting economic straits exacerbated a number of other contributing factors that led to a devastating depression four years after the accident. During this time the state did pay me a small fee for our sessions because Katherine was a victim of a violent crime.

At the time of her depressive illness, she was waiting for a permanent financial settlement from Workman's Compensation, a waiting process, by the way, which felt interminable and Kafkaesque. Nevertheless, Katherine, extremely frugal and inventive, somehow put amazing things together for her child, finding special schools and music camps and scholarships and even scraping together some extra pennies for spending money. The responsible Katherine never totally disappeared, but I confess that I helped Katherine out financially during this time, buying Eliza a violin, for example. Whatever traditional therapeutic frame still existed was severely cracked and compromised.

Now Katherine was tapped out, exhausted and suffering from battle fatigue. "Him," the man who has obsessed her for most of her adulthood, had intermittently been helpful to her during the first years after her accident. He had called regularly and visited her on infrequent trips to Los Angeles. However, newly divorced for a short time, he had apparently entered into a new love affair and abandoned Katherine for the umpteenth time in their agonizing relationship. Initially, she felt devastated but energized by rage, a moment exemplified in the dialogue that began this paper. Shortly, however, the heat of rage became frozen into paralysis.

Let me describe our pivotal appointment over five years ago. Her depression announced itself in Katherine's smell before I even saw her. In her unkempt, greasy hair and on her unwashed body, the strange sweetness of her scent had turned fulsome and putrid. Even on the phone, listening to one of Katherine's stinging "love songs," I could sometimes smell this strong and sickening scent. Katherine also looked ghastly, grey ghostly, and I found myself vainly searching her drawn face and skeletal body for the lost, exquisite girl. Unable to eat, sleep, or rouse herself from the couch, she had no heart for self-care. "This is what happens when agency collapses," I thought.

Today her suicidal plans required drastic action. "I want my medicine back," she said.

"But you gave it to me for safekeeping," I answered.

"You don't have to trouble yourself about it anymore."

I experienced a flash of knowing: "If Katherine leaves here alone, I will never see her again." My last threads of therapeutic restraint loosened; unbound ground rules splintered and flew to the wind; and I abandoned any effort to retrieve them. I left all remaining pieces of our shattered therapeutic frame scattered on my office floor. Cancelling all my day's appointments, I drove Katherine to the hospital; and as part of the agreement for her going, I made complicated arrangements for Eliza's care, mobilizing all of the family's willing social connections. Then I picked up the girl at school, explained about her mother, and bought her a burger. Bye, bye to analyst neutrality!

The hospital stay was fortunate. California, which had skimped on providing Katherine subsistence financial support, popped for a two-month hospitalization. There a creative psychiatrist devised a chemical concoction that included a stimulant along with a mood stabilizer and antidepressant and anti-anxiety agents. The combination worked; Katherine perked up; and for years she remained scrupulously compliant with the cocktail. During her stay I visited several times and engaged with her in conversation about life and death. Whatever the factors in whatever proportion—a needed respite from pressure and responsibility, chemical help, community response to her illness, my reliable presence—Katherine decided for the first time in her life to choose life consciously.

Here are some reflections that I wrote a year after Katherine's hospitalization:

> It is a year later, and some things seem dramatically altered while some things remain old and familiar. Most puzzling, Katherine has relinquished "Him." Despite some frantic courting on his part, he no longer exerts any emotional hold on her. Go figure! Katherine has also retained some of the inner quiet that she gained in hospital, and she has expanded her life horizons to include a regular exercise program, better nutrition, and new social activities. She has joined a singing group, and attends free jazz concerts every week. I like that she now initiates plans and makes choices. Her settlement with the state is pending and promises to leave her minimally safe financially. With me she is consistently appreciative and respectful, behavior that marks a radical change from the old unpredictable anger and sarcasm. It seems that she has erected and observes careful boundaries with me now, probably, I imagine, in response to the collapse of our frame last year. In turn, I am relieved that we have reconstructed a fairly traditional therapeutic frame.

178 *Katherine*

Yet—and this is the big yet—Katherine still hates being alive. She calls her life "purgatory," an ironic term, she notes, "… since I don't believe in any meaning and salvation beyond leaving behind a somewhat healthy child. I don't want to be here and sure won't be sorry when it's over."

If Katherine is a Job without faith, I wonder who I am to her in the face of her horrible misfortunes. Am I a friend, a comforter, or a thorn in her side, a tormenter who reminds her that there are fortunate people living in relative comfort, health, safety, and optimism? At times, I feel self-conscious and embarrassed that I live a good and lucky life. I guess I suffer from "Thrivers' Guilt," knowing that, if truth be told, Katherine must resent me.

And who is she to me? Toward her and her situation I carry a confused tangle of feelings, feelings whose colors often run together in a chromatic mess. When I can differentiate the colors, they sweep across a broader spectrum than my usual therapeutic range, and some of them wear the darker hues of anger, guilt, shame, and especially worry. Sometimes I feel compassion and sometimes pity for Katherine, but mostly I am angry. I feel enraged at her cruel and neglectful parents. I feel enraged at an uncaring social structure that allows a hard working and responsible adult to fall through the cracks of civilization into an invisible and impoverished underclass. I feel enraged at presumptuous people who, because she does not look neurologically impaired, do not see the extent of Katherine's injuries and suspect that she is a malingerer. Such folks proffer helpful advice such as, "You'll feel much better when you're back at work." And I feel especially enraged because I am Katherine's sole emotional support.

I worry about Katherine's future and about her daughter and frequently wrestle with impulses to help her beyond what is reasonable or possible given our therapeutic and my personal economic limits. And I struggle with both my peculiar feelings of responsibility toward her and my shame about my extra-therapeutic behavior, behavior that seems to me beyond the bounds of even the most relaxed or expanded therapeutic frame. I worry about what I will need to do for Eliza in the event that Katherine dies. Her birth father is an absent speck on the complicated map of her life. Yes, I worry about Eliza very much.

I also puzzle about how to be helpful to Katherine given the long, complicated, and compromised nature of our therapeutic bond. For example, I hate her bleak view and negation of life and wonder why our relationship has seemingly made no dent in her attitude. Sometimes I feel resentful that my hard work has produced such ambiguous and/or puny results. And, of course, my resentment raises questions about the very bedrock goals of my life's work: what is the moral thrust of psychoanalysis? For too long I have seen Katherine for a very low fee or, at times, no fee at all, and I also resent that. Worst of all, sometimes in my helplessness, I wish that I had never known Katherine or that she would magically disappear. I feel guilty about these thoughts. And I feel most ashamed when I wonder—and I do wonder—whether I did Katherine a favor that long ago New Years Eve.

Update and reflections

The early dialogue and this last narration should gracefully bracket the relational story of Katherine and me. But real life intrudes, and in six years the contexts and conditions of Katherine's life have radically changed again. Needless to say, our work together is in yet another iteration. We are currently doing serious recapitulation and reflection on our relationship in preparation for a termination in the yet-to-be-set but foreseeable future. In the process Katherine's buried memories and feelings are tumbling out with linguistic urgency and force that were previously unimaginable. Katherine has found her voice.

And there is a new depth and transparency in our interactions that surprise me in their realness and intensity. I'm even preparing to speak to Katherine about the dead kittens, a subject that in all these years I could never bring myself to address with her. The horror of it has always been too active and alive for me to speak about out loud. In its final chapter our therapy is finally a full-blown, recognizable contemporary psychoanalysis.

To put it briefly, Katherine's life has assumed a relatively peaceful and settled shape. After firing two incompetent lawyers, Katherine found an able Workmen's Compensation attorney, who fashioned a settlement that affords her a reasonable and secure standard of living. Given Katherine's lifetime of economic worry, the blessed effects of this security cannot be overstated. That she can provide for herself and her off-to-college child—and still have a few nickels in her pocket to attend a concert or buy a Starbuck's coffee on occasion—improves and regulates her moods and emotions and softens the lines in her face. The benefits from the change in her material life remind me that we analysts sometimes miss the profound impact of social, economic, and cultural conditions on our patients.

While she still has a dark view of the world, and probably always will, Katherine no longer wants to die. In fact, she has shown no serious depressive symptoms for about four years; and under her psychiatrist's supervision, she has weaned herself off medicine in the past year.

The family's more comfortable material circumstances and Katherine's improved moods and outlook coincided with Eliza's middle adolescence, which mother and daughter have both enjoyed. Eliza, independent, competent, and considerate by nature and experience—the periodic necessity of caring for a depressed parent—has grown to be a disciplined and talented kid. She loves her mother but is well into her own separate life. Not only does she have a more buoyant temperament than Katherine, she is also graced with her mom's good looks and a humorous and sweet presence that is attractive and endearing to others. She has just left for college on scholarship where she still plans to study music and violin. As Eliza's ersatz grandmother, I am breathing lighter and feeling great pleasure.

Because she is unable to work, Katherine is studying musicology. She also volunteers time, teaching and coaching disadvantaged children in a community

180 *Katherine*

music program. Except for some chafing relationships with fellow students and colleagues—lifetime patterns do not change easily—she is mostly pleased with her pursuits, has made some friends, and experiences enhanced self-esteem.

For two years Katherine has been seeing a new man, Mr. W. (for Wonderful) who is, paradoxically, like and unlike "Him." Another troubled jazz musician with little psychological sophistication, he nevertheless has a decent character and genuinely seems to love Katherine. However, his own economic pressures as well as parent, child, and work demands prevent him from committing to much beyond seeing Katherine a couple of times a week. Given Katherine's basically introverted temperament and her fear of and difficulty with intimacy, this mostly works for her. And though she still longs for more from him, she is loath to ask for anything. The power of repetition is awesome; and, of course, we explore the repetitive patterns recurring with Mr. W.

As the therapeutic part of our relationship draws to a close, I have written this in appreciation of Katherine's commitment to our work and for all that it has taught me about the analytic process. Before I was a psychoanalyst and through the most behaviorally-oriented periods in my work with Katherine; at those times when I observed strict analytic ground rules and at others when I bent and twisted the frame; and through my many roles with Katherine—that of young and interested therapist, worried and threatened therapist, parent consultant, grandma, career coach, booster, and mature analyst—certain enduring analytic attitudes about therapeutic action informed this relationship.

These include, first, that the empathic listening stance transcends theory and clinical choices. It matters to be in the company of another who wants to understand the world through your eyes; that is, someone who cares to experience the world through the lens of your percepts, experiences, memories, emotions, and values. No matter that empathy is subjectively qualified and imperfect, a reasonable approximation of empathy, consistently present and applied over time, can be psychologically transforming. Second, two minds working together intersubjectively—to understand and to know each and the other and the contexts of their joint beings—may create subjective and relational expansion and reorganization that cannot happen for either mind in solitude. The consequent ability to articulate and think about the unique place that one occupies in one's relational and social worlds fosters increased senses of coherence, solidity, choice, and agency. And, finally, once begun, the privilege of ending an analytic therapy belongs to the patient solely. A corollary: once committed, the analyst is bound to stay the course "through thick and thin."

Conclusion

In this paper I have tried not only to memorialize Katherine's and my relationship, but also to illustrate some of the things I learned about analysis from our work. I have tried to show that in our long and complex analytic process, what appears to be a single therapy was, in fact, multiple, related therapies. Katherine's and my changing therapeutic dyad embodied a host of relational configurations that each of us brought/created as well as innumerable separate and joint historical and contextual influences and experiences. As the contexts interacted and changed, it felt as though new therapies emerged unbidden, complete with new players and therapeutic tasks. It turned out that flexibility with theory and clinical procedure was a frequent challenge and necessity.

From my work with Katherine—and others—I am persuaded that rather than representing absolute truth about anything, theories have instrumental utility: an effective therapeutic approach in one context may not be helpful in another. A corollary is that therapy should provide needed affective responsiveness—regardless of theory—in order to foster an expanding relational matrix. What the needed affective response may be at any given moment is relationally and contextually organized and, therefore, always in flux and frequently subject to dramatic shifts. For example, early in our work, Katherine simply needed mirroring affective responses. A bit later, she profited from hearing titrated bits of my experience with her, profited from my taking what Fosshage terms, an "other-centered" listening stance (1997).

If the implied upshot of my thinking is an unwieldy mess of variables in play at any moment—all of these factors in recursive interaction with each other—it follows that each analytic relationship represents a continual transformative process. It is a process that reaches for some unique organization—or, at least, periodic soft assembly.

The metaphor that comes to mind is of a collaborative symphony. The development of a long-term dynamic therapy is similar to the construction of a musical symphony, in which innumerable complex musical elements and instruments organize around shifting and recurring themes, variations, tones, sometimes dramatically different but related movements, and a development and whole that are greater than the additive sum of the constituent parts. What issues emerge in analysis as relevant, what relationship configurations become not only manifest but salient, how the couple resolves individual and intersubjective glitches, where such resolutions lead the pair over time are all emergent phenomena. I have tried to illustrate this observation in describing Katherine and myself.

In our relationship, Katherine and I developed a tight and facilitative co-transference, in which, among my many roles, I have predominantly played "nurturing mother" and "wise woman" for Katherine and "loving grandma" for Eliza. These particular relationship configurations—the prominent themes—are ones that Katherine lacked and needed to experience in order to continue her growth and development. They are configurations that have emerged in the illusory space of our relationship. Although there have been many other co-transference configurations in our work—among them "bad mother," "helpless idiot," and "heartless bitch"—Katherine helped me to become mainly the nurturing mother, wise woman, and loving grandma to her eager and inquisitive, easily-hurt and quick-to-retaliate younger self. Her

182   *Katherine*

wish to be a successful parent has been a particularly strong inducement for her to remain in our therapy and do this work with me. And I feel honored that she has developed a strong trust in me, perhaps trusting someone for the first time in her life.

Since her financial settlement, our relationship has dealt with two different dimensions of experience. In one, we deal with practical matters—e.g., parenting an adolescent—and everyday events much as we did in the years before her accident. I find that my role is listener and encourager, encourager particularly when she exercises new choices and increased agency. In the second dimension, because we have the luxury of seeing each other three times a week, Katherine and I have reopened and delved deeply into her traumas and sorrows: her molestations, her rape, the death of her young sister, and the absence—until therapy—of a safe and protected grieving place. I have been surprised at the intensity of her work and believe that her new-found external and internal stability as well as her child's joyful flowering have allowed her the emotional space to visit and witness with me these primal and private agonies—and hopefully to place them finally in the past where they belong.

In closing, I have only one more observation on my role as therapist/analyst to Katherine, touching on my view of the moral-ethical dimension of the work. Simply put, once committed to a serious therapeutic relationship, one has the responsibility to hang in. After an early evaluation/exit period, we're hooked and hog-tied to our patients and should be. Many times with Katherine I felt that I couldn't stand one more second of silence, one more drama scene, one more personal attack, one more excruciating story of cruelty and abuse, or one more moment of witnessing her pain and vulnerability, of witnessing her depression and grief. Many times I felt relief when she was finally gone; and many times I wished that she would never come back. But what it means to be a person—and particularly an analyst person—is that we stay present to witness and to help if possible.[2] We stay present to witness especially when it's hard, and when the suffering that we witness stuns us as it emerges into daylight with shattering force. And sometimes, even beyond witnessing, we lend a hand if we can. Katherine has been my hard case because in its crucible I have learned that my charge and responsibility as an analyst is to help bear the burden of human suffering. What sane person would choose such a thing? Yet had I known this and chosen another profession, I might have missed work that is as close to sacred as any I can imagine.

Notes

1 There are so many teachers to thank for my analytic education, for giving me some words to describe ineffable analytic processes: luminaries like Kohut, Mitchell, Sander, Lyons-Ruth, Daniel Stern, the Boston Change Process Group, Beebe, Lachmann, Teicholz, Bromberg, Aron, Benjamin, Davies, Main, Target, Fonagy, Steven Stern, Stolorow, and Orange; and some shining folks closer to home like Shane, Pickles, Coburn, Bacal, and Hastings.

2 The French philosopher Levinas (1969) teaches that the ethical dimension of relationship precedes all knowledge and derives from the face-to-face encounter with the Other. The

epiphany of the face of the Other is revelatory and binding; it summons us, pulls us to it, and in its vulnerability demands our protection and responsibility. As a religious Jew, Levinas may be suggesting that the shock of the Other's face is a reminder that the Other is like me, and that we are both created in the Divine image.

References

Bacal, H. A. & Herzog, B. (2003) Specificity Theory and Optimal Responsiveness: An Outline. *Psychoanal. Psychol.*, 20:635–648.

Fosshage, J. L. (1997) Chapter 4 Listening/Experiencing Perspectives and the Quest for a Facilitating Responsiveness. *Prog. Self Psychol.*, 13:33–55.

Levinas, E. (1969) *Totality and Infinity: An Essay on Exteriority*, trans. A. Largis. Pittsburg, PA: Duquesnes University Press.

Index

AAI; *see* Adult Attachment Interview
accumulation, stories 10
"acknowledgment tokens" 48
Adult Attachment Interview (AAI) 10–1
agency 111; contemporary philosophy 121; human individuality 110; infant 116; and responsibility 105; self-agency 106, 115; subjective experiences of 106; subjective generation 9
aggression 58
Alexander, F. 155
American Psychoanalytic Association 58
analyst envy; *see* envy
analytic relationships 3, 6, 37, 46, 79, 91, 155, 158; attunement in 36, 41; dynamic complexity theory and 82–5; emotional "realness" in 159; envy, uses of 62; examines and deconstructs 19; expectations for rhythms 143; healing in 41; interactions 18; "in the transference" 36; non-verbal 26; repertoires of interactions 39; self-organizing 83; sensibility and 34
anger 22, 25, 28, 72–3, 76, 120, 166
anxiety 16, 21, 67, 68, 74, 93, 139; annihilation 126; betrayal and abandonment 91; castration 61; existential 122, 129
Arnetoli, C. 79
Aron, L. 23, 32–41, 43–6, 79, 83, 150, 155
artistic experiences 90
attachment theory 115, 139
attitudes 10
"attractor states" 103
Atwood, G. E. 79, 115
"authenticity" 38
authoritarianism 58
Axtell, R. 123

Bacal, H. A. 175
Beebe, B. 42, 45, 56, 79, 83, 116, 129, 151
behavioral dissembling 69
Benjamin, J. 39–40, 61, 113–14, 151, 159, 170
Beyerle, S. 48
bi-directionality 34
"Big D" determinism 108, 109; complexity 115; infant 115; intersubjectivity 115; stuckness 107, 110
"Big Tent" relational psychoanalysis 34
Bion, W. 147
"blank screen" analyst 34
blindness 46
Boston Change Process Group 39, 42
Bowlby, J. 45
brain 7
broader analytic theory 21
Bruner, J. 9, 9–10, 11
Buber, M. 113, 121
Bucci, W. 83

Cacioppo, J. 151
calcified stories 6, 13
Carleton, L. 89
cases studies (of patients): Briana 118–21; Elaine 117–18; Ella 16–22; Katherine 165–82; Lara 23–32; Sally 85–95
Cavell, M. 111–12, 121
choices: "Big D" determinism; *see* "Big D" determinism; chance 108; clinical work 110; complexity 109, 114–17; contemporary thinking 110; curiosity 119; existentialists 110–12; faith, bad 134; hyper-sensitiveness 119; infant 114–17; intersubjectivity 114–17; mind/brain people 110–12; recognition 112–14; sensibility 114–17; "stuckness" 106–7; "unreified" 105

Cilliers, P. 46, 79
Coburn, W. J. 46, 79, 84, 103–4, 109, 114–15, 121, 151, 159
cognitive: temporal disturbance 139; traditional emphasis 2
collisions, emotional 155
colorful stories 7
communication: complexity theory 89; verbal and nonverbal 39, 80, 150
"community mental health center" 54
complexity 6, 12, 18; choices 109, 114–17; communication network 89; disruption 91; emotions 89; future vision 147; intersubjectivity 89; mutual dissociative process 97, 102; neurons 80, 90; perturbations 81; recursive 81; reentry 81; selfishness 81; self-organization 80, 94; sensibility 82–5, 89–91, 93, 114–17; system changes 80–1; thinking 85, 104; trust 98; truth 81
comprehensiveness 8
confusion 2, 27, 92, 107, 122, 156, 159
connection: continuous 126; relational 130
consciousness: choices 112, 118; deceptions 58; loneliness 129; recognition 113; sensibility 84
constraining theory 56
constructivism 9
contemporary relational theory 19; conference 32–8; enactments 26–7, 30, 34; feminine 47; intersubjectivity theory 40; mutual relationship 34; perturbation 46; "prejudices" 34, 35; relational psychoanalysis 44; responses 38–49; sado-masochism 43, 44; sexual abuse 26; treatment 25–32; unarticulated patterns 26; unconscious 26; violence 30
contingent responsiveness 45
continuous connection 126
conventional expectations 63
"cosmological time" 8
countertransference envy 62
covetous feeling 62
creativity 67, 70
cultural paths 23
curiosity 6, 21, 30; choices 119; envy 65; future vision 148; mutual dissociative process 98–9; temporal disturbance 143
cybersex 98

Damasio, A. 84–5, 151
Davies, J. M. 37, 43
Davies, L. M. 155

Decety, J. 151
declarative memory 27
deconstruction 10
delinquency 57, 58; authoritarianism 58–9; community mental health center 54; conscious 58; dishonest behavior 58; dynamic systems thinking 53; envy 65; fear 57; human hostility 56; power tensions 54; Thalians theory 53; therapeutic neutrality 55; treatment programs 54; "truth claims" 57; unconscious 58
"demonic man" 31
depression 76, 146, 167, 168; mutual dissociative process 98; temporal disturbance 140
deprivation 26
destruction 159
destructive relationship 23
determinism 106, 108
"dialectical constructivism" 111
Dickinson, E. 125, 127
dishonesty: behavior 57–8; envy 65
disintegration 116
disorganized/chaotic stories 21
disruptions 91, 92, 121; temporal disturbance 141, 144
dissociated emotion 32
dissociation 24, 168
distress 22, 23, 27, 28, 74; emotions 92; temporal disturbance 142
distrust 69; temporal disturbance 144
Drake, T. 128
dyadic expansion of consciousness 39
dynamic systems: theory 103; thinking 12

eating disorder 17
Edelman, G. 46, 80–2, 84, 89, 151
ego psychology 2
Elliot, J. 151
e-mail 98–9
emotional attunement 36
emotional identification 26
emotions 2, 6, 17, 167; attitudes 34; brutality 117; co-created relational space 19; collisions 155; colorful stories 7; complexity theory 89–91; cortisol 7; disorganized child 27; distress 92; empathy 7; envy 61, 67, 68; faith, bad 136; intense feelings 155; internal reservoirs 19; intimacy 19–20; intimate emotions 155; life stories 10; mismatched emotional 27; music 142, 144; mutual

186   *Index*

dissociative process 97–9, 99–100, 102; non-verbal processes 2, 26–7, 48; oxytocin 7; passionate emotions 155; psychic mismatches 145; realities 158; recognition 113; temporal disturbance 139, 141, 142, 143; verbal processes 2, 26

empathy 6, 41, 86, 139, 152; capacity for 151; future vision 150; and human behavior 114; Kohut's 38, 150; listening 180; promoting 7; recognition 114; temporal disturbance 152

enactments 26–7, 30, 34, 83, 160

envy 60; –77; acknowledging valuable aspects or gifts 61; associated with grief 61–2; beauty and 172; being "green with envy" 63; countertransference 62; definition 62; emotions of 61, 67; feelings of 63, 69; Klein's concept of 61–2; malignant 61; "moment of meeting" and 61; penis 58, 61; raputation in psychoanalysis 61; uses of 62; at work 60

Epstein, J. M. 123

The Examined Life: How We Lose and Find Ourselves (2013) 12

existential-phenomenological tradition 110

"experience of the real" 159

exploration 10

facial and vocal expression 26

faith, bad: awareness 134; choices 134; definition 133; imagination 137; loneliness 136; self-interest 134; social isolation 135

fear 57, 144

feminine 47

finitude 149

focus relaxation 26

Fonagy, P. 113–14, 116, 121, 151, 158, 170

"forgetting" 141

Fosshage, J. L. 61, 150, 181

Frawley, M. G. 37, 43

Freud, Anna 58

Freudian positivism 9

Freud, S. 45, 57, 58, 107–9, 152

Frie, R. 110–11, 115

Fromm-Reichman, F 126, 128

future vision 141–2; collapse of 141; complexity 147; conjoint 146–7; construction of 146–7, 149; curiosity 148; failed 149; positive 149; self-destructive behavior 148; time 146–50

Gales, M. 79

Gallese, V. 151

generosity 25

Gentile, K. 146

Gergely, G. 83, 114, 116, 151

Gerhardt, J. 48

gesture, spontaneous 116

Goldin, Daniel 11–2

gossipy stories 7

Gottschall, J. 11

Grand, S. 155

Grey, Roger 54

Grigsby, J. 109

Grosz, Stephen 12

Harris, A. 61

Harrison, A. M. 79

Hastings, R. 116, 170

Hebb, D. O. 90

Hoffman, I. M. 111–12, 121

human hostility 56

Iacoboni, M. 151

Iatrogenic treatment 44

illuminating theory 20, 42

"illusion" 158

imagination 3, 7; complexity theory 80; envy 70, 72; faith, bad 137; future vision 147; reality 159; recognition 114; temporal disturbance 139; vision 26

immersion 38, 158

immigrant community 148

"implicit relational knowings" 103

impulsivity 162, 172, 178

indeterminacy 112

infant: caretaker system 116; choices 114–17; mutual dissociative process 99; recognition 113

Institute of Contemporary Psychoanalysis (ICP) 58, 59

intellectual intensity 33

interpretations: leading edge interpretations 42–3; trailing edge interpretations 42–3, 46

intersubjectivity 33, 139–40; choices 114–17; complexity 89, 93; recognition 114; sensibility 83–4; temporal disturbance 147; theory 36, 40

intimacy 19, 71

invitation 6

"I-Thou" 113

jealous 62

Jurist, E. 116

Kirsner, D. 57
Klein, Melanie 45, 58, 61–2
Knoblauch, S. 146, 151
knowledge 9
Kohut, H. 38, 41, 45, 150–1, 158, 168

Lachmann, F. M. 45, 56, 79, 116, 129
Lamm, C. 151
language: choices 112; intersubjectivity
    theory 36; metaphorical and narrative
    uses 3; self-definition 8
Leowald, H. 146
Levenson, E. 10
Levinas, E. 113, 182n2
"libido story" 13
Lichtenberg, J. 11
listener, imaginary 3
"Little Hans" 7
loneliness 24, 69; see also malignant
    loneliness; faith, bad 136; temporal
    disturbance 141
Lyons-Ruth, K 18, 42, 83, 116, 151

Main, M. 45, 151
"malignant envy" 61
malignant loneliness: attachment theory
    127; isolation 130; life-threatening 126;
    sadness 126; "trauma" 126; unremitting
    loneliness 126; vulnerability 129
Marks-Tarlow, T. 151
masochistic enactment 37
memories, positive 21
memory 3, 4, 35; complexity 81; curiosity
    6; empathy 6; expectations 12; painful
    memory 28; procedural 27; values 12
mental illness 28
mentalization 116; faith, bad 135; functions
    21; recognition 114; unconscious 19
Milner, Marion 26
minds 4
mistakes 25
Mitchell, S. 83, 151, 155
model scenes 11, 16; creativity 67; envy 64
"moments of meeting" 158–9
murders: complexity 76; faith, bad 135;
    psychoanalysis 54
mutual dissociative process: "attractor
    states" 103; complexity 97; curiosity 98;
    cybersex 98; depression 98; emotions
    97–8, 99–100; infant 99; "tipping
    point" 103
mutual love 163
mutual recognition 116, 159

mutual relationship 34
mutual rhythm development 21

narrative necessity 10
narrative rhythms 21
negative self-attributions 18
neglect 26
neurochemical brain process 7
non-interpretive interventions 37
non-linear dynamic systems theory;
    see complexity
non-verbal communication 2, 80, 83,
    89, 150
non-verbal emotional processes 2
non-verbally mediated memory 27
"nosebleed" feelings 31
nuance 6

ontological protest of subjectivity 117
open systems 89
Orange, D. M. 79, 115, 150–1, 151
orthodox psychoanalytic facility 168
Osuch, E. 109
oxytocin 7

pain 27, 162, 168
Pally, R. 151–2
passionate feelings 159
pathological accommodation concept 13
pattern recognition 143
penis envy 58, 61
perceptions 35
personal paths 23
perturbations 46; complexity 94;
    complexity theory 81, 91; sensibility 83
"phenomenological time" 8
"poison tumbleweed" 72–3
"prejudices" 34, 35
"present tenseness" 13
primal emotion 61
procedural memory 27
prosocial behaviors 7
psychic reality 9, 94
psychoanalysis: analytic tales 12–4; "Big
    Tent" relational psychoanalysis 34; brain
    7; clinical stories 4, 6, 21; "cosmological
    time" 8; curiosity 6; delinquency 58;
    empathy 6; "existential" 5; human action
    6; knowledge 9; language 7; memory
    stories 4; murdering 54; "mystery" 10;
    neurochemical brain process 7;
    "phenomenological time" 8; present
    tenseness 5; Ricoeur's epistemology 9;

188　*Index*

sensibility 9; theory stories 4, 6; traditional psychoanalysis 19; training 23, 33; truth 9
psychoanalytic relationship; *see* analytic relationships
psychotherapy 25

Ramachandran, V. S. 151
"Rat Man" 7
realities: cognitive patterns 157; confusion 159; emotions 155–6, 157, 158; enactments 160; external contexts 156; immersion 158; mutative process 158; strangeness 156; unconscious 157; vulnerability 156, 158
recognition: mutual recognition 159; realities 158
recursive interaction 18, 39
relational analysis 160
relational dimensions, in life tales 10–1
relationality 34
relational psychoanalysis 44; "Big Tent" 34
relational space, co-created 19
relations of mutuality 34, 40, 113
Renn, P. 151
responsibilities 69–70, 113, 167; loneliness 126
Ricouer, P. 9
risk 29
Ruderman, E. G. 61, 62
Rustin, J. 116–17, 122, 151

sado-masochism 37, 43, 44
Sampson, H. 90
Sandburg, C. 127
Sander, L. 151
Sartre, John Paul 133
Schore, A. N. 151
scripted story 20
Searle, John 109–10, 111, 112
self-consciousness 17
self-definition process 11
self-destructive behavior 148
self-experience 94; mode 48; temporal disturbance 151
selfishness 75–6, 79, 81
self-loathing feelings 167
self-organization 18, 39, 116; complex systems 80; sensibility 83
self-perception 111
self-restraint 25
"self talk" 160
sensibility 34; choices 114–17; complexity

82–5, 89–91, 93; infant development 83; intersubjectivity 83–4; self-organizing 83; temporal disturbance 142
"serotonin story" 13
sexism 47; cybersex 98; envy 63, 65; sexual abuse 24, 26, 29, 117–18, 167
sexual abuse 24, 26, 29, 117–18, 167
Shaefer, Roy 9–10
Shane, E. 23, 33, 46–7, 79, 89
Shane, M. 45, 79
Shared Circuitry 151–2
Shattered idealization 161
Shengold, L. 61
Siegel, D. 84
Skype therapy 14
"Sleeping Beauty"
Smith, L. 46
smoking 69
social attitudes 90
socially isolated childhood 24
Sorter, D. 151
"sovereign equals" 114
Spence, D. P. 9–10
Sroufe, L. A. 83
Stern, Daniel 10, 11, 42, 79, 85, 94, 116
stimulated imaginative associations 26
Stolorow, R. D. 23, 32–8, 41, 46, 79, 115, 149–51
The Storytelling Animal: How Stories Make Us Human (2012) 11
Strenger, Carlo 117
"stuckness" 117, 119
sub-symbolic emotional processes 2
suicide 24, 55, 87, 129, 166; antidepressant 173; depression 173, 176; "drop dead" 173; hospitalization 177; treatment strategies 174–5
Sullivan, H. S. 128
"surface mind" activity 26
surrender 39
symbolism 72
symmetrical analysis 34

Target, M. 116, 151
"temporal bandwidth 146
temporal disturbance: culture 147; disruptions 141, 144; distrust 144; emotions 141, 142; empathy 152; future vision 146; intersubjective systems theory 139–40; loneliness 141; musical unfolding 142–6; neurons 151–2; reading 146; self-experience 151; sensibility 142; thinking 146; time 139, 146–50; upset 146–50

Index   189

temporal horizon 148
termination 130
Thelen, E. 46
theoretical paths 23
"therapeutic neutrality" 55
time: constrained weekly therapy 25; temporal disturbance 146–50; travel 26
"tipping point" 103
Tononi, G. 46, 151
traditional psychoanalysis 40
traditional transference interpretation 27
traditional treatment programs 54
training 23, 33
transformation 28
trauma 13, 23, 44, 48, 91, 126, 130, 137, 143, 149, 172
Trump, Donald 81
trust 27, 98, 107
truth 9, 35; claims 57; complexity theory 81

unconscious: choices 112; deceptions 58; realities 157
uncovering process 20

"unknowability quotient" 44
unremitting loneliness 126

value: complexity theory 89; relational connection 130; stories 7
verisimilitude 9
violence 23, 30, 56, 172; faith, bad 136
vulnerability: emotions 155; future vision 149; malignant loneliness 129; realities 156, 158; recognition 113

Watson, J. S. 83
Weisel-Barth, J. 46, 151
Weiss, J. 90
Williams, H. 112–14, 116, 121, 128
willingness 29, 31
Winnicott, D. W. 39, 48, 62, 117, 170
Winnicottian theory 91
"Wolf Man" 7
"wonderbreads" 29
Workman's Compensation 176

Printed in the United States
By Bookmasters